DAN HANCOX

INNER CITY PRESSURE

THE STORY OF GRIME

WILLIAM COLLINS

William Collins
An imprint of HarperCollins*Publishers*
1 London Bridge Street
London SE1 9GF
www.WilliamCollinsBooks.com

First published in Great Britain by William Collins in 2018

1

A catalogue record for this book is
available from the British Library

ISBN 978-0-00-825713-2

Printed and bound in Great Britain by
CPI Group (UK) Ltd, Croydon

MIX
Paper from
responsible sources
FSC
www.fsc.org   FSC™ C007454

This book is produced from independently certified FSC
paper to ensure responsible forest management.

For more information visit: www.harpercollins.co.uk/green

'Grime is the sound of 21st century protest. *Inner City Pressure* is essential reading from a superb writer on the political awakening of a generation'
OWEN JONES

'The story of UK grime in the 21st century is a story that is bigger than just the music. This is the story of how young people achieved greatness against all the odds, how grime exploded from our urban, inner-city areas, how these artists gave a voice to those that were left behind, shut down and alienated and in the process of doing so took the music industry and the UK's popular culture by storm. UK grime was born in the areas where austerity hit hardest and was created by people who were ignored and maligned by politicians. Dan Hancox charts this remarkable story from pirate radio to the front pages. This is a story that deserves to be heard'
DAVID LAMMY MP

'Unputdownable and bristling with insights about grime and the city it was born in. Anyone with any interest in grime, you need to be reading this, trust me'
JEFFREY BOAKYE, author of
*Hold Tight: Black Masculinity, Millennials
and the Meaning of Grime*

'It says something about the last two decades that the first real history of 21st century London comes in the form of a book about grime. *Inner City Pressure* tells an astonishing story of a group of MCs who have gone from being ignored and effectively banned by the Metropolitan Police, to threatening to burn down the Prime Minister's house from the stage at the Brit Awards. Shifting constantly from the small details of a community music – school playgrounds, youth clubs, council flats, dubplates, FruityLoops – to the grand canvas of the transformation of a metropolis into a theme park for property developers, Hancox tells the story of a city and a music scene with restraint, humour and anger'
OWEN HATHERLEY, author of
A Guide to the New Ruins of Great Britain

'An amazing book ... phenomenal'
Mostly Lit Podcast

ALSO BY DAN HANCOX

The Village Against the World

For my parents, Helen and Rod: thank you
for bringing me up in London, among other things.

CONTENTS

DON'T HOLD
HIM BACK!

It's dusk on a spring evening in 2003, and the start of something exceptional: the hottest summer in years, a sweltering heatwave lifting temperatures in London above 100 degrees Fahrenheit. But it's cooler when you're high up on a rooftop, and windy, so hoods are up and beanies are on. Around 20 members of the legendary east London crews Roll Deep, East Connection, Boyz in da Hood and Nasty Crew are squeezed into a makeshift pirate-radio studio, the occupied box room being used by Deja Vu FM. The average age in the room is about 17. A few hangers-on lean against the walls watching, part-time MCs nodding their heads to the beat, hoping to be given some time on the mic or just there to witness, without realising it, a seminal moment in the history of British music.

On the decks is Roll Deep's DJ Karnage, who slowly builds momentum with his freshly cut vinyl, exclusive unreleased instrumentals unavailable to the general public, and the mic is passed from MC to MC, each of them spitting their bars over the new dubplates.

The MC line-up ranges from graduates of the jungle and UK garage scenes such as Wiley, Maxwell D, God's Gift and D Double E – each of them veterans already, by virtue of being in their early twenties – to early

Dizzee and Wiley in front of Crossways Estate, aka 'the three flats', 2002

grime heroes Demon, Sharky Major and Lady Fury. There's even a minuscule, half-squeaking, Tinchy Stryder, then only 16 years old.

The event is being filmed for an amateur DVD called *Conflict* by Troy 'A Plus' Miller, who has begged his girlfriend to borrow the camera from her university media department for the summer, to shoot some footage of his mates on the east London pirate-radio scene. Miller, from far-away Hackney, has met Bow boys Wiley, Geeneus and Slimzee in the nineties through their shared love of jungle, and become involved with their station, Rinse FM, Deja Vu's neighbour and rival. Wiley suggested he come down that day and film at Deja. 'No one had given me a tip, I wasn't expecting anything,' he says.

In its early days grime really was a scene, with its own institutions and infrastructure, friendships and rivalries, independent record labels and shops, as well as the pirate stations. It was also a community, in which the (mostly teenage) MCs and DJs all knew each other: if not from school, from youth clubs or just from hanging around the local area, then through 'doing music'. Their rejection by the older, more refined, aspirational and grown-up UK garage scene forged a unique camaraderie, and drove the music to new heights of innovation – the competitive bravado forcing MCs to keep writing new, bolder, better lyrics.

Like all pirate stations, Deja Vu FM is by definition illegal, and its secret studio location has been moved regularly to escape the Department for Trade and Industry. In summer 2003, it's in a grotty whitewashed box room – one window boarded up with chipboard, another blocked out with a bin bag – up on the rooftop of the same building that housed the notorious EQ Club, where numerous seminal UK garage nights took place. 'Deja was the maddest one,' MC Shystie says. 'Because the studio was on a rooftop, and the roof literally had no edge: so if you take one wrong move, you're dead. We should not have been up there! Because it would be late at night, and dark – so if someone gets pushed, or someone trips and falls back, they're going to fall off that fucking roof and die. It's mad when you look back at it now: nowadays the radio stations all look like how 1Xtra looks, all nice and shit – and they're all in flipping Shoreditch.'

When *Conflict* was filmed, the geographical horizons were as narrow as the sonic ones were wide: 'That's where I'm from, Bow E3,' Wiley boasts into the Deja Vu mic at one point. 'I'm like the 38 bus, because I never turn up!' he continues, shouting out north-east London's least reliable bus service. This closed-world intensity, bordering on claustrophobia, vibrates outwards from the crowded little Deja Vu studio, in the MCs' clamour for a turn on the microphone.

The *Conflict* video is grime at the point of its creative eruption – still unnamed, but undeniably alive – as the futuristic mutations of UK garage's slinky charm settled into the shape of an explosive new genre. This was the exact moment when the effusive charisma and hype of the MCs began to take over the show. Prior to that, anyone with a mic in their hand was first of all answerable to the beat, to the producer-DJ auteur, and pirate radio was all about 'rolling out' the instrumentals – building a steady, if restless momentum. The MC was a performer, and a host: a master of ceremonies, but also, in the parasitic sense, possessed by those pioneering early grime beats and their subdivisions – Wiley's 'eskimo', Jon E Cash's 'sublow' – all of them summoning a kind of macabre, horror-show minimalism.

There's D Double E, the lanky, cheeky fans' favourite, also known as the Newham General, not in military fatigues tonight but shrouded in a black boxer's hoodie, with a skippy, idiosyncratic flow and his own verbal audio-logo, 'the D Double signal', which is not easily transcribed, but sounds something like: 'Ooooerhhhhhh, ooooerhhhhhh – it's muuuuuweee, muuuuuweee.' There's Maxwell D, who in his early twenties has already been to hell and back, survived an upbringing of domestic violence, sheltered accommodation, hostels and foster care, been on TV – on *Crimewatch* – gone to jail for armed robbery, come out, become a major UK garage MC and a major drug dealer (at the same time), had hits and gone back on primetime TV, but as a pop star. There's Lady Fury, unmoved by being – as she often was – the only woman in a room full of jostling male egos, getting plaudits for her ferocity: 'I don't give head, but I give headbutts,' she spits, and the record playing underneath, 'Ho' by Dizzee Rascal, is wheeled back as her male peers throw their hands up. 'Dun no I represent for the ladies,' she says, as the stuttering gunshots of the instrumental start up again. There's Tinchy Stryder, still in school, expounding the strange wisdom of youth, 'brand new energy, same old Stryder,' he spits, like he's been doing this for years – he has – clutching the microphone with both hands like his life depends on it. And then there's Wiley, the godfather of grime, whose manic enthusiasm and hilarious non-sequiturs suddenly give way to moments of sublime clarity, like when he captures the whole bizarre and uniquely skittish practice of grime MCing: 'I'm futuristic, quantum leaping/there's no defeating E3 tiger/see me creep on the riddim like a spider/kill them with a 16-liner.' Grime 'spitting' is twice the speed of US-style rap: typically, you had just 16 bars to show your skills (or 21 seconds, in So Solid Crew's case), before passing the mic to the next MC – it is the most thrilling, exhausting, ADHD onslaught of a genre: a tension headache you can dance to. Andy Warhol's generation should count themselves lucky they got fifteen entire minutes to make an impact. But for all the idiosyncratic talents, they're in it together. The powerful conviviality and kinship in a genre where lyrical threats of violence are one of the primary means of communication may be surprising, but it's there all the same – a chain created between artists every time the mic is passed from one MC to the next.

As the energy of the set mounts, Crazy Titch is bopping with cartoonish energy, his face screwed up at the sheer meanness of the track playing underneath, his blitzkrieg of bars including the lyric, 'Draw for me, you'll be on the Ten O'Clock News.' Only three years later, he actually *was* on the *Ten O'Clock News*, when he was charged with murder: a moment when grime's casual lyrical brutality was horribly borne out in reality. 'When Titch came in, I could feel there was an edge,' Troy Miller says. 'He changed the dynamics of the room. Everything got a bit more serious, whereas it was all fun and banter before.'

Throughout the *Conflict* video Dizzee's voice has that lean, straining, high-pitched teenager's tone, altogether gone from his songs now that his throat's been fleshed out by success, and time. He is visibly defensive, an outsider even among his peers, the boy in the corner of the room, just as he was at school. Titch is much less guarded, happily lost in the music, grinning when he passes the mic to Dizzee, nodding his head to his rival's bars, adding a cheerful 'what!' to Dizzee's lyrics in choral emphasis.

There's no sense of a fight in the offing for the first, enthralling 35 minutes of the video – it explodes from absolutely nowhere. Dizzee asks for the mic, is refused by Titch, who is still in full flow, and somehow in a split second the two of them are yelling at each other and squaring up, fingers are pointed, and the music underneath cuts out abruptly, like in a spaghetti western; the card tables are flipped over, the piano stops playing and the saloon doors are left swinging in the breeze.

Wiley and Maxwell D are immediately in between the two young MCs – the elder statesmen who've seen this kind of bullshit before, and seen it get out of hand before. Wiley takes charge, the man who has always behaved like he cares more for the scene's collective success than his own. ('What's the highlight of your career so far?' Wiley was asked in 2017. 'Skepta making it.' 'No, *your* highlight,' the interviewer pressed. Wiley wouldn't change track: 'Skepta. I took him from a DJ to an MC.') He holds them back, instructing them to 'seckle, seckle', his eyes darting all around the room as other MCs move in to either help or hinder the rapprochement. Dizzee and Titch are pulled apart still shouting at each other, and everyone spills out onto the rooftop from the TARDIS-like studio, silhouetted against the dark blue east London gloaming, as friends attempt to calm them down.

'Don't hold him back, don't hold him back,' Dizzee yelps, as the struggle to defuse the anger continues. He was still so young at this point – still barking his anger out, straining passionately, defensively, hungry both on the mic and in the fight with Titch. 'I'M NOT A MOOK, I don't know what they told you but I'm not a mook!' he yells repeatedly at an equally aggressive Titch. He's scowling, livid – determined to defend his reputation. No one seems to agree on the etymology of 'mook' here (it might be a throwback to Scorsese's *Mean Streets*), but it's clear from the rage in Dizzee's eyes, and in his voice, that he's not one, right?

The clash looks serious, and is taken seriously by all the others present on the rooftop – and it was soon followed up by diss tracks from each MC to the other. As menacing as they both look when they're screaming at each other, the scrap is underscored by grime's quintessential, frequently comic tendency to the melodramatic. When the scuffle starts, it could almost be a scene from *EastEnders* – appropriately, given the location. When the music cuts out abruptly, amid the clamour of raised voices and bravado we hear 'step outside!', 'leave it, man'.

Three years later, Carl 'Crazy Titch' Dobson was sentenced to life imprisonment for his involvement in the murder of 21-year-old Richard Holmes, a crime that supposedly originated in a disrespectful grime lyric. In that Deja Vu show, Crazy Titch is captivating, going a hundred miles an hour on the mic, arms pumping, grinning ear to ear, wiping the sweat from his brow with his T-shirt. It's not a stretch to suppose that the gleeful, reckless energy he displays on the mic came from the same place as his manic, unhinged tendencies.

There's no blue plaque on the building commemorating this pivotal evening in the history of British music, because there is no building left at all. In 2003 Deja Vu was on the edge of an industrial estate, in a scrappy, marshy part of Stratford that was about to be wiped off the map – grime's machine gun snares and adolescent yelps were among the final, spluttering cries of the informal city. The pirate studio only lasted a few months there before moving on again, and the block that housed it was soon bulldozed to make way for the mannered and manicured London 2012 site, and the £486-million Olympic stadium.

Dizzee was back in the same spot that summer, nine years after his fight with Crazy Titch, to perform his number-one hit 'Bonkers' at the £27m London 2012 opening ceremony, to an estimated global TV audience of 900 million people. He wore a specially embroidered E3 baseball jacket, honouring the east London postcode that will forever be synonymous with grime.

'Forget all this, man, forget all this,' one MC is heard saying after the fight breaks out, attempting to subdue the rising temperature. He meant they should forget the beef – and soon enough, they did. But as this hyper-local rhythm began to reverberate beyond the narrow radius of the pirate transmitters, a great deal more was forgotten with it.

ONE

THE CITY
AND THE CITY

I'm from where Reggie Kray got rich as fuck
East London, who am I to mess tradition up?
Jellied eels, pie and mash, two pints of that Pride on tap
Polo top, pair of Stans, flat cap and a Burberry mac

Back when Lethal Bizzle was Lethal B
This is how we used to dun the dance in East
We used to spit 16s till they called police
Probably somewhere in a party or a dark shebeen

Kano, 'This Is England'

In the Museum of London Docklands, five minutes from One Canada Square and the shimmering glass totems of Canary Wharf, among the exhibits on slave owners and sailors' rebellions, tall ships and frost fairs, hangs a painting of the river made in 1883 by William Lionel Wyllie. It shows barge workers shovelling coal in the shadow of a clutter of trade ships, the river alive with noise, fumes and activity – the painting is titled: *Toil, Glitter, Grime and Wealth on a Flowing Tide.*

Canary Wharf and Limehouse, 2002

It's easy now to forget that London was, for most of its 2,000-odd years of life, not just a working city, not just an industrial city, but specifically, a port city. The world's dry dock; the shoving-off point for innocent expeditions and brutal subjugation. And as the title of Wyllie's painting suggests, port cities have a few consistent attributes: one is transience, a constant clamour of people leaving and arriving, drifting in and out with the tides. Another is inequality – rags and riches, a halo of insalubrious low-level criminality, insobriety and dirt hovering around the glittering cargo – or a halo of enriching gold around the squalor and decadence, depending on which way around you look at it. Either way, one travels with the other, one lives with the other. A hundred and twenty years later, Wyllie's namesake would use some cheap computer software and a microphone to document the same toil, glitter, grime and wealth flowing through twenty-first-century London, at 140 beats per minute.

Some cities are divided between distinct geographical binaries. North and south. The centre and the suburbs. Uptown and downtown. The shanty towns and the gated communities. London is not easily disentangled: it weaves its divisions into a fine mesh, like the netting that stops pigeons gathering underneath railway bridges. The council tower blocks are mingled in with the multimillion-pound mansions. The greasy-spoon caff that's been there since the seventies stands next door to the refurbished gastropub charging £15 for a Sunday roast. The grandiose seventeenth-century church faces down the night-time den of iniquity.

When widespread rioting erupted across London and several other English cities in August 2011, the writer James Meek reflected on an incident that he'd witnessed a few years before in one of Hackney's most prominent new bouji enclaves, Broadway Market – when a group of 30 tooled-up black teenagers, chasing two enemies with a hand gun, suddenly entered (and quickly departed from) the lives of the white middle-class people sipping wine at the outdoor tables. 'It is as if the council-owned tower blocks and estates behind, around and in-between the gentrified patches, where less well-off and poor people live, belong to some other dimension,' he wrote. 'Loving the cultural diversity of London as a spectator-inhabitant is not the same as mingling with it.

The yuppies don't go to the white working-class pubs, and the white working class don't go to the yuppie pubs … this isn't mixing. It's the ingredients for something – nobody knows what – laid out side by side and not being mixed, not touching.[1]

London was in an unsettled temper at the start of the new millennium. It had survived the much-feared but unknowable threat of the Millennium Bug, but suffered the embarrassment of the Millennium Dome, and the damp squib of a Millennium Eve 'river of fire' on the Thames that was supposed to be visible from space, and wasn't even visible from the Embankment. The clock ticked over from 1999 to 2000, planes did not fall out of the sky, and the world didn't end – but some more slow-burn changes were starting to take shape. In May, the British capital acquired an elected Mayor for the first time in its history: Ken Livingstone shook off the contempt of Prime Minister Tony Blair, resigned from the Labour Party, and ran as an independent against the Conservative Steve Norris, and the candidate from his own party, Frank Dobson – beating both comfortably. London had a new City Hall, and a maverick left-winger and newt obsessive in the Mayor's chair.

Two days after Livingstone's victory, to the annoyance of maturing dance music sophisticates everywhere, Oxide and Neutrino's frantic 'Bound 4 Da Reload' – with a chorus built around the theme tune from TV hospital drama *Casualty*, sampling a silly line from gangster flick *Lock, Stock and Two Smoking Barrels*, and peppered with gunshot noises – entered the charts straight at number one, flicking a V-sign at the music establishment. The UK garage scene which the two young south Londoners had emerged from had previously prized refinement, romance, aspiration and an urbane multiculturalism above all else. But clean lines, shiny shoes and champagne were being replaced with something much darker, and murkier – just as the city itself was about to start moving in the opposite direction. A new sound was about to muddy the waters of UK garage's infinity pool, just as the new Labour government, indeed the New Labour government, were hatching grand plans to drastically smarten up the inner city forever.

* * *

In the late 2010s, we tend to look at the cranes going up around London and assume they sprouted from the city's chalky soil, or we gaze wearily upon the prettified glass towers of luxury flats, the pop-ups and the hipster cereal cafes and assume they landed out of the clear blue sky. But urban change is not like the weather, and gentrification is not organic, inevitable or natural. The new millennium began with grime's inner city on one side, and an entirely different, largely new kind of inner city growing rapidly to take its place: expensive, monocultural, private, surveilled and planned from the very top by Tony Blair's government.

At the time, inner London was the richest region in the European Union, yet alongside citadels of banking wealth like the City of London and Canary Wharf were some of the most deprived council estates in the country. Long-standing economic and social divisions were intensifying, as the changing winds of late capitalism induced the middle classes to begin moving back from the suburbs and the home counties. They were about to get a big push from the government, who wanted to make the inner city the engine of bourgeois modernity, cosmopolitan culture and aspiration – the essential spirit of what was self-consciously referred to as the New Labour 'project'.

The reality on the ground as Blair took office was not good. After 18 years of Conservative government, social problems and hardship were thriving in British cities, and in the country at large. By the mid-nineties Britain had more children growing up in unemployed households than anywhere else in Europe, and the highest teenage pregnancy rate. Child poverty had trebled between 1979 and 1995, the number of drug addicts quadruped in the decade to 1996, and the number of homeless people sleeping on the streets had soared.

Since the deregulation of the City in the late 1980s, London's role as Britain's primary economic engine had been greatly magnified: by the millennium, earnings in the capital were on average a third higher than the rest of the country. But the divisions were greater, too: Londoners had a higher unemployment rate than the national average, and a much higher proportion of children growing up in households with no income: 36 per cent of children in inner London lived in workless homes in 1999 – compared to 17 per cent nationally. London households were also more likely to be overcrowded: 16 per cent compared to 6 per cent in other English cities.

In east London, the area that will always be most associated with grime, the boroughs of Hackney, Tower Hamlets and Newham have consistently appeared among the most deprived local authorities in the entire country; in 2000, the government used a new, complex model for analysing different aspects of poverty, from housing to health, which they called Indices of Multiple Deprivation. Across all of England, the grime boroughs were ranked at 1, 2 and 3. A medal-winning podium of poverty.

'East London is in need' has been the received wisdom of London local government ever since it was first introduced in 1888. A century and a half ago, Tower Hamlets was home to the disease-ridden squalor, vice, filth and overcrowded warrens of the infamous Old Nicol slum, before it was finally demolished in the 1890s, following the Housing for the Working Classes Act. The slum clearance programmes continued for decades, both before and after the devastation of the Blitz; some residents moved out to the suburbs, others were given low-rent social housing in the modern new council estates being built. Between 1964–74, the last of the slums were demolished and the Greater London Council built 384 tower blocks of ten storeys or more, providing 68,500 new flats. They were accompanied by utopian rhetoric about a new way of living and 'streets in the sky', changes that would finally grant the dignity London's working-class communities deserved, and dramatically lift the quality of life. In 1981, at the peak of the social-housing boom, there were over 75,000 council homes in London, housing nearly 31 per cent of the capital's population. It is no coincidence that they were heavily concentrated in exactly the boroughs where grime and UK rap would later thrive: 42 per cent of London's social housing was in 'Inner East London': the boroughs of Hackney, Newham, Tower Hamlets, Islington, Haringey, Southwark, Lambeth and Lewisham.

London has historically been a fairly low-rise city, with relatively few skyscrapers, landmark blocks of luxury apartments, or high-end hotels and offices – it has not looked like Manhattan, or latter-day Dubai, Hong Kong or Shanghai. Largely this was by design: planning laws have prohibited tall structures which obscure certain 'protected views' of iconic old London landmarks like St Paul's and the Palace of Westminster, as seen from certain high points on the fringes of the capital, like Parliament Hill, Richmond Park and Alexandra Palace – it's not the specific views themselves which matter so much, but their utility as insurance against a cluttered skyline.

But at the start of the new millennium, a new kind of high-rise building started arriving in the capital: one much less likely to produce exuberant forms of youth culture, clad in glass rather than concrete. Most obvious amongst them was the Shard – Mordor-upon-Thames, owned by Qatar, an obscene 72 storeys high, built with the enthusiastic support of Ken Livingstone, and the backing of New Labour. This directly contravened the 'protected views' regulations; English Heritage objected at a public inquiry, and were ignored. At the time of writing, five years after opening, all ten of the £30–50m flats on the tower's upper floors remain unsold, and empty. Even a visit to the viewing deck costs more than £30. Since then, the trickle has become a flood: in 2017 a survey found that 455 new high-rise blocks were either planned or already under construction in London: 'safety deposit boxes' for wealthy investors, expensive hotels, high-end office space and luxury flats. Blocks like the ickily-named Manhattan Loft Gardens in Stratford followed the Shard's lead and caused controversy by ruining another sight line of St Paul's. More importantly, not a single one of the 455 was being built to provide housing for London's poorest.

The Shard started a bold new trend – building hideous neoliberal obelisks which London didn't need – but the major precedent had already been set: the planting of Canary Wharf's towers of misbegotten riches, right in grime's back yard, in place of the city's abandoned docks. Today, underneath the white office lights and CCTV cameras of what is sometimes known as the 'second City', teem the ghosts of empire, hard labour, hard liquor, opium dens, sailors and sex workers. Even as it enters adolescence, Canary Wharf's cluster of gleaming skyscrapers still feels like a life-size artist's impression, rendered in three dimensions; free from clutter, free from litter – and free from heavy explosives, you presume, if the security presence is anything to go by.

Look closer, and some of the police aren't actually the police at all – they're private security guards, in uniforms designed to look exactly like real police uniforms. The whole area is unnervingly clean. As close as it is, Canary Wharf is almost completely sealed off from its neighbours to the north, where grime erupted into life – Poplar, Limehouse, Bow, and eventually Hackney and Newham – separated by the huge A13 and A1261 dual carriageways, and a no man's land of train lines, Docklands Light Railway sidings and buildings, business parks, car parks, blind alleys and dead-ends, all of which act as further barricades. It is almost as if the builders of Canary Wharf wanted it that way. 'That's where all the yuppies are,' MC Breeze from Roll Deep says in a 2003 documentary, pointing up at One Canada Square. 'We're just over the road, and it's one of the worst boroughs in England.'[2] On the south side of the skyscrapers, in a part of the Isle of Dogs which used to be known as 'The Land of Plenty' during Britain's colonial heyday, the Anchor & Hope pub (Est. 1829) sits boarded up and unloved, its business perhaps swallowed by the two-storey Thai restaurant next door – the hope is gone and the boat is adrift. Commerce spares little attention for sentimental attachment to the past – even its own.

East London's past is weighed down with poverty, and weighed down with heavy industry: the docks, of course, but also gas, railways, manu-facturing, textiles, mills – and, a rare example which is still clinging on today, the Tate and Lyle sugar refinery. It has always been the city's work-ing quarter, with an abundance of low-paid, physically punishing jobs, and was not just the arrival point for immigrants and internal migrants, for centuries, but also the place where many of them made their first homes in the capital: always more multicultural than the rest of London, and almost entirely working class.[3]

East London's industrial history continued to loom over the area once all the industrial work was gone. Even without the factories coating nearby buildings in a layer of soot, and the industrial pollution and jetsam from the docks, east London remained associated with grime, dirt, grit and debris. The connection between the word, the music genre, and the places where grime came from has always been understood to be obvious. 'Most grime tunes are made in a grimy council estate,' MC Nasty Jack told an American documentary crew in 2006. 'Mum ain't got enough money, everyone's just angry. You need a tension release.'[4] The name of the genre aside, grime has featured a whole range of lyrical tropes in which dirt is lionised: tunes are praised as mucky – mucktion, as a noun – dutty (dirty); Shystie even proclaimed one of her tunes was 'muddy'. Partly this is about paying tribute to the sonic 'bottom end', the sub-bass, but it's also a testament to the music's geographical origins.

The East End had been very literally grimier in the past – as in the great smog of 1952, where coal smoke and bad weather conspired to kill around 12,000 Londoners. Regeneration and grime are oppositional forces in the urban arena: in the recent vernacular of urban planning, the word 'regeneration' has always been understood as a response to grit, grime, disorder, clutter and failure or decline. It has a Christian moralistic aspect, a sense that the city too can be born again, that it might – with the right purpose and guidance from above – dunk its head in the water and repent its poverty and sin. Indeed the first recorded use of 'regeneration' in English is from the Wycliffe Bible of 1384, describing the kind of rebirth that Jesus's disciples can expect upon reaching heaven. It was the perfect word for New Labour and the secretly evangelical Prime Minister: grime was old Labour, 1970s, strikes and coal, rubbish piling up in the streets, sin and concrete; regeneration was pastel colours and cheery post-modernism, IKEA urbanism that would make the city look like a kids' play centre – and entice the middle classes to come and live in it.

The East End's underdog mentality, marginality, poverty and history of industrial squalor are all interconnected. Macho resilience and physical and mental toughness have long been fetishised as traits specific to east London, and that kind of grittiness is prominent in grime's vernacular. Dizzee Rascal's single 'Graftin'' addressed listeners inside and outside the capital, and proposed grimy London as a more honest alternative to the scenes on the city's tourist postcards:

> *Young hustlers, London city, stand up*
> *L-D-N, they know us in the world*
> *You know what time it is*
> *I swear to you it ain't all teacups, red telephone boxes and*
>   *Buckingham Palace*
> *I'm gonna show you it's gritty out here*[5]

Almost everyone involved in making grime since its early days has, at one point or another, said something along the lines of 'I don't know where the name came from, I didn't really like it, but it just kind of stuck.' Musicians will almost always do this anyway – disavow all genres and taxonomy, unwilling to let their free-flying creativity be pinned down behind glass and labelled. It's understandable. But there is another (equally understandable) motive for rejecting the name. Unlike UK garage, grime wasn't explicitly aspirational in its fashion or its ethos. But all the same, when it first emerged, the word 'grime' seemed to undercut a basic need for respect. What you can hear in the disavowals of the name is 'We're trying to push ourselves out into the world and show we're worthy of respect, because we don't get any – and this word marks both us and our work as unsavoury. Why would you be proud of being dirty?'

Legendary UK garage DJ EZ is thought to have – semi-inadvertently – named it on his KISS FM show, describing some tracks as 'grimy garage', until the word 'garage' eventually fell away. No one's entirely sure. What is certain is that EZ wasn't alone: describing the music that way was fairly normal among DJs and MCs in the early 2000s, before anyone agreed that grime was called grime – you can still hear it now, on classic recordings like Slimzee's 2002 Sidewinder tape pack set with Dizzee and Wiley (often, correctly, hailed as the greatest mixtape ever made). 'This one's dirty, this one's mucky,' says Dizzee as Slimzee wheels in another tune – Dizzee, of course, named his label Dirtee Stank.

'East London's quite a poor area,' DJ Trend, aka TNT, told a BBC Radio 1 documentary about the still-unnamed emerging scene, broadcast in 2004. 'So a lot of the kids, they don't find nothing else to do, so it just leaves one thing: MC and listen to pirate radio stations.' The music being made by these young people was a reflection of 'what you see when you wake up in the morning,' he continued. 'Most people that's what they're seeing: a lot of grime in the area, a lot of grimy things happening.'[6]

Throughout its history, the East End was the impoverished edge of a wealthy city; but it was also, as the twentieth century drew to a close, the home of the largest piece of urban regeneration in Europe – a project that would help set the tone for all development projects in London in the years that followed. After thriving for centuries, London's docklands collapsed in the space of about two years in the late 1960s, when the work was moved further east down the Thames, to Tilbury docks in Essex. The standardisation of shipping containers ushered in a new phase of global capitalism – it suddenly became ten times as fast to load and unload ships, and could be done with far fewer hands. 83,000 jobs were lost in the docklands boroughs in the 1960s alone, and as people left in search of work, the area became a desolate post-industrial wasteland: the 'wild east' of classic British gangster film *The Long Good Friday*, filmed around what would eventually become Canary Wharf, during its long interregnum of abandonment and decay. The docklands were indicative of the 'developing sickness of our society' Conservative Shadow Chancellor Geoffrey Howe said in 1978, adding that 'the dereliction is itself an opportunity'. Three years later, the Thatcher government set up a mega-quango called the London Docklands Development Corporation (LDDC) to take charge of what was at the time the largest urban regeneration in the world. After more than a decade of urban planning tug-of-war, and substantial protests from parts of the local community, in the nineties Canary Wharf slowly began to take shape: a district of skyscraper-dwelling superbanks and legally dubious white-collar profiteering, patrolled by private security guards. A new kind of urban space for a new London and a new millennium.

One Canada Square, the actual name of the fifty-storey, pyramid-topped building often identified as 'Canary Wharf', was completed in 1991, and became the UK's tallest building, the most visible legacy of Thatcherism, towering over London. It was not until the first years of the new millennium that Canary Wharf really fulfilled its destiny as 'the second City', and took on a life of its own, outstripping the old City of London (the capital's traditional financial centre, around Bank and St Paul's, with its antiquated heraldry, liveries and rituals), and becoming the home of the newer, much more dangerous unregulated financial speculation that would be instrumental in creating the global financial crisis of 2008. Peter Gowan called it 'Wall Street's Guantánamo', a lawless bolt-hole where firms like Lehman Brothers could get away with complex debt-repackaging and trading they would never have been allowed to pursue in Manhattan.[7]

In a neat example of the laissez-faire capitalism which led to the financial crisis itself, the building of Canary Wharf itself benefited from special government exemptions on rates, tax and a speeded-up planning permission process. No questions and no regulations. It was to be the Big Bang of urban regeneration – creating not just the bankers' skyscrapers that watched over the grime kids, the yin to the estates' yang, but also a new airport aimed at business-class customers (London City Airport, opened 1987), the Docklands Light Railway (1987), the Jubilee Line Extension (1999) and the ExCeL conference centre (2000). The LDDC was the flagship of the hyper-gentrification that would follow across British cities, legitimising New Labour's urban renaissance, of which the renovating and demolishing of council estates was also a vital part. Canary Wharf's tower blocks were barely a couple of miles from the council blocks where the pirate radio aerials were going up, but 'the second City' was never designed to have a relationship with its neighbours: the attention was turned towards its rival and parent. Canary Wharf was deliberately laid out so its 'central axis' – a gap in the two tower blocks facing One Canada Square

– looks out across a fountain, and lines of trees, towards the City of London.

The arrival of Canary Wharf coincided perfectly with changes in the financial world, as greater deregulation, coupled with new technology, created new markets for global capital and financial services. London was especially well placed to take advantage of these – not just because of Britain's historic global and colonial power, and the corollary dominance of the English language, but also because it was in a critical time zone between New York and Tokyo. The likes of the Bank of China, Bear Sterns and Morgan Stanley moved into One Canada Square, while next door, the Lehman Brothers were housed in the 30-storey tower at 25 Bank Street.

It is largely forgotten now, but there were protests against the LDDC throughout the eighties and nineties by local people, especially in the Isle of Dogs, as well as alternative 'people's plans' for developing the area in a way that benefited the communities who lived there, rather than itinerant hedge-fund managers who would move in for a couple of years, before going on to Hong Kong or Frankfurt. The locals were ignored. 'There may well have been other ways in which the regeneration of the area could have been secured,' admitted the LDDC in 1997, but these 'would have perpetuated rather than solved the problems of east London'.

The 'problems of east London'? Social housing and social housing's fellow traveller, poor people, who unfortunately placed 'added pressures on the resources of the local authorities'. Instead, the regeneration had transformed the area from somewhere previously 'isolated both physically and emotionally from the rest of London' and placed it 'well and truly in the mainstream of metropolitan life'.[8]

The LDDC spent £3.9 billion of public money on the Canary Wharf regeneration, only to seal it off from its disproportionately sick, unhappy, overcrowded, addicted, jobless and impoverished neighbours.

For those Londoners too young to remember the area before the skyscrapers of Canary Wharf, it feels like it's always been there, with One Canada Square's blinking top-light our city's modern lighthouse. Canary

Wharf is less than two miles from the notorious 25-storey, three-tower block Crossways Estate where Dizzee Rascal and Tinchy Stryder lived as children ('the three flats'), and less than a mile from Langdon Park School, where the former wrote the beginnings of *Boy in da Corner* in music class. Interviewed in 2010 for a BBC London radio programme about 'the best and worst of the capital', Dizzee was asked to nominate his favourite building in London, and unhesitatingly chose One Canada Square:

'It means the most to me, I could see it from all angles as a kid. That was the highest building I could see from my bedroom. And when I see it from south London, when I'm coming over from the Blackwall Tunnel, it always gets me excited, especially at night – it feels special. I love that and the buildings around it – you see a little mini metropolis being built up … It's not quite as impressive as New York or Japan, but it's *ours*, innit? I remember when we were little, we had a conspiracy, we thought that thing on the top of it was like aliens, and they were about to fly off – loads of little theories like that. We'd blink and think they had lasers up there.'[9]

It's not a stretch to suggest that Canary Wharf was the source of grime's unique incarnation of Afrofuturism; the African diasporic aesthetic that takes science fiction as a tool for discussing oppression and freedom – where spaceships might be a metaphor for slave ships, subverting the journey to make it one of escape, not damnation. It's a futurism you can hear in the constant injunctions in grime to 'push things forward', to 'elevate', to make music – and to *be* – 'next level', and it dovetails with the competitive rhetoric enshrined in Canary Wharf's giant totems to late capitalism. Contrary to American hip-hop's rootsy rhetoric about being 'real' and knowing and respecting your history, grime is a year-zero sound, which – in its early days, at least – asked only what's next, and sought to get there first.

You can hear this Afrofuturism most of all in the sonics of grime production – the stark, unfiltered minimalism of the kick drums, the interplanetary weight of the bassline, the sleek raygun zaps and zips of a synth, the way the whole edifice shines sleekly like a spacesuit. It's the sound of the future kids have dreamed of for decades, even while grime's lyrics describe with molecular detail the dirt of the MCs' vividly quotidian lives; MCs who were not universe-traversing spacemen, but teenagers growing up in the poorest boroughs in the country. The real meaning of Canary Wharf, rather than its laser-shooting sci-fi potential, was not lost on Dizzee's peers in the east London grime scene.

'Canary Wharf is like our Statue of Liberty,' Roll Deep's DJ Target told the *Guardian* in 2005: 'It pushes me on. It's like all the money is there and it's an inspiration to get your own.'

Target is now a BBC 1Xtra DJ, which might seem like a token victory for the twin myths of trickle-down economics and climb-up philosophy that Canary Wharf and Britain's political classes so aggressively pushed. New Labour's architect Peter Mandelson infamously defined what was 'new' about the party when he said, in 1998, he was 'intensely relaxed about people getting filthy rich'. British politicians have long perpetuated fallacies about social mobility, the 'aspiration nation' (a favourite slogan of David Cameron when he was PM), or the £9-billion 2012 Olympics 'inspiring a generation' out of poverty, but there is no clearly articulated British equivalent of the American dream – for which US rap music has been such a strong shill. In the UK, the relationship is less overt than the familiar American alliance of multimillionaire 'ghetto' musicians and multimillionaire financiers: the kind crystallised in *The 50th Law*, the self-help book by 50 Cent and best-selling 'power strategist' author Robert Green. But it is there. For the teenage Dizzee, Canary Wharf's blinking white light held the potential for an alien getaway, but it was also perhaps east London's version of the green light at the end of the dock in *The Great Gatsby*, a symbol of 'the orgastic future that year by year recedes before us', the tantalising dream of escape into a brighter tomorrow.

Slimzee, perhaps grime's greatest ever DJ, with his childhood friend Geeneus one of the founders of Rinse FM, tells me they had other dreams for the tower. 'We always used to look up at Canary Wharf, when we were growing up, and I wanted to go up to the top and put an aerial up there.' He pauses, amused at the obviously flawed teenage ambition. 'But you couldn't: it's got that sloping pyramid roof, it wouldn't work.'

Tinchy Stryder, who grew up in the Crossways Estate, says Canary Wharf dominated the skyline. 'When I was growing up you could see it everywhere. We felt like, "Oh, wow, do we get to go there one day?" It felt really close, but far away at the same time; like, it wasn't really anywhere for us to be. Everything felt fresher and cleaner than where we grew up; it felt like a different world. It felt like when you go there, you had to be on your best behaviour.' And he was right – the paved terrain around the skyscrapers was a paradigm for what have become known as 'POPS', privately owned public spaces: where private security guards can ask you to leave just based on looking at you. If Detroit techno captured the metronomic industrial rhythms of the city's car factories, grime's sonic palette describes the dystopian scene in millennial east London: the view from the decaying tower blocks down onto the de-cluttered spaces and privatised plazas of Canary Wharf – gleaming, futuristic, and glowering with menace.

When the BBC filmed a short profile of Dizzee to be broadcast as part of the 2003 Mercury Prize TV show, they caught him looking out of the window of the Crossways Estate with a less light-hearted attitude to the second City than he would display by the end of a decade, once he'd reached a state of monied grace: 'That is Canary Wharf,' Dizzee explained to the camera. 'It's in your face. It takes the piss. There are rich people moving in now, people who work in the City. You can tell they're not living the same way as us.'

New luxury flats and gated residential blocks were sprouting rapidly in the foothills of Canary Wharf throughout the 2000s; like Target, Dizzee was under no illusion about the lesson to be learned from Canary Wharf, malevolent or not. He was asked in the same BBC Mercury Prize interview what motivated him. He stared straight at the camera. 'Money motivates me. I'm motivated by money.' A year later, on the B-side to 'Dream, Is This Real', he summed up the ethic of the age:

We was kids, we was young, used to love having fun
Now we look up to guns, and the aim's only one:
Make money, every day, any how, any way
I tried to choose the legal way[10]

Those rich people who 'don't live the same way as us' (and don't always choose the legal way, either) arrived in droves, to the point that by the 2010 election, the Tory candidate for Poplar & Limehouse, Tim Archer, an HSBC banker on sabbatical from his office in Canary Wharf, was the bookies' favourite to win. It would have been the Conservatives' first victory in any Tower Hamlets seat in decades. Intrigued by this daring incursion of the banking set into their grimy new neighbourhood, I went on the campaign trail with Archer and his team. To the surprise of Conservative HQ, they failed to win Poplar & Limehouse. One of the main reasons for their defeat was that they couldn't get access to the new blocks of luxury flats; there were so many entry-phones and security gates they weren't able to canvass and recruit the very people who were supposed to be helping them win. It was almost as if the new arrivals didn't give a toss about the area they'd moved into. One of those new luxury blocks for the international super-rich, a development called Pan Peninsula, promises buyers 'a view that few will share', and that unlike the teenagers gazing up at Canary Wharf's blinking eye, residents will 'look up to no one'. The spiel on their website promises you will:

Inhabit a private universe. Where luxury apartments combine with a spa, a health club and a cinema to create an urban resort. Where service is tailored to need, and bends to individual will, effortlessly and invisibly. Where business and play happen high above London. Live at Pan Peninsula, exist in another world.

It perfectly articulates the mentality of Canary Wharf: where everything – and everyone – bends to the will of those who can afford it.

'Coming from where I come from, you didn't feel a part of London,' Dizzee told BBC London in 2010. This is the essence of what it means to be marginalised; on one level, your hometown brings you pride – there are numerous grime songs paying homage to London as a whole, rather than just the local neighbourhood – but you are excluded from its most famous parts, the parts the tourists see, the parts the middle classes negotiate with ease and confidence. In this sense, grime both *is* London, but also excluded from its official narrative, invisible in the face the city shows to the world.

To prove London wasn't all 'teacups, red telephone boxes and Buckingham Palace' as Dizzee put it on 'Graftin'', its music video was shot on top of, around, and beneath the three tower blocks of the Crossways Estate. The estate had been nicknamed 'the pride of Bow' when it was built in the 1970s, but bad upkeep of the buildings, untreated poverty and overcrowding meant that the alias did not stick around for long.

The video is shot almost entirely at night time, on grainy analogue film, the Crossways blocks looming over Dizzee's head, studded with occasional lights. It's a classic US rap-style 'hood video', with Dizzee surrounded by members of Ruff Sqwad, one of the most identifiably 'Bow' of crews from grime's golden age, and assorted other local teenagers. At times he delivers his bars with Canary Wharf's light blinking in the background. Twice, towards the end of the video, the director splices in a brief, split-second cut-shot of One Canada Square, like a subliminal message – a suggestion that subconsciously, Canary Wharf is always there, when you're living in and talking about 'the grime'.[11]

When vines grow on a hill facing the ocean they pick up the brine on the wind, and the taste of the grapes is suffused with a salty tang. When black British music was pouring, melting hot, into the crucible of a new genre in the early 2000s, New Labour were polling 57 per cent to the Tories' 25; it was the apex of the blind hubris that led to our current malaise: reckless, wild-west capitalism in Canary Wharf, and New Labour's carefully controlled vision of modernity and unapologetic social conservatism. This is the tang in the air: tough love, zero tolerance, ever-growing inequality, CCTVs, ASBOs, and an 'intensely relaxed' attitude to what was fuelling the economic bubble they said would never burst. In Dizzee Rascal's first ever interview, he described

New Labour's transformation of the inner city even as it was happening around him. He was only 17 years old in July 2002, sitting on a wall in Bow, with the third of Canary Wharf's three towers still being finished overhead. 'There has been bare change around here,' he observed. 'It's all about adapting. Like all the cameras, sly little cameras everywhere, more police, drugs, crime ... everything is changing.'[12]

'There will be no forgotten people in the Britain I want to build,' Tony Blair said in a photo call at London's notorious Aylesbury Estate a month after the 1997 general election, launching the government's 'new deal for communities'. British cities were riven by intense geographical inequalities between rich and poor neighbourhoods. New Labour's concern was that the latter were falling ever further behind the rest. 'Over the last two decades the gap between these worst estates and the rest of the country has grown. It has left us with a situation that no civilised country should tolerate,' Blair said in 1998.

Such estates had 'become no-go zones for some and no-exit zones for others', according to a government report published that year, which blamed this crisis of bad housing and social exclusion on mistakes by previous governments: in particular, the concentration of the poor and unemployed together in neighbourhoods where hardly anyone had a job. At the time, around 5 million households nationally were in council- or housing-association homes, and the maintenance backlog was upwards of £20 billion. New Labour's response was to advise councils to seek PFI funding, and to demolish many of the blocks altogether – too many of them were 'sinking ships', Blair told the *Daily Express*:

'Some estates are beyond rescue and will never be places where people want to live. That could mean moving people to new homes, levelling the site and using the land for something the public wants.' The idea that the public might want – first and above all – decent, affordable new social housing did not seem to enter into the conversation.

New Labour set up an Urban Task Force, and appointed a Regeneration Tsar, the architect Richard Rogers (aka Lord Rogers, aka Baron Rogers of Riverside – a man with as many alter-egos as a half-decent MC), who delivered a report in 1999 which would shape the future of London: *Towards an Urban Renaissance*. The report found that one in four people living in urban neighbourhoods thought their area had got worse in recent years, compared with only one in ten who said it had got better; and that unemployment levels in Britain's inner cities were more than double the national average. The Urban Renaissance strategy proposed to tackle inner-city poverty and 'sinking ships' by doing what has now become the norm, and a euphemistic byword for gentrification: they would 'create neighbourhoods with a mix of tenures and incomes, including opening up council housing to more of the population'. Rogers' report also called for faster Compulsory Purchase Orders (to get people out of blocks they wanted to demolish), 'streamlined' planning procedures, and greater access to PFI funds. Make it easier, make it quicker, and bring in the private sector.[13]

New Labour promised a 'lasting urban renaissance' to 'stem urban decline' brought on by the neglect of previous governments. They quoted Tsar Rogers: 'People make cities but cities make citizens,' which, like most New Labour slogans, sounded clever without saying anything of substance. The strategy was framed around the goal of arresting and reversing middle-class flight to the suburbs: 'encouraging people to remain in, and move back into, our major towns and cities' would be central to the Labour plan, said another report in 2000. These were complex, big government strategies – the Urban Task Force made no fewer than 105 recommendations: one of them was estate renewal, using the private finance initiative. From the outset, New Labour's plan had been to 'modernise' (or indeed, dismantle) the welfare state as it stood, to introduce private finance into everything on the basis that, as the Home Secretary David Blunkett said in 2001, 'government could never do it all'.

Not everyone was impressed. Two academics at the annual Royal Geographical Society conference called New Labour's Urban Renaissance strategy a 'gentrifiers' charter'. Leading academic expert Loretta Lees agreed, and suggested the strategy might be called 'the cappuccino cave-in'. The Blairite view was that government had lost control of

Britain's inner cities under Tory rule, who had made urban environ-ments uninviting and unloved.[14] Their proposed solution was to encour-age the middle classes to move back into the inner city, 'drawn by a lifestyle where home, work and leisure are interwoven within a single neighbourhood'. Rogers' report envisioned new middle-class enclaves, populated by people with more time 'to devote to leisure, culture and education', wealthier communities that are more mobile and flexible – freer. 'In the twenty-first century, it is the skilled worker, as well as the global company, who will be footloose. Cities must work hard to attract and retain both.'

Local and national politicians, when they talk about gentrification, often speak of the need to create 'balanced' or 'mixed' communities. Mixed communities sound good, don't they? They sound diverse. They sound like they would welcome everyone, and that everyone would benefit from the mixing – by class, by race, by age. No fair-minded liberal would advocate for the opposite: because the opposite is an enclave, or a ghetto. And that's exactly how – when you push them to reveal themselves – architects of gentrification characterise the inner London that is being rapidly dismantled: a series of social-housing ghet-toes, holding back the people living in them – held back not because they are poor, but because they are surrounded by other people who are poor. They're a bad influence on each other. Bring in the middle classes, and everyone will learn from one another, and thrive. The problem with all this, the deception buried in the rhetoric, is that urban regeneration is almost always a zero-sum game: for some people to 'come back' to the inner city, others have to leave.

A decade later, I asked a leading property developer whether building blocks of luxury flats in previously poor inner-city areas was the essence of gentrification. 'Hopefully we are getting blended communities,' he replied. 'In the poor parts of London where we've been working in the past, they have been – and I use this term politely – but they have been social enclaves. No one buys homes there, because your money will probably depreciate. But that's changing. It's not gentrification, it's just becoming a more balanced community.'[15]

In one sense, New Labour and grime should have been allies from the start. The elevation and intermingling of culture and business was integral to the Urban Renaissance strategy: regenerated, modernised cities would be created in part by monetising art and culture. The nature of work was changing faster in London than anywhere else in the country, as the last of the factories disappeared. Following the flag-draped nineties nonsense around 'Cool Britannia' that was synonymous with the early years of New Labour, their Cultural Manifesto for the 1997 election was called 'Create The Future'. 'Creativity' became a crucial signifier of Blair's entire political project, and the New Labour vision of modernity.[16] Treating culture as a business connected New Labour to their Thatcherite predecessors, and this 'creative' enterprise culture was bound up with urban regeneration, in part by stimulating tourism. As Britain's de-industrialisation rapidly continued, New Labour was determined to 'modernise' everything – from the Labour Party itself, to the NHS, to the workforce, to architecture – and free the party from its electoral reliance on the industrial working class, 'a class rapidly disappearing into the thin air of the knowledge economy', as Robert Hewison put it in *Cultural Capital*.

'Most of us make our money from thin air,' wrote Charles Leadbetter, a friend of Mandelson and Blair, capturing the spirit of the times – as music switched from heavy pieces of wax and shiny plastic discs to the intangibles of mp3s, and capitalism moved on from buying physical products with coins and notes to buying and selling complex, abstract 'financial products' like collateralised debt obligations, futures and derivatives. By 2007, the character Jez in the sitcom *Peep Show* would be summing it up in more day-to-day language: 'I'm a creative. We don't make steam engines out of pig iron in this country anymore, yeah? We hang out, we fuck around on the PlayStation, we have some Ben & Jerry's, that's how everyone makes their money now.'[17]

But even while New Labour were placing culture and creativity on a pedestal and garlanding it with £50 notes, other government changes were making it harder than ever for working-class people to develop careers out of their creative impulses and talents. In March 1998, changes to unemployment benefits that came in with the New Deal made it much harder for artists to live on the dole while honing and improving their craft – a part of the welfare state that had historically been a lifeline for working-class musicians. The *NME* ran a cover story about the threat to grassroots music, arts and culture these changes posed, with the banner, 'Ever get the feeling you've been cheated?' Inside, Jarvis Cocker recounted that, without the dole during the eighties, Pulp never would have made it as far as the nineties, and their vastly better and more popular albums. There were countless other musicians, artists and writers like him. Free education, a strong welfare state and affordable housing had given working-class creativity the space to breathe in the post-war years. For New Labour, it was too much like a hand-out: money for nothing.

The grime kids went without those state subsidies – but still never succumbed to the rampant individualism of their neighbours in Canary Wharf, or their political masters. For all that we should celebrate their independent, DIY spirit and sheer self-motivated perseverance – teenagers with nothing, making something more dazzling and millennial-modern than anyone could ever have imagined – they did so with the help of youth clubs, school teachers, and a collective, communitarian spirit that was being pummelled by a government determined to dismantle it, in the name of remaking the inner city.

TWO

IN THE ROOTS

The irony of grime being derided as antisocial by its critics – all that clatter, hostility and bad attitude – is that it has always been community music: invented and developed collectively and collaboratively, by people whose lives and roots are deeply entwined, and who made music because it was the sociable thing to do. Community can mean a lot of different things, but whichever way you draw the diagram, grime emerged from a spider's web of intergenerational influences, schoolmates, neighbours, friends, family, and people who knew people – from school, from the estate, from the local area.

The more you dig into its past, the more you realise grime's social networks precede the music entirely, not just by years but by generations. Grime is black music (even if it's not always made by black people), and its roots spread across London, and the world. While east London has for centuries been one of the most multicultural parts of the country, and a first port of call for new arrivals, the generation of Caribbean migrants who began arriving in Britain after the *Empire Windrush* docked in the Thames in 1948 tended to settle in Notting Hill in the west, and Brixton in the south. But with east London depopulating rapidly in the post-war decades, owing to decay, bombing, slum clear-

Notting Hill Carnival, 1999

ances and degeneration, housing became relatively cheap. Manufacturing jobs in places like the Dagenham Ford car plant, and Tate and Lyle, Unilever and ITT around the docks, encouraged newly arriving Caribbean nationals, now British citizens, to look to the east.

In the tightly bound geography of working-class inner London of the 1960s, 70s and 80s, many of the grime kids' parents, and in some cases grandparents, knew each other before the kids even arrived – and as a result some of east London's most important foundational MCs actually played together as children. D Double E's dad went to school with Jammer's dad. Jammer's dad and Footsie's dad were at Sunday school together. Footsie's dad was in a reggae band in the 1980s with Wiley's dad, and taught young Richard Cowie Jr how to play the drums.

'We've known each other *before* before,' Footsie says.[1] A ridiculous number of MCs, DJs, producers and key behind-the-scenes figures met as children, at school or a playscheme; or playing football, or in someone's aunt's house, or at a party, or night fishing in the Hertford Union Canal, between Wiley's estate and Victoria Park. Roll Deep's first paid job was working for Wiley's dad's patty factory (they were subsequently fired when Richard Cowie Sr caught them having a food fight). 'It's so deep,' Footsie continued. 'Sometimes I think I'm not doing nothing special, other than carrying on what was already done.'

Grime's lineage is suffused with this sense of kinship that precedes any sense of desire to make music – of being mates first, and lyrical sparring partners second. It's easy to romanticise, but not easy to romanticise well: Kano's nostalgic 2016 album which signalled his return to grime, *Made in the Manor*, does so brilliantly, telling sincere and evocative stories about his youth in his childhood home, 69 Manor Road in Plaistow, E15. On 'T-Shirt Weather In The Manor', Kano vividly describes multigenerational summer barbecues where the kids are listening to UK garage titans MJ Cole and Heartless Crew, and 'the olders want some [reggae singer] Dennis Brown', a prelapsarian community idyll, before fame, beefs and adulthood came along and complicated everything.

That kinship was formed, in part, out of marginality. Crazy Titch says he knew brothers Mak 10 and Marcus Nasty when they were children because 'there was like three black families in Plaistow when I was growing up, and theirs was one of them'.[2] In parts of inner London with more substantial black communities, grime's originators were bound through pre-internet social networks formed by geography and background, by a sense of being marginalised by poverty, or racism. 'It was a nice little community here,' Kano recalled, smiling, in a short documentary accompanying *Made in the Manor*. 'There was definitely a feeling that we weren't supposed to be shit, or have shit, or become anything great. An underlying attitude that people grow up with, from around here.'[3] Those narrow horizons enforced by poverty keep people down, but they bind people together, too – and when the kids at those barbecues started making music, by themselves, for each other, those bonds provided the foundations for something powerful, and lasting.

Sometimes grime's ancestral links didn't become apparent till years later. Footsie recently told his dad who Wiley's dad was, and he responded that they'd played together as children. 'I was there with Will, running around as kids, I just don't really remember it.'[4]

Sitting in a pub beer garden in Bethnal Green in 2017 with Roony Keefe, creator of the seminal *Risky Roadz* DVD series, he told a story about Devlin, who he first filmed for his DVD in 2006, when he was a teenage MC from Barking, still only 16:

'I've known Devs all these years but … my dad went to this funeral last year, and he was talking to one of his old mates there, and he said, "Oh, how's your boy?", and he said, "Yeah all right, still doing the music." My dad was like, "Oh yeah, what music does he do?" Turns out my dad grew up with Devlin's dad in Hackney, they've been mates all these years. But we didn't know that until last year. It's a really tight-knit kind of thing.' Devlin wrote lyrics to describe this story of their dads drinking together in their favourite Hackney pub, before its gentrification-make-over, in a freestyle for Keefe's YouTube channel: 'Oi Roony, do me a favour and let 'em all know we've been around from day: like mine and your old mans, down the Kenton pub before it sold grub, just beer and grams. Funny how it all turns out … damn.'[5]

Wiley would watch his dad's VHS copies of famous Jamaican sound-clash events like Sting, where rival sound-systems (with a team of engineers, hosts and selectors) would compete by offering up their biggest dubplates – also known as dubs, or white labels, because the vinyl was freshly cut from a new recording, and specially made for the occasion, rather than released to the general public by a record company. These did not have a sleeve or any artwork, just the naked simplicity of the record, its title inscribed on the white label in marker pen.

'I sometimes heard my dad listening to Sugar Hill and the Gang,' Wiley recalled in 2016, '[there was] some American rap. But it was minimal compared to all the reggae.'

Wiley had already learned to play the drums, and began to try and copy some of his dad's reggae jams, using a Yamaha CX5, 'the one with the big stick-in cartridge thing on top. I would go on there and see if I could play what he had just been playing.' Reggae suffused the general atmosphere that the grime generation grew up in, tracing direct ancestral links from Britain's pre-acid house reggae culture, some of it imported from the Caribbean, some of it created by black Britons. South London grime and dancehall MC Doctor – known for his 'yardie flow' – was managed by one of London's most famous sound-systems, Saxon. Dreadlocked grime icon Jammer – a stalwart behind the scenes, a pioneering producer and a zany presence on the mic – grew up in a house immersed in this culture: his parents ran the ELRICS (East London Rastafarian Information and Community Services), which helps Rastafarians with housing, and incorporates work with young people (Jammer himself has spoken at schools and colleges, and been involved in their mentoring programmes). Iconic black British dub poet Benjamin Zephaniah was a family friend. The connections go on: Spyro's dad is St Lucian reggae singer Nereus Joseph, Scorcher's dad is jungle MC Mad P from early nineties crew Top Buzz.

It's not just a family connection, or an abstract component of the musical bloodline: grime echoes its Jamaican reggae heritage in its structure, in its tropes, in its slang, in the way it's performed, and stylistically: particularly harking back to the 'fast chat' reggae style of the likes of Smiley Culture, a black British MC who made it into the charts two decades before Dizzee Rascal did the same. Grime is a direct product of Caribbean sound-system culture. The legacy is more implicit than explicit a lot of the time, but it's there in so much of what is integral to grime: in the dubplate white label culture of exclusive new tracks, in the competition of rival sound-systems or crews, in the MC responding live to the selector or DJ's choices of instrumental tracks, or riddims. It is there in the song structures, in the sense they often do not have clearly demarcated structures: rather than the verse-bridge-chorus-verse architecture of the traditional three-minute pop song, MCs begin their careers 'riding the riddim', usually a steady tempo from beginning to end, that only changes when the next one is faded in.

Academic Nabeel Zuberi makes the point that MCs are middle points between the music and the audience – they have to ride the rhythm but also 'conduct the choir' on the dancefloor, and move the crowd to respond. In this sense the MC's voice is 'a social voice that includes the voice of others', Zuberi writes.[6] The performance function is more complex than simply, 'I'm going to talk, and you're going to listen'.

There's a unique and productive cultural tension at the heart of grime that comes directly from its inner-London geography, of working-class cultures from the African and Caribbean diasporas intermingling with working-class London slang and culture, rubbing up against each other, borrowing, collaborating and adapting freely and fruitfully. It's a tension familiar to fans of 1980s British reggae, where the duality is referred to as 'Cockney and Yardie', taken from Peter Metro and Dominic's 1987 tune of the same name. In this song white reggae MC Dominic, born in west London, and black MC Peter Metro, born in Kingston (Jamaica, not Surrey), trade and translate slang from Jamaica ('yardie') and east London ('cockney').[7] Smiley Culture's 1984 single 'Cockney Translation' had performed the same ludic act of cultural elaboration, and become a surprise hit.

Grime has often been described as dazzlingly innovative, alien, groundbreaking, avant-garde, and it is all those things; one factor which explains its newness, perhaps, is not just the individual and collective daring of its creators, but the exact point at which it arrived: in a new millennium, from mostly second- or third-generation black Britons who were just estranged enough from their cultural roots in the Caribbean, or Africa, or both, and far enough along the lineage of unique British dance styles – acid house, jungle, drum 'n' bass, UK garage – that they could draw from them all, while never being too in thrall to any of them. Just the right amount of respect for what had gone before, and just the right amount of healthy disregard for it, too – a mingling of conflicting and cooperating identities.[8] 'This is something new for your ears,' runs the chorus of Roll Deep's 2007 track 'Something New', 'you ain't heard beats or spitters like this: no American accents, straight English.'

Grime lyrics and vernacular – grime grammar, even – draws on a wide range of roots and influences, but Caribbean English is unsurprisingly prominent, along with grime's own neologisms, cockney rhyming slang and other pieces of what is known to linguists as MLE (Multicultural London English). There is a minority of grime MCs who use what's known as a 'yardie flow', a proudly Jamaican, often ragga-influenced, gruff, patois-heavy delivery, but a more musical one too – and some, like Riko Dan, who switch in and out of cockney and yardie as they feel the rhythm demands. Meeting cheerful Pay As U Go MC Maxwell D in a pub in Peckham recently, he lists off the MCs who would deliver 'that extra bashment, yard vibe' in the grime scene: 'There's Riko Dan, myself, Jamakabi, Flow Dan, Armour, Doctor, Durrty Goodz, God's Gift ... but the top MCs in grime were not dancehall, people like Wiley and Dizzee. My style, the dancehall reggae style, grime doesn't sit on it, the way it's meant to, because it's an English way. It actually helped me develop another style, because I started doing less of the bashment style and more of the English style, because I realised the kids, the black kids, weren't really in tune with their culture no more, it was like an English culture. In my opinion even garage was more dancehall-orientated than grime, it was still rootified. But when grime came along, Dizzee and Wiley, they changed the lyrical style.' He barks an impression of Dizzee's halting, staccato flow: "'Take that Nokia! Get that, what!" It was like rap, but an English vibe.'

While the roots of grime's vocal style and a great deal of its slang and idioms travelled across the Atlantic with the *Windrush* migrants, it's a telling part of grime's unique flavour that its accent is so often London English – especially as 'UK hip-hop' (a genre in itself, distinct from grime) has often borrowed not just the genre tropes – turntablism, a fetishisation of 'realness' and roots – from the United States, but its accent too.[9] 'I thought it would be heavy to sound English,' Dizzee Rascal told *Sound on Sound* magazine in 2004. 'I listen to a lot of US hip-hop, and I know that is how they talk in real life, but a lot of UK hip-hop doesn't do that. My influences are from jungle, and many of those artists still keep their English accent, and I respected that.'

Indeed, some of Dizzee's biggest early singles, tracks like 'Fix Up, Look Sharp', 'Stand Up Tall' and 'Jus' A Rascal' were not only the grimier precursors to hits like 'Bonkers', that made him Britain's first black pop superstar, but in their boisterous, playful style, they also reproduced a kind of east London barrow-boy charisma, even perhaps music hall in its sensibility. How many Top 20 hits can claim to have opened with a battle-cry of 'Oiiiiii!' and a *Carry On*-style cackle? Too few, certainly. Dizzee's delivery was so English, in fact, that it actually tripped him up on the road to international success. When he toured the US for the first time in 2004, appearing on Los Angeles' famous rap station Power 106 with DJ Felli Fel, he spat his yelping, double-time flow over classic US rap beats from Brooklyn's M.O.P. All was well until the end of the slot, when, chatting with Felli Fel on air, there was a telling obstacle: the DJ could literally not understand Dizzee's accent. He asked Dizzee to repeat the name of his debut album no fewer than three times in a row. Eventually Dizzee, sounding slightly exasperated, just spelled it out: 'B-O-Y ...'

First-wave grime MC Bruza, also from east London, is the name that first comes to mind for 'cockney grime': for his especially boisterous delivery, frequent use of cockney rhyming slang, and proud claim that he is 'brutal and British'. And then there are the white MCs: crews like

OT Crew, from Barking, created what you could call 'geezer grime' – MCs like Syer B and Dogzilla, repping 'Barking and Dogenham', had some underground success with tunes charting their heartfelt quests for the finer things in life: 'Where's All The Beer?' and 'Where's The Money?'. Dogzilla is one of those overlooked first-wave MCs who may not be to everyone's taste, but he is evidence that, in the early days, distinctive voices, flows and vocal styles abounded on pirate radio. Dogzilla flipped the MC's typical self-aggrandisement to a new level of lyrical honesty, too: 'I'm obese, white, I smoke too much, I'm a bum, I'm a drunk … I live on strictly takeaways … I like girls in PVC, I support West Ham, UFC … here's my fat white arse, I bet it makes you laugh.' The pinnacle of white-boy geezer grime was a track called 'Straight Cockney' by an MC called Phenomenon, who it seems no one has heard of since, but whose legend lives on with over a million views on YouTube, where comments mock him to this day.

US rap has had numerous discussions of the phenomenon of the 'wigga', and the disproportionate media prominence and industry support given, Elvis Presley-style, to white rappers from Vanilla Ice to Eminem, by an at best cynical and at worst racist music industry. But grime has seen relatively little discussion of racial tension or cultural appropriation. It might be that the genre's long languishing on the underground meant that, if you were a white DJ or MC taking part in the scene, your participation was implicitly understood to be out of authentic love for the music, rather than calculated profiteering or co-option – the same goes for Mr Wong, a much-loved first-wave MC and producer, the self-described 'rude boy Chinese wigga'. It might be that the relative lack of racial segregation in Britain's council estates and poorer areas, compared to the black ghettoised geography of 'the projects' in America's big cities, had something to do with making race less of an issue. It might simply be that – while the likes of Geeneus and Slimzee were instrumental from day one – the biggest talents and cross-over stars produced in grime's early days, for several years, were all black British: Dizzee Rascal, Wiley, Kano, Shystie, Lethal Bizzle. With the exception of Lady Sovereign in 2005 – always a bit of an outsider to the scene in any case – and some years later, Devlin, the few white MCs weren't the ones getting record deals.

There is something utopian in grime's collectivist origins, of 'kids hanging out together making something they enjoy', as Jammer described it to me recently, and this is a rich part of its musical roots too. Academic Jeremy Gilbert has said that the relative weakness of neo-Nazi street thugs in British cities in the nineties, while such groups were on the rise elsewhere in Europe, owes a lot to the 'cosmopolitan hybridity' blooming (and booming) out of the speaker stacks and pirate-radio aerials where hardcore, jungle and UK garage were created. State-led multiculturalism takes the form of abstract government initiatives and directives, more progressive school curricula and better community and arts funding – and these things are all essential, and should be done right – but in terms of creating a more harmonious society, its impact looks fairly tepid compared to what young, working-class people of different ethnic backgrounds cooked up together on London's council estates. In fact, to tweak James Meek's pessimism about our class-riven, divided city, where the ingredients are laid out side by side, not touching, not mixing, perhaps the solitary demographic where multiculturalism is an organic, lived experience, rather than an idealised illusion, is in young, working-class communities where schools, youth clubs, estates and later workplaces make a shared and convivial culture not just realistic, but the unforced reality.

'I was one of the only white kids on my estate growing up,' recalled Nyke from white UK garage and grime duo Milkymans (humorously named, they explain, by a Caribbean bouncer, surprised to see them at a mostly black nightclub). 'The Irish community had moved out, and me and Nikki grew up in the Afro-Caribbean communities in Peckham and Stockwell – so I lived between Ghanaians and Jamaicans; if I couldn't smell fufu, I could hear Capleton blasting. My radiator used to shake off the wall! And even if I didn't know what some of the artists meant, in a kind of black culture context, I was still feeling the vibrations of the music from young. I remember I used to wash my mum's car, and I'd be blaring Kool FM – if I think back to it now, I'm lucky it was a noisy estate, because I love jungle, but that was *noise*. Like that was not easy listening.' He laughed. 'But when you're a 13- to 14-year-old obnoxious, rebellious kid, that's all you want to hear. It's kinda the equivalent of someone listening to really dark heavy metal. That was our version of that.'

As with punk's extensive late-seventies love affair with reggae, and the 'two tone' ska of the early 1980s, jungle saw urban multiculturalism manifested in youthful conviviality. It channelled a mixture of cultural influences into a novel, fiercely experimental form, created by a rich ethnic mix of producers, DJs and promoters, and enjoyed by a similarly diverse assembly of ravers. It transcended the difference in junglists' backgrounds, but it did not forget those origins – something you can hear in the music, with soul and ragga samples and fierce basslines high in the mix.

In a 1994 BBC jungle documentary, UK Apache, the MC behind the superlative jungle anthem 'Original Nuttah', highlighted the power these styles had in forging a sense of belonging for second- or third-generation immigrants. Growing up as a working-class child of an Indian-South African mother and Iraqi father in Tooting in the 1970s and 80s, when the National Front were a menacing presence on the streets of south London, Apache made friends with kids of Jamaican heritage and went to reggae sound-system dances with them in some of the same estates in Battersea from which So Solid Crew would later emerge. He told the BBC documentary crew:

'Jungle, because it's from England, I can really relate to it, it's important to me because I'm born here. I'm from England, and London, and nobody can tell me I'm not from here. Once I was ashamed of being British, but it's like the jungle's drawn me back into my roots, where *I'm* from. Although my parents are – I'm half Arab, half Asian, African – I can relate to those countries only up to a point. When I talk to my children, I say, "You're born in England, be proud of it," and don't let nobody tell you different, no BNP or anything like that.'

There is another key cultural lineage to grime that is too easily overlooked. Long before Afrobeats (with an 's') and its rap, R&B and bashment hybrids made their way into popular consciousness in the UK, the children of African migrants to the UK, in particular from Ghana and Nigeria, were making grime, and slipping in references to this heritage. Among others, Dizzee Rascal, Tinchy Stryder and Lethal Bizzle all have Ghanaian parents; there were musical links from London to West Africa too – genre-hopping producer, singer and MC Donaeo and grime-adjacent rapper Sway were performing big shows in Accra and collaborating with Ghanaian rapper Sarkodie in the late 2000s. Skepta, in particular, made it clear in his most well-known early radio and rave bars, that he was 'Joseph Junior Adenuga, from Nigeria, not St Lucia – big lips, African hooter'. This didn't preclude an upbringing in which he obsessed over Ninjaman and Jamaican sound-clash culture, but it coexisted with the West African music he heard at home. By the time I interviewed him for a second time, in 2015, black British youth culture was changing – a diasporic shift in emphasis away from Caribbean dominance had been slowly taking place in the UK. 'When I was a yute, to be called African was a diss,' he recalled, sadly. 'At school the African kids used to lie and say they were Jamaican. So when I first came in the game and I'm saying lyrics like "I make Nigerians proud of their tribal scars/my bars make you push up your chest like bras", that was a big deal for me.'

Even saying his full name in his lyrics was an act of defiant pride with a very personal context. 'In school, when a teacher would try and read my name, as soon as she goes to try and say it, I'd be trying to say it first, to stop the embarrassment of her not being able to pronounce it. Eventually I grew up. I remember one day when I was about fifteen, my mum told me, "Junior, your name *means* something – just because your name isn't some standard English name." I remember going back into school and it started to power me up. Bare self-hate vibes was pushed into me as a kid at school, trust me. That's why it makes me happy to see all these kids today just love Afrobeats, because since the start I've been trying to fucking fight this ting, for them to be able to stand up.' He mentioned 'Sweet Mother', his single released in 2007 for Mother's Day, a reworking of Prince Nico Mbarga's 1970s hit of the same name, an early pointer to the way black British music might be going next, with Nico's sweetly sung, Nigerian-accented chorus sitting alongside Skepta's grimy London beats and MCing.

The 'Black Atlantic'[10] pathways between Africa, Britain, America and the Caribbean have seen cultural exchange, revision and refinement in numerous iterations, but it should be no surprise, given their histories, that black British MC culture has evolved along very different lines to American hip-hop culture. South London rappers Krept and Konan, schoolmates of Stormzy, are situated very much on the rap side of the rap-grime divide, in terms of the slower, hip-hop tempo of their beats and rhymes: and yet, they explained to me, there wasn't that much of a divide at all – that just as black Britishness embraced its diverse roots, it also produced a family of different, coexisting genres. I'd been sent by the *Observer* to ask them what separated British microphone culture from its American equivalent. Konan didn't hesitate in saying that it was essentially 'everything' – fairly or not, he viewed American hip-hop culture and identity as monolithic in a way black British culture never was:

'What's different? Our accents, our lifestyle, our culture. When we was in America we'd say "Where are you from?" and they'd say "America". But over here if someone said where are you from you might say "Jamaica", or "Africa" or something else – maybe "British" and adding something else. We bring different cultures to our music, and different slang, a different way of doing things. And there's different-sounding beats: in their clubs there's a lot of just hip-hop, in our clubs you'll have house, dance, Afrobeats, bashment, you've got a blend of styles.'

Jungle was the teenage apprenticeship for the pioneers of grime. They snuck into the raves while still underage just to hear it, persuaded mums and dads to let them go with older brothers or sisters, obsessed about it on pirate radio (usually Hackney's Kool FM, the leading jungle station), made tapes in their bedrooms and swapped them at school and college, and through that shared community forged friendships that would last into the end of the nineties, to the evolution of 2-step garage and later their own sound. The family tree is robust enough that many of grime's first wave of MCs started out in music spitting over jungle – it was their first experiences in writing rhymes, performing in a dance. D Double E started out MCing at jungle raves aged only 14. Wiley did too, and Riko Dan. There are recordings now on YouTube of the three of them spitting at jungle's frenetic tempo – these items themselves a beautiful low-fidelity chronology of the last 20 years of technology and urban music: an illegal and unofficial pirate-radio broadcast, recorded onto a tape cassette, stored in an attic somewhere presumably, and then years later linked up via a cable to a computer, the audio converted to mp3, then uploaded to YouTube. Many of the personnel playing jungle at house parties, raves and on radio in SS (Silver Storm) Crew – the likes of Wiley, Maxwell D and Target – would go on to form seminal garage-into-grime crew Pay As U Go Cartel.

I remember listening to a Ruff Sqwad show on Rinse FM a few years later, in 2005, in which, for the first hour and 45 minutes of their two-hour set, they followed their usual formula: DJ Scholar beginning with a few US R&B and hip-hop (vocal) tracks, followed by half an hour of the biggest grime vocal tracks of the day, and then around the hour mark, switching to brand new grime dubplates and instrumentals, for the gathered MCs to spit their bars over. And then, for the final 15 minutes, the MCs, still only around the age of 20, MCs who would have been about ten when jungle was in its prime, switched up the pace for a final, hectic flurry of junglist ske-be-de-bi spitting. The overwhelming sensation you get from listening to them passing the mic to have a go is just sheer, infectious joy, as they fall about laughing.

The affection most of grime's foundational figures have for jungle, then and now, is something to behold. Grime may have come directly from UK garage, and have mutated from it, but its creators speak of jungle like a first love, or a first high, an experience that will be refined, but in some wistful sense, never bettered. 'Jungle,' Wiley sighed fondly, when I interviewed him for the fifth time, in 2016. 'That's my favourite. You know jungle, it's the only genre that didn't get exploited? Because the people weren't dumb – they just didn't care! A few went to labels, got money, and realised, "You know what? Majors are a waste of time – I was earning more money on the white label." They learned that trick, very early. But then it wasn't an MC-led thing, from the point of the business. It is in the rave, but when it came to the records it wasn't MC-led; it was more producer-controlled. So that's why they weren't gassed [carried away].' The implication is that the purity and community of the underground scene were never sullied by the ego of MCs-turned-superstars – never capitalised on unduly by the suits from the industry, or the biggest names from the scene.

For Skepta, his musical youth had been primarily 'reggae in abundance' – the likes of Barrington Levy, Gregory Isaacs and Half Pint – and that was followed by an instinctive and deep-rooted sense of connection, or ownership, to the frenetic ragga jungle playing out of cars and pirate radio stations in nineties Tottenham. 'When I first heard jungle, I understood it immediately,' he recalled in 2015, as we sat parked in his car in Palmers Green, his eyes glazing over with stoned awe. 'To make something this bless sound this hype was just sick. I think it resonated with me because of the reggae basslines, but also because I'm British and I'm around dancey music – in Europe our ears are set towards like, high synthy sounds and fast speeds. We're accustomed to that.'

It's not a controversial point that deep in its spirit, jungle is grime's true antecedent. Its aesthetics – a hard, scowling, dark side that is counterpointed by ludic, transcendent expressions of joy – were essential to the mutation of UK garage as it became grime. 'Coming from jungle, you're always going to be a little more into the darker stuff,' recalled Troy 'A Plus' Miller, describing the garage days as a kind of stylistic interregnum. 'Even though you like the light and the happy – you and your crew out in a rave, all the girls are here, we're all having a nice time – you're still going to lean towards things that are a bit darker.'

A Plus's friend and founder of Rinse FM, Geeneus, is unequivocal about the power of that junglist passion; that passion would lead them to a collective mistake that would help change the course of British music. He told a podcast in 2016 about the influential UK garage instrumental 'Cape Fear', a welcome (re)turn to the dark side, which the Pay As U Go MCs could spit over with the speed and aggression of jungle lyricism. It wasn't the way things were done in UK garage. 'I was the last person to get involved in [UK garage], because I loved jungle so much,' he recalled. 'We started getting involved in it, but we was bringing along what we learned from jungle into the garage. But we got it completely wrong. And because we got it completely wrong, we ended up with grime. We thought we was making garage: getting garage beats like Cape Fear, and putting MCs on them, and they were spitting their heart out.' On other occasions, to fit the Bow boys' lingering passion for super-fast jungle with the contemporary 140bpm sound of 2-step, Slimzee would play Mampi Swift's jungle track 'Jaws' at the wrong speed, at 33 instead of 45rpm, and the MCs would spit on it.

They had, Geeneus continued, 'railroaded' the UK garage scene 'into something completely different. Where they're bubbling along having a nice time in the party, looking nice, we've come in with tracksuits on, spitting lyrics everywhere, MCs everywhere, me and Slimzee just DJing for the MCs really.'[11]

As summaries of UK garage go, 'bubbling along having a nice time in the party' is pretty spot-on. The subject matter of the tunes – love, sex and relationships – narrated in smooth, soulful vocals from an even balance of male and female singers, reflected a much more grown-up, stylish swagger and refinement than had been seen in the wild days of British rave music previously, from acid house through jungle and drum 'n' bass. It was as if, with the nineties drawing to a close, rave itself was moving beyond adolescent zeal and striving for a kind of adulthood. Garage as a form did not begin in the UK, but the US, and as Simon Reynolds records in *Energy Flash*, to begin with, in the mid-nineties, garage in the UK had 'slavishly' followed US production style. Then the junglists 'entered the fray', and created a 'distinctly British hybrid strain that merged house's slinky panache with jungle's rude-bwoy exuberance'. The UK underground brought that edge, even as it was swapping a tracksuit for smart shoes and an ironed shirt.

Indeed, maturity was reflected in the aspirational dress codes in UK garage clubs, where shirts and shoes (no trainers!) would often be a compulsory component of the door policy, and where the narcotics of choice were champagne and cocaine – even while the music's primary creators and ravers were from the same humble inner London backgrounds as the junglists before them, and the grime kids who would follow. No hats no hoods! Only two school children may enter the rave at any one time.

It's a tension that was a rich seam for British underground dance music more than once: the wicked and the divine, the debonair and the scuzzy, rubbing up against one another. In the first two years of the millennium, UK garage was being stretched in two directions at once – a process which is always likely to make something break in the middle. On the one hand, the poppy, commercial end was thriving, and producing numerous hits: singer-MCs like Craig David, Ms Dynamite and Daniel Bedingfield became stars, and tunes like Sweet Female Attitude's 'Flowers' and DJ Luck and MC Neat's 'With A Little Bit Of Luck' were ubiquitous.

But something was pulling hard in the opposite musical direction – to the dark side. On this side of UK garage's personality split, mostly male MCs dominated instead of crooning singers; the instrumentals conjured not a glitzy VIP area but a low-lit council estate. It was inner London's millennial aspiration and promise versus the grim reality that persisted when those aspirations failed to materialise. Darker garage that was built around breakbeats and accompanied by jungle's hectic lyrical energy was thriving on pirate radio, while the more established, soulful tracks dominated the charts and high-street clubs. When catchy, sample-heavy novelty records like DeeKline's 'I Don't Smoke' started to take off in the garage clubs, and the likes of Heartless Crew, So Solid Crew and Pay As U Go Cartel started to have hits themselves, the divisions deepened. For the old guard, there was a 'last days of disco' feel to the new millennium: the resplendent purity of one of the greatest periods in British music history having to come to terms with its own looming mortality – these were the best days of our lives, and this is how it ends? With some hyperactive teenagers chatting about guns and drug dealing, instead of a smooth, 2-step shuffle and some sweetly sung love songs? With a song that samples the *Casualty* theme tune and a Guy Ritchie film? No wonder they were upset.

Bizarrely, the tensions between the old guard and the new wave came to a head in the unlikely context of the UK garage committee meetings. It sounds somehow reminiscent of the kind of sit-down familiar from *The Sopranos*, where representatives of the mafia families would thrash out their differences, negotiate and cut deals. A similar thing had happened in the jungle scene too, when prominent figures had attempted – in some cases, successfully – to blacklist General Levy's raucous party-starting anthem 'Incredible', after he had claimed to be 'runnin' jungle'. The substance of the tension at the turn of the millennium was that the new guard were sullying garage's grown-up reputation, both musically and in terms of the rebellious gangster pose they sometimes presented to the world; they didn't like the chat about gats and violence, and they didn't like the exuberant use of novelty samples either. The straw that broke the camel's back was Oxide and Neutrino's 'Bound 4 Da Reload' going to number one in May 2000, and 'I Don't Smoke' following it in to number 11, after months as an underground smash. Prominent gatekeeper DJs like Norris 'Da Boss' Windross and Radio 1's The Dreem Team refused to play either record. 'I don't like many of those records of that style,' DJ Spoony from the Dreem Team told the *Guardian* at the time. 'I like music with more soul and groove in it.' When So Solid Crew appeared on their Radio 1 show that winter, the atmosphere was frosty to say the least: 'Give the youth of nowadays a chance to bust through that barrier,' Romeo told them, 'cos you lot have been there for so long, and it's our time now.'

In the meetings, there was some discussion of whether the darker, 'breakbeat' garage would also attract more undesirable elements to the clubs. 'I was always bearing the brunt of it,' recalls Maxwell D. '"Who's this crew, Pay As U Go, talking all this gangster stuff? We don't want them in the dances, they're thugs, they're this, they're that ..." They really didn't want to give us the mic.' (Unfortunately for him, Maxwell found himself on the sharp end of exactly this kind of condescension and obstruction again, years later, when he made a light-hearted funky house tune about his mobile phone called 'Blackberry Hype' – the kids loved it, the grown-ups, less so.)

For Matt Mason, editor of *RWD* magazine from 2000–05, who also DJed on garage station Freek FM, the combative, transitional period was exciting, even if the end result was inevitable: 'There was a real sense the new guys were doing something different, that a chasm was opening up in garage. It's interesting because it really crept up. First there was just some really weird records, I think from about 1999. There was the Groove Chronicles tunes first, like okay, that's different, and some MJ Cole records, like … all right, some different thoughts have gone into this. And then there was a record by Dem 2, under the alias US Alliance, called "All I Know", and "Da Grunge" remix of it was this fucking mutated thing, that had mutated out of garage, and I remember hearing it at Twice as Nice and just thinking, "What the fuck is that? That's not garage."

'At first I really didn't want to see garage splinter, because I liked that you could play a weird breakbeat record into a Todd Edwards record, into an old school, Strictly Rhythm house record, into a DJ Zinc record at 148bpm, I felt this was such a good thing, don't let it break into a thousand pieces and die. But obviously it did, and that was great too.' Mason attended the UK garage committee meetings, which were hosted and coordinated by the old guard, with Norris Windross as chairman, Spoony as spokesman, and well-established DJs such as Matt Jam Lamont and MCs such as Creed on one side; positioned against them, the likes of Mason, Maxwell D, producer Jaimeson and MC Viper:

'We went along because we wanted to give the new generation a voice,' Mason tells me over Skype from his home in California. 'I really liked all the guys on the other side, but at the time I butted heads with them, especially Matt Jam; I remember him having a go at us for putting a grime artist on the cover of *RWD* – it was one of the MCs from Hype Squad, this young crew who were on Raw Mission FM. This was still only 2001, it was a kid sitting on a bike and he was making gunfingers. And they all said, "You're promoting violence, you shouldn't be promoting these artists, this isn't garage," and I said, "Well, look: they're playing it in garage stations and garage clubs, and they're buying the records in garage shops, from the garage section. And I think you're right, I think maybe this isn't garage, and it's becoming something else – but, we absolutely should be fucking covering it, of course it's going to be on our front cover."'

Oxide and Neutrino, as members of So Solid Crew and also a very successful duo in their own right, responded to the ire sent their way for their scrappy, cheeky 'Bound 4 Da Reload' tune with an appropriately punk follow-up, called 'Up Middle Finger', describing the garage scene's jealous whining about their success, and bans in clubs and radio stations on playing their songs. 'All they do is talk about we, something about we're novelty, cheesy ... did I mention we're only 18?' They had sold 250,000 copies of 'Bound 4 Da Reload', and 'Up Middle Finger' became their third Top 10 hit in a row. That record scratch was the sound of the old guard being rewound into the history books. 'Garage didn't really want us involved in their scene,' as Lethal Bizzle said years later, 'so we started making our own thing.'

That's not to say there wasn't some fluidity between the two camps, or some overlap in taste and affection from the kids for the old guard: just that in that intense moment, the Oedipal urge to shrug off your elders and gatekeepers requires a bit of front, if you're going to claim the stage. Even within Pay As U Go – really the critical proto-grime crew, in terms of its personnel – there was a slight difference in aesthetics. You can see it in the video to 'Champagne Dance', Pay As U Go's one proper chart single, where Wiley and the rest of the crew are dressed in tracksuits, and Maxwell D, who, following a tough upbringing, wasn't about to let the opportunity to dress like a star pass him by:

'I had money from the street from selling drugs, and then I went straight into music, and was living like a drug dealer, legally. That's why I stood out a lot in the crew. That's why when people saw me they were like, "Rah he's dressed in all these name brand, expensive clothes." Even in my music videos I'd say to the stylist woman, "Look, I want a fur jacket yeah? I don't want to wear what I wear in the street." The rest of the crew were all like, "Why are you wearing a fur jacket?" and I'm like, "Because it's a music video! I'm going to go all out, I'm going to make myself look like a pimp." That was the garage style thing: dress to impress.'

During their brief time in the limelight signed to Sony, Pay As U Go were given the major-label rigmarole to promote 'Champagne Dance'. Wiley was given the surprisingly high-profile job of remixing Ludacris's 'Roll Off'; they appeared on CBBC with Reggie Yates, and on Channel 4's *Faking It* programme, advising the lawyer-turned-UK-garage-MC George on how to be less of a 'Bounty' (black on the outside, white on the inside), and get a bit of street cool. The most unlikely of these promotional activities was a tour of school assemblies around London and beyond, in Birmingham and Reading too; Flow Dan and Maxwell D took the helm, and the other MCs, including Wiley and Dizzee, would join them too. On one occasion, the disjunction between urban stars in the hood and a pop-friendly, public-facing crew reached a nadir. 'Sony made them go out on a schools tour,' Ross Allen told Emma Warren. 'I was like, "Nick [Denton, their manager], how's the tour going?" He was like, "I just had Wiley on the phone and they're well fucked off," and I was like, "Why?" They'd been sent to this school and they were playing to five-year-olds – they're on the mic and these little kids are doing forward rolls in front of them.'[12]

There was a baton being passed, and in spite of the £100,000 advance the crew received from Sony, and 'Champagne Dance' reaching number 13, Maxwell D was in a minority with his inclination for a fur coat. 'I wouldn't ever have said, "Take that Nokia!"' Maxwell reflects, referencing the Dizzee lyric, as emblematic of the new generation's hunger, 'because I could already buy five Nokias if I wanted – it wouldn't have made sense. But Dizzee, he'd just come off the street, he had that mentality.' And of course, if you're a 15-year-old, especially a poor 15-year-old, there's no financial barrier to becoming an MC – you've seen Pay As U Go, Heartless and So Solid do it and become stars, why not do the same? The same was not true of DJing: several hundred pounds on a pair of Technics, a couple of hundred more on a mixer, more on some decent headphones, and then, after that, all the records: £5–10 for each new 12 inch, and about £25 to cut a dubplate. DJing isn't cheap. MCing is free. 'Everybody wants to be an MC, there's no balance,' as Wiley's Pay As U Go-era bars observed. The posing, luxury brands and pimped-out stylings of the UK garage scene were being replaced by something much less aspirational, more raw, more hungry. In his autobiography, Wiley describes some of the few, frosty meetings in this transitional period between his rising east London crew, and south London's reigning kings of UK garage:

'Imagine seeing So Solid with all that fame, all that money, and then these bruk-pocket half-yardie geezers from east turn up with an even colder sound. There was no champs, no profiling, no beautiful people. Just us raggo East End lads in trackies and hoods, hanging out in some shithole white-man pub on Old Kent Road. We were realer in a way. We were just about spitting and making beats, that's it. South must have thought we were on some Crackney shit.'[13]

Those bruk-pocket geezers from east would change everything. 'I do sometimes wish more people respected what Pay As U Go did for grime,' Maxwell D says. 'Because Pay As U Go, that's the grime supergroup. That's like a grime atom bomb, exploding into all those little molecules.' You can see what he means. Even though their album was never released, and 'Champagne Dance' was their sole official release, the personnel involved would go on to transform British music. Geeneus made piles of stunning instrumentals (under his own name and as Wizzbit) and was the chief architect of UK underground super-pirate Rinse FM, stewarding sibling genres dubstep and UK funky along with grime, signing Katy B and creating an ever-expanding collection of related businesses. Slimzee would become grime's biggest and most respected DJ, the dubplate don par excellence. Maxwell himself would go on to join East Connection and later Muskateers. Target would make a number of sterling instrumentals for Roll Deep, and become an influential DJ on BBC 1Xtra. And then there was Wiley, the godfather of grime, who sprang from the short-lived excitement and disappointment of Pay As U Go to start Roll Deep, bring through Dizzee Rascal, Tinchy Stryder, Chipmunk, Skepta and create his 'Eskimo sound', perhaps the sonic palette most identified with the genre.

'Don't get me wrong, we weren't there in isolation,' Maxwell continued. 'So Solid Crew were a big part of influencing the grime culture, but they were already superstars, and they were garage superstars. And Heartless Crew, they were doing garage and sound-system stuff, playing a bit of ragga, a bit of darker stuff – but for me, Heartless were always happy, they were about love and peace, whereas we always used to bring a lot more street lyrics. And underneath us, you've got all of east London immediately turning over to grime music. Because after us, who was next? East Connection, More Fire Crew, Nasty Crew, Boyz in da Hood, SLK. All these crews started emerging.

'After Pay As U Go, that was when it all went dark,' he smirks. 'We turned out the lights.'

THREE

THE NEW ICE AGE

I f it takes a village to raise a child, it definitely takes a village to raise a scene. It's one of the fallacies of the bedroom-producer trope in grime's origin story, that a wild and pioneering auteur creativity was born out of solitude. Grime was created in bedrooms – but not alone, or in isolation: it didn't allow for eccentric hermits, because the London it came from didn't either: boroughs of densely populated flats on densely populated estates, where a tower block is itself a kind of vertical community, and both in it and around it, everyone knows everyone's business – and their bars. The inner-city kids who came up through jungle and UK garage in the nineties learned how to DJ it, how to MC on it and how to dance to it together.

When they were ready to make their own sound, they taught each other, vibed off each other, and absorbed each other's ideas and idioms, hanging out in vital if unglamorous hubs like Limehouse basketball court and Jammer's parents' basement. Shystie only started to write lyrics because her friends at sixth-form college pushed her to. 'They taught me how to put words together, which instrumentals to spit over, and I'd spit in front of them. There was no YouTube, no Twitter, no SoundCloud, there was nothing – instead it was word of mouth: it was

Pass the mic. Chrisp Street Youth Club, Poplar, 2005

about getting big in your own area, your friends bigging you up, practising at sixth form with them – then you have other local schools, they would kind of support you too, because you're seeing them on the way home; you're building up your local fanbase, really. I started performing locally at parties, and my name got around more. I'd do little local raves, and it just spiralled and domino-effected and spread like wildfire. Those practice hours were so important man – I put in so many hours, it's not a joke.'

School outside of classroom hours was instrumental – it was a key location, a vital node in the network, in an embryonic scene populated largely by teenagers and exclusively by under-25s, where local connections were everything. In a sense, it might be said to be the last truly local scene: these were the final years before social media and web 2.0 collapsed distances between strangers, and forged brand new kinds of instant networks across geographical boundaries. In grime's formative years, it was the people who you knew from the area – neighbours, schoolmates, brothers and sisters – that created the platform on which a scene was built. Crews like Ruff Sqwad were formed through school in the first place, and MC practice took place in a group, in the playground – after school, during lunch break, whenever there was time. There's a reason all those hood videos and 'freestyles' show the MCs with their crew and their mates gathered around them, whooping and popping gunfingers: because that's how the bars are written, refined, practised and improved to begin with: it's not so much a gathering for a performance, to camera, as an – albeit slightly exaggerated – mirror on the day-to-day reality of where the music comes from.

The story of grime in east London in particular is a dense family tree of friendships that initially preceded music, and then as the protagonists' teenage years proceeded, developed because of it. When I asked Target about the lineage that led him to Wiley, and the rest of Roll Deep, it went back to primary school: by the age of ten, they were playing with the vinyl decks in Wiley's dad's flat in Bow, ten minutes from Target's childhood home. 'We literally didn't leave the bedroom all weekend, we were just playing on these decks. We couldn't mix or anything, but we were just having the best time ever.' By the final year of primary school they'd formed a new jack swing meets rap group called Cross Colours, inspired by Kriss Kross and Snoop Dogg, and Wiley's dad was taking them to meet an A&R.

By the mid-nineties, still only in their mid-teens, they were already veterans, and Target and Wiley formed SS (Silver Storm) Crew with Breeze, Maxwell D and others. They would hang out on Limehouse basketball court and practise their jungle bars, or go to each other's houses to record tapes, streaming up the stairs of Slimzee's mum's house, where Geeneus and Slimzee were for a while broadcasting Rinse FM, illicitly – the authorities didn't know, and nor did Slimzee's mum. 'She kept saying to me, "What's going on up there?" Them times I was only young, so they didn't really want me to go out – it weren't a bad area, but … things was going on, you know? So they'd rather me stay in, than go out, taking drugs and all that stuff.'

More than one MC or DJ has recounted that, as much as grime would soon lyrically reflect the trials and tribulations of petty crime, drug dealing and violence, many of their parents supported their teenage musical experiments for the very reason that, if they were all making a ruckus in the bedroom, they weren't out on the street getting up to no good. Tinchy Stryder's older brother was a DJ and had turntables in the bedroom they shared in the Crossways Estate. 'We all used to come back to my mum's house and practise there. I'm always grateful to my mum and dad, because I don't know if many people would've let loads of boys come in the house and make that noise,' he laughed. 'Because grime ain't nothing calm, and it wasn't a big house.' So much was developed in childhood bedrooms with hand-me-down decks, or even less. In Shystie's case, her mic skills were developed as a teenager with a karaoke machine and a £9.99 microphone from Argos.

That neighbourhood scene in the nineties thrived via word of mouth, pirate-radio broadcasts, and one critical performance arena: 'The root of all this grime business, of grime MCing, was house parties,' Wiley said to me in 2016, while recording *The Godfather*, his eleventh album (or fortieth, if you count all the mixtapes). 'Proper house parties, with a proper system, all across Bow and Newham when we were teenagers. We'd go and jump on the mic, and clash each other.' SS Crew would get invited to perform at any house parties around E3; they'd be walking around Bow carrying their decks and boxes of records.

'That was the first taste of when you get that energy back from the crowd,' Target recalled. 'We couldn't believe it, like, "Whoa, this is sick!" At that stage we didn't ever think we could get paid, there was no future plan: just the excitement of participating. It was a sense of community, definitely, it was. At the time we wouldn't have used words like that, but that's what it was. We were all from the same area, loads of us were into music, DJing or MCing, and when Rinse started we actually had a base, and the chance to be heard by people who didn't already know us. Going on Rinse and having a text from say, Stacey in East Ham, felt incredible – it was like going international. It was like having your track go Top 10 in Spain or something, it was that exciting.'

As London's millennium wheel first began to turn, the sun began to set on UK garage, its glossy pop moment cast in shadow. The younger generation of MCs and DJs had had years of training on the mic and on the decks, but if they were being pushed out by their elders, the response was to turn their outcast status into something they could be proud of and control. Before it had acquired a genre name, grime's young talents, those too young or too angry to feel UK garage was theirs, began creating a new sound, riffing on some of that weirder, darker garage, the kind with broken beats instead of 2-step's shuffle and swing: the kind that was too awkwardly shaped to wear designer-label shirts and smart shoes to the club. They would eventually overwhelm British pop, doing so with the barest minimum of equipment, and in most cases with almost no formal musical training. They taught themselves and each other, and used software like Napster, Kazaa and Limewire to downloaded illegal 'cracked' versions of simple music production software like FruityLoops Studio. To begin with, that was the closest grime's pioneers would come to a studio.

Grime, in its first years, sounded as if it had crash-landed in the present with no past, and no future – a time-travelling experiment gone horribly, fascinatingly wrong; a broken flux capacitor glowing amidst the smouldering wreckage, a neon light pulsing in the mist. While on one side of the A13, Canary Wharf's tenants enriched themselves to dizzying new heights, the sounds emanating from the tower blocks barely a mile away declaimed through the airwaves that there was more than one east London. There was an alien futurism to a lot of the computer-generated aesthetics – the reason why some of the bleeps and bloops sounded like noises made by spaceships from computer games was because they were in fact made on games consoles: most famously a piece of software for the first PlayStation, called *Music 2000*. A lot of So Solid Crew's first album was built on this very elementary software; as was Dizzee's 'Stand Up Tall'. Producers like Jme and Smasher made their first tunes on it, recorded them to MiniDisc, and then had vinyl dubplates cut straight from the MiniDisc – without going anywhere near a recording studio.

Mixdowns are usually seen as a crucial stage of the recording process even for the most entry-level producer, where the elements created are refined and balanced out to create a clean and coherent whole – but with grime they sometimes didn't happen at all, before the tunes were cut to vinyl and released, either as dubplates or for general release to record shops. This applies even to the instrumental frequently cited as the first proper grime tune, Youngstar's 'Pulse X'. The spirit of the period echoes the famous punk mantra, 'Here's a chord. Here's another. Here's a third. Now form a band.'

DJ Logan Sama, for one, was happy enough with the devil-may-care approach to technical proficiency. 'I don't give a shit if a record is mastered well or not,' Sama said to me back in 2006, then a new graduate from the pirate-radio scene to the legit world and new sofas of KISS FM. 'All I care about is the reaction it gets when I play it in a club. How technically well-made art is doesn't matter: it's art. Why would you want to analyse it on its technical merits? It's not an exam. My white label of "Pulse X" still has the hiss from the AV-out cables from the PlayStation they took it off to record it onto CD, when they took it to master it. You can hear it! The '*bawm*'s are all distorted. That record sold over 10,000 copies; it was fucking massive. Half of So Solid's first album was produced on *Music 2000*, they then took it into the studio on a memory card to re-engineer it. That album sold over one million copies. A lot of people loved jungle when it was shit – when the quality of it was shit! Personally I like "jump up" stuff, and if I get that out of a technically well-made record, then cool; if I get that out of a record that's been made on FruityLoops and not mixed-down properly, so be it.'

Grime's canon of cult classics is full of music made by producers who were unwilling or unable to do things 'properly'. One of Ruff Sqwad's most famous instrumental productions, 'Functions On The Low' by XTC, took on a life of its own when, 11 years after its release, Stormzy used it as the instrumental for a freestyle recorded in his local park. That freestyle, 'Shut Up', would go on to take the charts by storm and propel him to pop superstardom. XTC is one of many of grime's ephemeral geniuses[1]: for most of the crew's existence, he was barely even in Ruff Sqwad; more just a mate from the area who made a few tunes and spat a few bars, and the older brother to MC Fuda Guy. XTC finished only a handful of tracks, and only ever released one 12 inch of three tracks with 'Functions' on the B-side – it just happened to be a masterpiece. It's a breathtaking five minutes of longing, like a fleeting glimpse of the love of your life disappearing into the Hong Kong night – neon lights seen through a torrent of tears. It's so heartbreaking, and yet so addictive, so humane, that the moment it stops, you're desperate to have it back. It took him half an hour to write, on FruityLoops, one morning before college, while the rest of his family were still asleep. He used the computer keyboard in place of an actual keyboard, never got it mastered, rendered the audio file, burned a CD, and took it straight to the vinyl pressing plant.[2] And that was that.

Other more prolific producers, like Dexplicit, who made the instrumental 'Forward Riddim' that would be used for Lethal Bizzle's 'Pow!', an underground smash and later a Top 10 hit, began writing music on even more basic equipment: a pre-app, pre-internet 'brick' of a mobile phone. 'When I was in secondary school, everyone used to get me to create ringtones of their favourite songs on the old Nokia 3310's,' he laughed, when I interviewed him for a piece about 'sodcasting', the much-maligned mid-2000s phenomenon where people (usually young teenagers) would play music off their phones on public transport. Grime's birth coincided with the popularisation of new kinds of cheap, low-end, unsophisticated audio technology. Of course there had been TDK cassettes and home-taping off the radio in previous decades, but the explosion of rapidly evolving mobile-phone technology, mp3 players and cheap ear-bud headphones skewed a lot of listening towards treble-focused audio – a paradox for grime, with its 'bass culture' lineage through reggae, jungle and UK garage. I asked Dexplicit if the techno-logical and consumer changes were conditioning how he made tracks. 'My primary focus is how it's going to sound on a club system,' he replied, 'but I am aware there are sections of the frequency spectrum that won't be picked up well via iPod headphones, TVs and phones. I make "heavy-bass" music. And listening to a 50–100hz, very low bass on a iPod is like trying to hear ants walking. I've always tried to create a balance in my music, and often have "pretty" melodies going on upstairs, the treble, accompanied by a kind of nasty low end.'

Ask 20 different grime fans what they consider to be the first grime tune, and you'll get, if not 20 different answers, probably about ten: a good half of them will either say 'Pulse X', or Wiley's 'Eskimo'. I actually carried out this test, entirely unscientifically, on Twitter. Other answers included a smattering of late-garage crew cuts: More Fire Crew's 'Oi' (2001), So Solid Crew singles 'Dilemma' and 'Oh No' (2000), as well as one shout for Danny Weed's 'Creeper' (2002). Rinse FM founder, grime svengali and long-standing producer Geeneus, who ought to know, maintains that the first grime track is Pay As U Go's 'Know We', the crew's under-ground anthem released in 2000. 'Wiley was the one who was like "we're going to put the MCs on the songs", and I was like "MCs on songs, that's a bit mad innit? No one does that,"' Geeneus said in 2016. The aggressive tone of the MCs, and the unsettling, urgent momentum of the keyboard riff all mark the track out as grime, but most of all it was the structure which shifted the paradigm: tracks like 'Know We' created clearly demarcated space for MCs to fill with complex rhymes – to tell stories and to dominate proceedings, rather than merely accompany an instrumental. They weren't hosting the rave for the DJ/producer anymore: this was their show. The Pay As U Go MCs brought the track straight from the studio to Rhythm Division on Roman Road, where it was played out at top volume to the two dozen people hanging around there. 'I was like "What is this music?"' Geeneus recalled. 'It was 16 bars, then chorus, 16 bars, a chorus. We just went off on one. Every tune was formatted like that after that. That's grime! That was the template. And it's still going now, same format.'[3]

Youngstar's 'Pulse X', released in January 2002 but on the airwaves for some time before that, offered its own template: it was arranged in functional 8-bar segments, switching quickly and with little variation – which briefly led to '8-bar' as the designated genre name for this new, untested mutant strain of UK garage. The format was vital for grime's evolution as an MC-led genre, in that they would write lyrics in either 8, 16, 32 or 64 bar sections, with the style varying for each of those lengths. 'Your 8s are your reload bars,' Shystie explained to me recently, 'or it can even just be a 4, repeated twice': they had to be memorable, crowd-pleasing and catchy – held in reserve for when the DJ brings in a particularly brilliant instrumental. These are your silver bullets, your punchlines, powerful and simple shots of lyrical adrenaline – the bars that could make you underground-famous. 16s and 32s are for your more detailed or thoughtful content, 'for spraying', and they need more space to breathe: they're better suited to slower burning, less sugar-rush hectic instrumentals – but because they'll take longer, you need to start them at the right time, too, early on in a track, unless you're confident about continuing them over the hump of two tracks, during the DJ's blend. Judging the mood, and the rhythm, and anticipating the DJ can be fiendishly difficult, especially when you have to make split-second decisions about switching up the pace while also in the middle of spitting. It requires a pretty remarkable level of mental dexterity, the more you think about it. Eighteen-year-old MC Streema from latter-day Lewisham crew The Square explained the challenge to American podcast *Afropop Worldwide*: 'There could be a hype beat coming in, and you're already spraying a 32, and not really know what 8 to spray ... The person listening is going to think, "All right, cool, this beat coming in is gassed, this beat is a hype tune, I want to hear someone do a madness on this," so if you're on your own at the [radio] set, it would be good to draw for your 8 ... but sometimes it's better to wait, to get into the beat, to then drop the 8, because it doesn't always work instantly as the beat comes in.'

It's an under-explored facet of grime's playful theatricality that as well as a canny knack for inventing its own slang and idiolects, often the MCs would push the boundaries of language altogether – although this has its own history too. Simon Reynolds, describing pirate-radio MC patter in the early nineties, points to the sensual thrill of hearing 'an arsenal of non-verbal, incantatory techniques, bringing spoken language closer to the state of music: intonation, syncopation, alliteration, internal rhyme, slurring, rolling of 'r's, stuttering of consonants, twisting and stretching of vowels, comic accents, onomatopoeia.'[4] It's a legacy carried down the continuum of pirate sounds into grime's cast of players – especially in the early years when their faces weren't so well known, and MCs had to make their voices stand out on crowded pirate sets, with familiar bars but also stylistic tics, accents and affectations. Like characters in computer games, most MCs developed their own overblown catch-phrases to help identify themselves, bat signals beaming from the pirate transmitters into the night sky over Bow. Scratchy had his self-described 'warrior charge' ('brreee brreee!'), Jammer a range of absurd and playful nonsense poetry ('are you dhaaaaaaauum?!' [dumb] 'Seckk-kulllll – draw for the neckk-kulll'), Jme the comically over-pronounced 'Serious!' and 'Shhhhut Yuh Mouth', and in a category of his own was Flirta D, whose extraordinary rhythmic sound effects and imitations took in computer-game noises, explosions, snatches of sweetly sung R&B, jungle-style trilling and more – somewhere between scatting, beat-box-ing and a malfunctioning sample pack.

We've already heard about D Double E and his 'D Double sig-a-nal', the immediately recognisable announcement of his arrival, like a music hall performer peering his head around the side of the curtain, before stepping out onto the stage. Written non-phonetically, in standard English, it looks camp and comical – 'Ooh! Ooh! It's me, me!' (where, we might ask, is D Double E's washboard?) – but it's spread out over about seven or eight syllables, a visceral vocal exorcism from somewhere deep in the lungs. 'That's very original – never heard that from another individual,' runs another old-school D Double bar, in meta commentary on his own idiosyncrasy. 'At raves, sometimes I don't even have to MC,' he told the *Guardian* in 2004. 'I just go on stage and hear the echoes coming out the crowd. It's a deep signal.'

Skepta (pirate radio catchphrase: 'Go on then, go on then!'), by contrast, very deliberately chose the most clear-voiced, discernible flow he could – 'put me up against gimmick, sound effect or skippy-flow man,'[5] he taunted (and I'll merk all three of them). On diss tracks 'Swag MC Burial' and 'The End', he took on several rival MCs in sequence, mocking them by imitating their flows and quoting their catchphrases. A pre-planned live MC clash on Logan Sama's KISS FM show in 2007,[6] with Skepta facing down the super-fast skippy flow and 'technical' lyricism of Ghetts, highlights an interesting tension between different styles of MCing. Speaking about himself in the third person, Skepta goes after Ghetts' technique specifically: 'Skepta how did you kill him like that, when he's skipping all over the riddim like that? You will never hear me spitting like that … I like the basic shit, I don't like too many words in a sentence,' he announces. Skepta is punk trashing prog rock: why is long and convoluted inherently better? 'Go on then, spit a 32-bar lyric, I'll rustle up an 8-bar lyric, to dun your lyric,' he tells Ghetts, dismissing his crew The Movement's fondness for complex lyricism, punning and wordplay. He castigates this kind of borrowing from US hip-hop (and Kano) – it's foreign, and intrinsically inauthentic for a London grime MC: 'I make the best grime music: some man run up in the booth and lose it, start spitting like Dipset, D Block and G Unit/Kano brought a new flow to the game, now I look around: 10 million MCs in the grime scene want to use it/It's my job to make them look stupid.' The counter-point is put by a fan in the YouTube comments on the audio clip, who prefers Ghetts and his crew: 'Skepta just has basic one-line flows.'

For all grime's non-verbal and semi-verbal vocal dynamism, the significant break in the tradition of rave-based British MC culture was the grime generation's turn away from the functional role of (party or radio) host towards storytelling. And as the MCs developed their voices, producers began their own world-building, too – sketching out new rules, and changing the entire emotional register of what had gone before. (Significantly, in the beginning, there was a huge overlap; in fact the overwhelming majority of MCs have recorded and released at least one instrumental record as producers, at some point.)

Alongside transitional darker garage instrumentals by the likes of So Solid Crew, in 2001 and 2002 there were also beats being made that sounded like nothing that had gone before.

After learning the drums as a child, experimenting with copying his dad's reggae jams on the keyboard, and dabbling – quite excellently – with making the sweetest of straight-up vocal UK garage on 'Nicole's Groove', under the pseudonym Phaze One, Wiley moved on to making his own sound. Geeneus and Slimzee had bought a Korg Triton, a new synthesiser that went on sale in 1999, a piece of equipment that would become synonymous with the quintessential grime sound, and Wiley would pop around and use it. In the first years of the 2000s, he created a sound, 'eskibeat' or 'eskimo', that was characterised by its sparse arrangements, futuristic, icy cold synths, devastating basslines and awkward, off-kilter rhythms. Like UK garage before it, it was generally 140 beats per minute – the consistency was important for DJs to be able to mix records seamlessly. (Dubstep and grime producer Plastician is not the only one to have observed that FruityLoops' default tempo is set to 140bpm, which 'may have a lot to answer for'.) But the world it conjured – the same city, from a totally different perspective – had a completely different atmosphere.

In this crucible moment, around 2002–03, the taxonomy of what would become 'grime' was greatly contested – and even debated on one of Wiley's first label-released singles, 'Wot Do U Call It?'. ('Garage? Urban? 2 Step?' he speculates derisively, without providing a definitive answer.) Eskibeat quickly became a one-man sonic empire, a distinctive sound all branded with an arctic theme: the track titles from that era include Ice Rink, Igloo, Ice Pole, Blizzard, Ice Cream Man, Snowman, Frostbite, Freeze, Colder and Morgue. 'Sometimes I just feel cold hearted,' he said in 2003, by way of explanation. 'I felt cold at that time, towards my family, towards everyone. That's why I used those names … I am a nice person but sometimes I switch off and I'm just cold. I feel angry and cold.'[7] The narcotically-enhanced, loved-up bliss of the eighties and nineties rave predecessors, and the giddy utopian place-making that made raves 'temporary autonomous zones' had been wiped off the map. Wiley offered another explanation in 2005, which pegged the claustrophobia, emotional dislocation and rage of his and his peers' music to the city around him: 'The music reflects what's going on in society. Everyone's so angry at the world and each other. And they don't know why,' he told American magazine *Spin*. 'As things went bad, away from music, the music's just got darker and darker.'[8]

'Eskimo' was the first of his eski-oeuvre, the most game-changing, and the most enduring: a few minimal drum skirmishes, some artificial synth stabs, and the sound of a hollow metal pole rolling around a construction yard. Docklands after the docks, and before Canary Wharf – just a wasteland – but maybe with a hint of the bankers' blocks' futuristic glint, too. During the Pay As U Go school tour, they would play 'Eskimo' as an instrumental bed, and the kids would come up and freestyle over them. 'The kids were going mad over that beat,' Maxwell D recalled – this alien soundtrack was appropriate to the mood of the age. Its sheer newness is startling, and unsettling: it is easily situated in the context of millenarian anxiety, with all the apocalyptic fears that had accompanied that mystical calendar change, made worse by an ambient sense of dread about the new era that lay ahead. The frosty wastelands and open space reaching out ahead in the twenty-first century provoked a kind of psychic agoraphobia, triggered by the seismic jolt of the 9/11 attacks on the World Trade Center in New York, and the rush to war that followed, with the growing likelihood of unavoidable climate catastrophe ahead. Wiley wrote one of his formative eskimo tracks, 'Ground Zero', on the day of the attacks. 'Imagine travelling through the streets, through all that dust. I want [Americans] to understand that I understand. I felt it,' he told Martin Clark in 2003. 'If we were in West End and the BT tower fell down and we were on that street. The fear – you can't imagine the fear that would be in someone. "Am I going to die? Am I going to live?" Your heart would pop out of your chest. I've had that feeling: where you feel like death.'[9]

There is a case for saying that grime's sonics are grounded in the material experience of east London life, that grime sounds like its environment; as Hattie Collins says in the documentary *Open Mic*[10] – producers sample snippets of police sirens and gunshots, and perhaps in some of its clanking metallic sounds we can hear the heavy security gates on council flat front doors closing. But beyond this quotidian, literal testament to urban claustrophobia and noise pollution, is a sense that a historic rupture is happening, and that is audible in the music. You can hear it in some of Dizzee's instinctive ad-libs on radio sets and Sidewinder mixes with DJ Slimzee in the 2001–03 period, his off-the-cuff reactions to the year zero tunes being faded in by his DJ: 'two thousand and slew ... this is the new ice age', 'playing all these end of the world beats ... all these tunes sound like judgement day', 'this is divine intervention stupid ... now we're going to start getting space age'. Embracing those unknown frontiers was a mark of pride for the grime generation: 'Millennium time!' one of the Diamond Click MCs announces as the tectonic bass drops on Jammer's 2003 classic 'Don't Ya Know' – millennium time for those brave enough to be ready for it, even though 'nuff man still stuck in 1990s'.[11]

There is a kind of shlocky horror show melodrama to many of grime's formative instrumentals, often reflected in the naming as well as the sonics: Danny Weed's seminal and irresistible 'Creeper', a kind of prancing Halloween ghoul lurking in the shadows, Target's 'Poltergeist', tracks by Macabre Unit, or Terror Danjah's work, tracks like 'Creepy Crawler' and 'Gremlin', stamped with his trademark sinister chuckle. The same goes for much of the sublow sound of west London's Jon E Cash and his crew Black Ops, where, on 'Spanish Fly', a 1950s B-movie quality is granted by an unnerving tickle of Spanish guitar, before the glowering bassline kicks in. Other pioneering producers like Waifer and Young Dot created maximal, militaristic instrumental assaults, turning strings, hiccups and other sound effects into deadly weapons – anthems like the former's 'Grime' and the latter's 'Bazooka VIP' left little space for the MC; or at the very least, demanded a huge effort and big lungs to keep up.

What is unnerving and uncanny and which differentiates grime's sonics from darker garage, is the sheer alien newness of the bass sound (dark bass was not invented by grime, as any junglist will tell you) and frequently off-kilter arrangements, all jolts, awkward gaps and juddering surprises. Wiley's eskimo creations were perhaps the pinnacle of this: taken to the extreme on his 'devil mixes'. These were remixes of tracks like 'Eskimo', 'Colder' and 'Avalanche' made even more sinister by stripping the drums out, inspired partly by the dub versions his dad's reggae sound system had created, but so named because they 'sounded evil'. As if to highlight the ungodly power they had, the devil mixes sold really well, and Wiley used the proceeds to buy a car, which he then crashed. Convinced that his creations were cursed and too powerful to control, he insisted on calling them 'bass mixes' after that.

Before it hardened down into the fabric, Jammer, Dizzee, Danny Weed and Wiley drew another strain of futurism into this creatively molten moment: what's come to be known as sinogrime, a glitch of Chinese instrumentation in grime's normally stable sonic geography (the UK and Jamaica, with a bit of US rap swagger, house from Chicago and syncopation from West Africa). Grime's instinctive (and functional) tech-positivity is what always helped it feel like sonic futurism incarnate: rejecting the organic clutter of live instrumentation in favour of empty space, dehumanised synths and cyborg basslines. I was unlucky enough to see Roll Deep play a one-off show with a live band at the Stratford Rex in 2005, and it was all kinds of wrong – the wholesome twang of the live bass guitar the antithesis to grime's aesthetic (let us not even deign to discuss Ed Sheeran's strumming collaborations with grime MCs). Grime is situated in the future aesthetically, and perhaps embedded in sinogrime's Chinese elements is a sort of intuition about where the future lies, geopolitically. In looking east beyond the blinking light of One Canada Square, sinogrime producers were offering a kind of accidental socio-political prophecy, taking grime's acquisitive tendencies and sending them east on a journey beyond Britain's pre-2008 bubble.

Following the history of slum clearances, Luftwaffe bombing, empty warehouses and managed decline, by the early 2000s east London had become the archetype of the post-industrial city. The future had gone to China, and grime instinctively followed. You can hear it in the delicate sino scales on Dizzee's 'Do It', a minor lament, as the rough and tough drums try and put a brave face on the poignant instrumentation and deeply depressive lyrics ('Feds don't understand us, adults don't understand us, no one understands us', he mumbles, forlorn, on the intro[12]). On the stunning 'I Luv U Remix', what might be a MIDI (digitised) version of a *guzheng* or *guqin* – Chinese stringed instruments – is used to play out a light but intensely melodic bed for the MCs' heartfelt lyrical sketches, accompanied only by the sparest, subtlest snatches of bass and drum. Wiley and Danny Weed's 'Blue Rizla', Jammer's 'Weed Man', and Kode9's 'Sinogrime Minimix' are all in this category. Of course, there is a direct influence from the staple teenage boy's cultural diet of Wu Tang Clan, kung-fu movies, and video games like *Mortal Kombat*: indeed one of Dizzee's best teenage productions, 'Street Fighter', was lifted directly from the game's theme tune.

Another pinnacle of emotive sinogrime built this connection in a more direct way. Watching a video of the 1993 Jet Li film *Twin Warriors* with his dad, Jammer was struck by the heartstrings-tugging theme music, in particular one ear-worm of a snippet. He was determined to sample it, and after playing around with TV leads and Scart plugs, he managed to wire the VHS to his mixing desk. 'It came straight off the VHS,' he told me, justifiably proud of his teenage ingenuity. 'That's why it sounds so grainy – but it kind of adds to the emotional power of it.

Now music's very digital and very focused, and cleaner – but in those days, that's what you had to do, to improvise to build the sound you wanted, and it was rougher, but had a lot of heart too. Like a lot of the records I made at that time, it was emotional, orchestral stuff – when that underground sound was flourishing.' The MCs didn't miss an opportunity to respond to the emotional vulnerabilities in the instrumental, 'Chinaman', built around a beautiful, elegiac flute loop – there's a clip from Deja Vu in 2003 of MC Stormin spitting: 'Where do I go from here? Shed a little tear for my friend that I lost this year, back in the day we used to go everywhere/Same things that make you love make you cry, everybody that you seem to love seems to die.'[13] 'Chinaman' became the instrumental to Sharky Major's 'This Ain't A Game' – the perfect partner for Sharky's soul-searching lyrics. 'I feel like I'm not as good as people say I am, I know I can spit ten times better than I've ever done – see me rise with the morning sun,'[14] he pleads. He's surrounded by criminals, cops and people who've 'never seen a day's work', and the dream of 'superstar status' is his only possible option. He never did get there, or even very close, but he did make one of the greatest reflective grime tunes of all time.

Swept up in the creative ferment of the early millennium, other young producers who had grown up on jungle and UK garage started making music that sounded nothing like them. Skepta's first release, more than a year before he ever picked up the mic, was a reworking of 'Pulse X' and 'Eskimo', released in 2002 on Wiley's label as 'Pulse Eskimo'. It's an utterly ferocious instrumental track, and accompanied by an appropriately grimy conception story. It was built with *Music 2000* on the PlayStation One (at this stage Skepta and his brother Jme were even making beats using the game *Mario Paint*) – and before Wiley signed it up, Skepta was playing it on his show on a pirate-radio station in Tottenham, Heat 96.6 FM. 'I gave it to a few DJs in the hope they'd start playing it,' Skepta recalled, 'and one of them, I don't know if it was Mac 10 from Nasty Crew, or Karnage from Roll Deep, well they played it at Sidewinder, and when they played it, on the drop, someone started letting off gunshots in the dance.' Chaos ensued, mercifully no one was injured – and ever since, the tune has been known by the nickname Gunshot Riddim. It's an appropriate testament to the sheer power of a grime instrumental.

While these new creations were honed by more experienced former junglists like Wiley and Geeneus, a younger generation, still in their mid-teens, were just starting out with making music, developing the new sound and their mic skills in schools and youth clubs. Grime as a genre, and a scene, was built on an astonishing level of youthful auton-omy and self-sufficiency – but for all its entrepreneurial, DIY vigour and self-starting rhetoric, the state played a little-noticed role in some of its earliest developments. For one thing, there was the youth clubs. Dizzee describes an informal circuit of them as his apprenticeship on the mic, 'going from youth club to youth club, it started there' – they would travel to youth clubs in Canning Town (east London), Deptford (south-east) and further east to Beckton, Kano's local. It was at Lincoln Arches youth club in Bow (long since closed down), part of the Lincoln North Estate, where Wiley, Dizzee, Nasty Crew and Ruff Sqwad among others would hang out, play table tennis and pool, and then sometimes be allowed to have raves, where they'd practise spitting over garage and proto-grime. 'Friday night after school you'd think, "Yes, I need to go to the Linc, I need to go clubbing, I need to impress everyone and the girls there,"' Tinchy Stryder recalled a few years later.

Another youth club, across the other side of Canary Wharf in the Isle of Dogs, was responsible for financing Ruff Sqwad's first ever release, the squalling, punky 'Tings In Boots'. 'Obviously you needed money to put out a song, and we were still in school. Jeff and Jo, who ran that youth club on the Isle of Dogs, they were sort of the unsung heroes of grime,' Rapid said. 'They saw our talents, they sort of managed us, they thought yeah we'll put a couple of hundred quid into actually bringing this out.' Other times they'd pool their dinner money to fund their early vinyl releases. And the elders on the nascent local scene were always there to help them too, with advice, practical hands-on tips and financial support: 'When we got further down the line with our productions, we used to go down to Jammer's basement and give him the parts, I remember he was like, "Raps, Dirt, your tunes are banging, but you have to get mixdowns," and we were like, "What's that?" We didn't know what that was! We were like "What do you do?" – by then he was already well into making grime and releasing records. From people like Jammer and Wiley we got a lot of energy around then.'

And then there was school, as a meeting point for practice, socialising and developing musical skills. Shystie's transformative experience, taking her from hobbyist MC with a 9–5 job she hated, was the decision to study sound engineering at FE College, '[where] I realised: I could really do this!' – after a whirlwind year, she signed to Polydor, and didn't go back for the second year of the course. The most famous example of the importance of school comes from Dizzee Rascal's teacher Tim Smith, who garnered some press attention after *Boy in da Corner* won the Mercury Prize in 2003; the story resonated as a redemptive one, of the singular faith of a mentor who refused to abandon hope – Dizzee had been expelled from two secondary schools already, and was placed at Langdon Park in Poplar, where Tim Smith was Head of Arts; he gave him the space to get on with his music, even after he had been expelled from all his other classes. Sent home from school one day for misbehaviour, angry and frustrated, Dizzee wrote some of his most well-known rave bars: 'lyrical tank, box an MC like my name was Frank/going on dirty, going on stank.'[15] 'You could vent, I think that's why I loved MCing,' he told Radio 1 recently. The school was, like most state comprehensives, chronically short of resources, and the music department's PCs had been donated by Morgan Stanley, and some of the other major banking corporations in Canary Wharf – via the LDDC, in fact.

On Dizzee's first day, Smith left him to his own devices, sitting at a PC playing with Cubase. 'After about 20 minutes, one of the pair of teachers said, "You've got to come over and see this." Most kids are happy to have got a few bars down, but he had already zoomed ahead. He could quickly get information down, but what was most unusual was he would then spend a lot of time refining it – a lot of youngsters wanted to create music, but weren't as interested in total refinement of a sound. He could string quite a complex rhythmic pattern together, in 20 to 30 minutes, but then be quite happy to spend a week refining and editing.' On Monday evenings after school, a drop-in session funded by Tower Hamlets Summer University gave him a further opportunity to work on beats; Smith loaned Dizzee Philip Glass, Steve Reich and John Adams CDs, minimalist composers and favourites of his – there was some connection there, in the use of space, he thought. (Hyperdub founder and musical and academic polymath Steve 'Kode9' Goodman once said of dubstep that you should 'dance to the gaps', a sonic architecture which was shared with some of the more sparse early grime instrumentals, when neither had 'taken the name'.)

Towards the end of Year 11, Dylan Mills was excluded from all his lessons, after more misbehaviour – but a forgiving headmaster knew that three expulsions, statistically, would most likely lead to a bad downwards spiral, and asked Smith if Dizzee could just sit quietly in the music room with him. So Dizzee would sit alone and work on his music for those last months, and occasionally help Smith teach Cubase to the Year 7s.

'The music was awesome,' Smith told me, who has retired from teaching, but now sits on the board of Rinse FM. 'Nobody else had written music like that, with those really sharp, intricate beats, but sometimes just dropping out to nothing. And that is the hardest thing in music, to create space. And that showed particular talent, especially for someone so young, and you can hear it on *Boy in da Corner*, to know that you shouldn't overload it. In Cubase you get quite a visual image of what you're going to hear – and he would colour code, so you can see when something's going to be repeated.'

Boy in da Corner was a significant development from the music he made at school, but those basics of creating space were definitely learned there. 'The giveaways were the very very sharp beats,' Smith told me. 'He would compose at about 80bpm – most youngsters were into about 120 – but he would have a deliberately slow beat, so that you could sub-divide each beat, not into 2 but into 4. That's where you get the really sharp, interesting sound. He would draw it in, so it was filled, and erase certain bits of it, so it had a gap. That's where that unexpected break in the music came from.'

Many of Dizzee's instrumental creations in his mid-teens were unfiltered, unvarnished beats, breaks and synths. He spun gold from the most basic and unadorned of sound palettes: the songs he wrote in Langdon Park School were constructed from their kit of a small mixer and Cubase software on the second-hand PCs, using the Cubase sound pack. Simplicity, and the idea of having the beat already ringing around his head, seemed to lead to a very methodical, straightforward composition process. It was the least of experimental techniques to achieve the most 'experimental' of sounds – an inborn tendency to the avant-garde, no oblique strategies required:

'I was always fucking about with some weird noise,' he said to me a decade or so later, in a break from rehearsing the *Boy in da Corner* revival show. 'All the samples were just lined up on the keyboard, I never used an MPC, so each key is a different sample. Those times I would usually start with the drums. "I Luv U", I definitely started with the drums, and then built around it.' On both *Boy in da Corner* and *Showtime* there are moments that reject not only simple pop structures and sensibilities, but any 'songiness' at all – part of his desire to move London electronic music on from UK garage, Dizzee once said, was because it was 'all too nice-sounding'. Even the regularity and order of a simple 8-bar grime track is absent from tracks like 'Knock, Knock', on *Showtime*, a beat that constantly splits off at awkward angles and refuses to settle down. On 'Brand New Day', from his debut, Dizzee juxtaposes the most desperately depressive, real-world lyrical narratives with production of breathtaking otherworldliness. It is almost indescribable: effortlessly light, like someone running their finger around the rim of a glass, but it also makes you queasy, like you're spinning down a plughole, out of control. In Dizzee's teenage hands, the Japanese three-stringed *shamisen* becomes something between an earworm and an inner-ear infection.

'I think it's really important that you shouldn't be afraid to use something if you like it, no matter how fucked the sound,' Dizzee told *Sound on Sound* magazine in 2004, explaining his use of the *shamisen*. 'Some people process sounds too much, but to me, that defeats the object ... I felt that it was a really interesting sound, which didn't remind me of anything else. I like using sounds that are about as "out there" as they come.'

Tim Smith noted that when Dizzee arrived in his GCSE music class at 14 he was already very comfortable with creating clear structures, and balancing rhythm, bass and melody – that he knew what the song sounded like in his head already, and the only challenge would be making it a reality. Tellingly, and unusually, many of the vocal recordings on *Boy in da Corner* were first takes: Dizzee's pirate-radio training – as well as the street hustle of practising in the playground or around the estate – meant he could just walk in and get it right first time. But that one-take skill also helps explain the album's vocal rawness, and its freshness. 'I'll never forget da way you kept the faith in me, even when things looked grim,' he wrote in tribute to Smith on the album sleeve. Smith casually mentioned to me that he still had 33 tracks Dizzee composed back then. 'I couldn't pass them on to anyone,' he said, seeing the glint in my eye, but reassured me they were at least fully backed up (many classic instrumentals have been lost over the years in hard-drive meltdowns). We agreed maybe some kind of donation to the British Library sound archive would be in order.

It takes a village to raise a scene, and it gives that scene an extraordinary power and coherence when everyone in the village suddenly becomes obsessed with it. Appearing on Commander B's Choice FM show in 2002, Wiley was asked about his ongoing beef with Durrty Doogz (later Goodz) – who did the fans think was winning, of the two of them? He told the radio host he 'wasn't really interested' in what listeners in the world at large thought – there was only one audience which counted. 'Home is where it matters,' he said. 'I care about my own area, I'd rather be the top boy in my own area – I want to be the top boy in east.'

MC Griminal, one of the younger of several members of the Ramsay family to become a key figure in the grime scene (older brothers Marcus Nasty and Mak 10 were founders and legendary DJs with Nasty Crew), tells a story of being an 11-year-old at St Bonaventure's School in Forest Gate, when Tinchy Stryder, several years his senior, and already well known on the local scene, approached him, handed him a CD of his tracks, and a £10 note for his troubles, telling him to make sure Mak 10 got it. 'None of my mates could believe that Tinchy was coming up to me, or that Dizzee was at my house,' Griminal told local paper the *Newham Recorder* eight years later, in 2010. It was the era of hyper-local celebrity, even while almost all of the celebrities in question were living in cramped council homes with their parents, or sharing bedrooms with their siblings. When Slimzee's gran went to the Woolworths on Roman Road, five minutes walk from their house, to buy his *Bingo Beats* CD, she saw two teenage girls enthusiastically pawing it. 'That DJ Slimzee is my grandson,' she told them, much to their excitement.

'We started to become local-famous,' Kano recalled in the *Made in the Manor* documentary. These years of dedicated community-based under-ground music making, in youth clubs, pirate-radio sets and house parties, made for a unique kind of apprenticeship, and a quietly confi-dent mindset, once the stage unexpectedly became much bigger a few years later. 'What helped when we broke through,' Kano continued, 'was the practice hours that we put in, performing in front of like, 20 people.' When he was signed to 679, and was booked to do his first proper gig outside the manor, opening for The Streets, he wasn't overly worried. 'It was my first time performing in front of that many people, but I had put in so much hours, and made all my mistakes behind closed doors, that it was cool. We got to make our mistakes in someone's kitchen, on a pirate radio.'

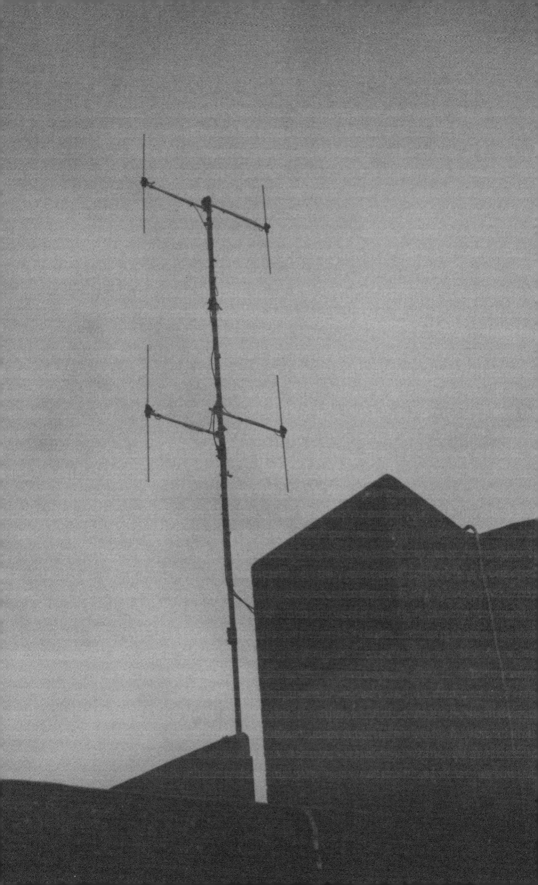

FOUR

THE LAST OF
THE PIRATES

The first few years of the new millennium were also the end of an era. Grime's first flush of youth, before it took the name, took place in the last days of a wilder, rougher metropolis; before a swathe of council estate regenerations began and others were demolished altogether. The demographics in areas like Bow, Stratford and Lewisham would grow ever more affluent, as richer people moved in, and New Labour plastered London with CCTV – a change intimately connected to their Urban Renaissance strategy to bring the middle classes back to the inner cities.

Until that point, illegal and semi-legal economies, black markets, cottage industries and thriving sub-cultures circling around inner London were essential to the informal city. In east London in particular, coping strategies in the face of entrenched poverty had long been part of the fabric: ducking and diving, wheeling and dealing, while the proximity to the Thames and docks meant historically the black market was always thriving.[1] There is very little left of the informal city now, and pirate radio in the grime era might be the last bastion of truly autonomous, urban working-class self-expression – autonomous in the sense that it is possible to make a living from it, without the approval, or profit extraction, of the whiter, wealthier established British culture industries.

'Let us know you're locked.' Rinse FM aerial, 2009

Mostly, it wasn't about making money at all. In fact, DJs would pay monthly 'subs' of £20 or £25 for the upkeep of their station, and broadcast to a narrow radius of only a few miles, for the sheer love of it – although, in return for their subs, equipment and dubplates, came rave bookings, record sales, and a just-about-sustainable living. It's hard to overstate how vital the pirates have been to the incubation and growth of eighties and nineties dance genres, from acid house and soul through ragga, jungle, happy hardcore, dubstep, UK garage, bassline, funky house, and so much else of the UK dance family tree. Their proliferation had reached a high point by the early 2000s, and they were the lifeblood of grime in its embryonic period: a meeting point; a testing and rehearsal ground for new and established talent, live on the mic and on the decks; a place where hits and stars were made; a communication channel and a binding agent, for the community contained within earshot. 'I came from nothing. I came from the underground, the pirate-radio scene,' Dizzee Rascal said in his Mercury Prize acceptance speech in 2003. 'If you don't acknowledge it, it will creep up anyway.'

Some arms of the British establishment were more than happy to acknowledge the pirates. Using the 1949 Wireless Telegraph Act, the government's Radiocommunications Agency (part of the DTI), and later Ofcom, were the Wile E. Coyote to the pirates' Road Runner: always on the hunt for their secret locations, shaking their fists, threatening prosecutions, raiding studios, shutting them down, or more often just seizing transmitters (worth a few hundred pounds) to disrupt and penalise their activity. DTI operations more than doubled between 1991 and 2002, reflecting the spread of pirate stations as the equipment got cheaper, and the music evolving live on the broadcasts flourished. In 2002, the Radiocommunications Agency raided 209 pirate stations, 181 of them in London. It's hard to imagine how grime could ever have developed without them.

It's also hard to convey to people who've never heard them just how exciting and unpredictable listening to the pirates could be. Unexpected guest cameos, collaborations and musical detours were commonplace: they worked to reasonably consistent, though changeable schedules –

but you never quite knew who was going to be brought along to 'touch mic' on any particular set; or whether your favourite station might suddenly disappear completely, without, of course, any warning or explanation. The premiere of a new anthem on pirate radio could be a genuine event: the jaw-dropping sonic newness of some of the hot-off-the-vinyl-press dubplates, the sheer hype of the latest club banger being reloaded, two, three, five times or more – with no prospect of hearing it anywhere else until the next rave featuring the same crew, possibly no prospect of hearing it again full stop. Each show was a unique broadcast, especially when the MCs were inside: it's why so many fans had a TDK recording while listening. It helped that as a listener, you too could be a participant in the hype: by joining the 'phone line crew' and quickly texting in or dropping a missed call, or a 'one dinger', to show approval (one ding, because you only let it ring once, so it displayed on the screen of whatever Nokia 'brick' phone they had in the studio).

'I want ten missed calls for the reload' would be a common injunction as the DJ flicked the cross-fader to a new dubplate: they would be strict about this, too – if the tune got about a minute or so in, with only eight or nine, they'd chide the audience as a group for their decadence: 'You're too slow man … nah sorry you're too slow, it's not coming back now – I can see you still ringing in, yeah big up the 392, but it's not coming back.' It was a conversation: a peculiar, imbalanced conversation, but a conversation nonetheless. Sometimes the conversation was more detailed, or even stretched to call-ins: I dimly recall the banter during the African Cup of Nations, maybe in 2006, as two MCs of African descent debated the relative merits of Ghana and Nigeria's chances and abilities with each other and the audience. Shystie first got her break from ringing in to her local station Heat FM and spitting bars down the phone, live on air. Eventually another aspiring female MC called in to do the same, and they had a slightly stilted clash, taking it in turns to call in. 'It was literally just hunger,' she told me later, 'I practised and practised and practised and I wanted people to hear me.'

The pirates developed very specific codes, rituals and semantics, bringing listeners closer into the in-group – the one ding for the reload, the shout-out via three final digits of a mobile-phone number, 'hit us up on the text', 'hold tight the Plumstead massive', 'this one's a persie' (personal favourite) – even down to knowing to tune in at 20 past the hour, because there will usually be 20 minutes of continuous adverts at the start of a two-hour show, but then none after that. The slang evolves between the MCs, DJ and the listeners with little managerial input or oversight, with the exception of some stations prohibiting swearing – ostensibly confusing, given the whole thing is illegal – or the need to read out information about a rave organised by the station. There are times when requests to 'let us know you're locked' takes on a plaintive air – because without that, how would you ever know anyone was listening? There are no official RAJAR figures (those used by legal stations to determine listenership), and there's always been a chance some scruffy herbert has nicked or broken a vital part of your £300 rig during the night.

Listening to the pirates can be a romantic experience, as anyone who has waltzed around their bedroom with the aerial clutched in their arms can attest – all the more so when the signal plays hard to get, and you can hear the unique, one-of-a-kind musical moment you were looking forward to all week being swallowed up by static and crackle, the MC holding the mic aloft as the ship tragically disappears beneath the waves. Then there is the beguiling patter of shout-outs, and the adverts for raves voiced by MEN WHO MUST HAVE SOME KIND OF HEARING IMPAIRMENT, THE WAY THEY'RE SHOUTING. Most of all it is the sheer gusto the DJs have for the music they play; molten-fresh new music direct from the artists themselves, tunes that would maybe become the club, or even, occasionally, mainstream hits of weeks, months or years hence. Turning that mind-bending innovation into mainstream money would often take a comically long time; turning it into cash-in-hand wads from club promoters, or sale-or-return deals with independent record shops, much less so.

* * *

Pirate broadcasting has always been a perilous business. The stations have been positioned against cultural gatekeepers, state authorities and dodgy rivals for their entire history – and have always been stoically determined to broadcast to their public, no matter what, ever since the broadcasting was done from actual boats. One early pirate station, Radio North Sea, was attacked by fire bombs in 1971, lobbed aboard from a small boat owned by a rival station, and had to be rescued by the Dutch navy – with the ship ablaze, the DJ on air broadcast a Mayday call while pop music continued to play underneath.

Famous 1960s nautical pirate stations like Radio Caroline transmitted pop music from the sea to European listeners when there were only three stuffy BBC stations on the legal airwaves in the UK; as the voice of the establishment, the BBC was hostile to youth culture in general. Like latter-day dance and black-music pirate stations, the subversive activity of the pop pirates of the 1960s and 70s was always at risk of co-option or assimilation – when the big ships on the mainland finally conceded defeat, and offered young people at least some of what they wanted to hear. The point is that the pirates have always been the site of rebellious or marginal culture, operating outside managed or official creative avenues, and often ending up changing them – when the music, DJs and even the stations themselves move from the pirates' rickety schooners to HMS Culture Industry. Famously, Radio Caroline's illicit success led directly to the creation of BBC Radio 1. 1980s acid house pirate station KISS FM became a legal station in 1990, and today is a well-established media brand and platform (because that's what we have these days) – it also hosted Logan Sama's weekly grime show from 2004–14, for most of that period the only grime show anywhere on legal radio.

Even while they remained hounded by the establishment, and illegal, pirate stations effectively became the feeder stations and cultivation grounds – of new artists, DJs and entire genres – that would sustain their commercial counterparts, and the entire 'legit' music industry, in years to come. And while the grand histories of the pirate stations that made it big – KISS FM and Rinse, primarily, or Kool FM, during the jungle era – are told in documentaries, with justification, there were literally hundreds of others, some short-lived, others not, some amateurish, some bound up in criminal activity, but most just doing it for the love, never making any profit. Rinse FM founder Geeneus got his first show on east London jungle station Pressure FM, and met his fellow founders Slimzee and Wiley at Chillin FM; it was an ever-changing constellation of cheap, illegal hubs for new music.

When Geeneus and Slimzee were both kicked off Pressure FM, still only in their mid-teens – they didn't like the fact Slim, even as a teenager, had all the best records, and was embarrassing the other DJs – they set up Rinse FM. Rinse has been a legal station since 2010, after years of dogged bureaucratic work and lobbying by Sarah 'Soulja' Lockhart – and has become more than a station: an urban-music superbrand, encompassing several record labels, club nights, an annual festival in Hackney, and, as part of its legal 'community licence', a range of youth and community training programmes. It was not, of course, always the sleek vessel it is today. Their first broadcast, in September 1994, was from the 18-storey-high Ingram House, five minutes from Slimzee's flat, five minutes from Wiley's flat, five minutes from Roman Road. They paid the brother of a friend £30 to broadcast from his flat for the weekend, set the decks up in the kitchen, and, not really knowing what they were doing, attached an aerial to the TV, and dangled it out the window.

The world of the pirates was appropriately dangerous and swashbuckling – staying one step ahead of sometimes dodgy rival stations, and the authorities, looking for better blocks to raise an antenna on, or a new studio to use. Even with entryphones at ground level and locked doors to the roof, accessing the tower blocks themselves to put up transmitters was never too hard; you'd steal or buy a fire-brigade key from a dodgy firefighter, or a lift engineer, or someone who worked for the council. The critical thing was looking inconspicuous when you were setting up the rig – so that was usually done at night, or in workmen's clothes, as a disguise. There was always the danger that rival stations, or just local criminals, or addicts, would get wind of where your studio was, boot off the door, and steal the decks and equipment – you could hardly go running to the police if it happened. In the informal city, different rules apply. Wiley was threatened with a shotgun outside Deja Vu in Stratford. Geeneus had a sword held to his throat in a studio in Nesbitt House in Hackney. The folklore and mythology around stations like Rinse and Deja Vu is as extensive as befits that surrounding any great cultural institution: such as the highly entertaining hour where Wiley ridiculed former friend God's Gift on air, only for Gift to turn up at the studio mob-handed while the show was still on air, and bring it to a premature and possibly violent close. You can hear Wiley shouting 'outside!' amidst the ruckus in the background, while Gift takes the mic to announce drily there are 'technical difficulties'. There are mythical tales of DJs booting doors off studios after disagreements with management, and crews turning up with shotguns because they felt slighted that they hadn't been given a slot. More benign (and verifiably true) are historic and hilarious broadcasts like Wiley's drunk Christmas show with DJ Karnage on Rinse FM in 2004, where his meandering monologue includes him idly slagging off numerous friends and peers, and even Christmas itself. 'Easter's better innit?'

Studios were often located in squats – walls tagged up with sharpies, bin bags or cardboard in the windows for privacy – or in an under-used flat with no one living permanently in it, with a bit of rent money thrown in for access. On one occasion, in the Crossways Estate in Bow (where Dizzee and Wiley are photographed on the cover of this book), Rinse effectively bought a council flat off an ageing alcoholic, in return for a £130 plane ticket. 'He was an old geezer, always drunk, and had a flat on the eighth floor – and he just wanted to get home to Ireland, he didn't care about the flat,' Slimzee recalled. 'But he had no money to get home, so he said we could have it for a few months if we paid for a ticket to get him back home. We were squatting in there for about a year.'

This was in grime's critical year, 2003, and the growing popularity of Rinse, and the music, meant MCs were turning up from across London to showcase their skills; the station's management tried to institute a rule of only two MCs at a time – like a newsagent with rowdy school kids –

because the neighbours were getting increasingly, unsurprisingly, suspicious, as people traipsed in and out at all times of day or night. Eventually, exasperated, Rinse temporarily banned all MCs from the station, and the entire east London scene decamped, many of them to Deja Vu FM, where the seminal night of *Conflict* between Dizzee Rascal and Crazy Titch took place. The Deja studio was then in Club EQ on Wardens Road, a couple of miles to the east of Bow in Stratford, which wasn't in a residential block, and so there was more freedom there.

'It was like a madhouse, there were like a hundred people in there, all smoking, fights would kick off, crazy things would happen,' recalled Matt Mason. 'There were stations like that, and then there were stations like Ice FM and Mac FM, where it felt like we were part of the SAS. You would be standing in a little broom cupboard, like basically an airing cupboard on the top floor of a council block, and it's always dirty – you know, mould on the walls, and the carpet smells of God knows what – and the tricky thing was making it sound like you were at the best fucking party in the world for the listeners, while keeping the music down so as not to alert the neighbours. At other times, when we were really struggling for a studio, someone would say, "Okay look, we can do it at my house for a week," – so the turntables would be on an ironing board in someone's living room, and the guy's missus is all pissed off because of all the people in there.' Rinse furtively broadcast both from Wiley's and Slimzee's childhood homes, either side of Roman Road, at various points. Wiley's dad was not impressed when he worked out what was going on.

'It's crazy to think back about pirate stations now,' said Skepta as we sat in his car in 2015, shortly after filming the video for his hit 'Shutdown', and well on the way to becoming a superstar. 'Obviously I'd seen proper radio stations on the TV, so when I'm hearing these people on pirate radio I'm thinking, "Ah shit, when I get there it's gonna be so sick." I remember the first time I went to a pirate station, and I walked in, and I'm walking into a house! And I'm thinking "this is crazy" – I turned the corner, the pirate radio is in the kitchen, fam. It's in the kitchen, decks just on the side! It was a kind of mad realisation, it was like finding out the tooth fairy wasn't real. So so greazy.' But for Skepta's £20 subs to Heat FM, even in the short term, it was easily an investment worth making: he sold 'literally thousands' of white labels like 'DTI', his second ever release, a tongue-in-cheek homage to the Department of Trade and Industry. The video for 'DTI' – it is one of the few instrumental tracks of its kind to ever warrant its own music video – follows two hapless DTI officials trying to make a bust, while our heroes run the track from a small temporary studio on a council estate. 'It was a priceless hustle, man. Pirates were like the sickest, most rebellious type of pop-up that you could ever have.'

The problem was that the more successful these rebel hustlers got, the more they would get noticed – and a government with major, top-down urban renewal on its mind did not have space for informal or illicit ways of doing things. It is no coincidence that, alongside their Urban Renaissance strategy for transforming the inner city, in the late nineties and early 2000s, New Labour helped turn London into the most surveilled city in the world. It has more recently been pushed into second place by Beijing, but there are still, at the last estimate, 420,000 CCTV cameras in London. Many of these are on private property, of course: but it is a transformation that was led by the state. A House of Lords report published in 2009 found that, during the nineties, 78 per cent of the Home Office crime prevention budget was spent on implementing CCTV – and a further £500 million of public money was spent on it between 2000 and 2006. We are, as Dizzee noted on 'Graftin'', the most watched society on earth: 'living in the Big Brother cameras' view, keep an eye out for the boys in blue.'[2] Kirstie Ball and Frank Webster's study, *The Intensification of Surveillance* (2003), concluded that it was the 9/11 attacks in America which 'stimulated and … legitimated the acceleration and expansion of surveillance trends', helping to 'promote especially acute disciplinary forms of surveillance'. These included more CCTV cameras in public places, and innovative facial recognition technology like the Mandrake system, which was trialled in the grime heartland of Newham, just to the east of Bow.

New Labour also outsourced security, probation and youth-justice services to inexperienced private security firms like Serco, Securicor, and Group 4 (now G4S) – giving them contracts for initiatives like the electronic tagging of offenders, which increased dramatically during the first years of the 2000s. The use of tags, with associated curfews, was also extended for use on 12–16-year-olds in 2002. As public space in the city was increasingly privatised under New Labour, especially in 'privately owned public spaces' (POPS) like Canary Wharf, so more public (i.e. council) housing was being bought up under the 'right to buy' scheme Thatcher had introduced, leading to more and more poorer Londoners renting from private landlords rather than the state – and now even parts of the policing of the city were being handed over to profit-making firms. New Labour's urban renaissance was taking shape.

Grime's ascendancy coincided with another central element of New Labour's frequently controversial, authoritarian approach to law and order – and another one that was deeply bound up with their urban regeneration strategy – the Anti-Social Behaviour Order, introduced in 1998. ASBOs were a wide-ranging, rather elastic tool which allowed police and the courts to discipline the kind of day-to-day delinquent behaviour that would not be significant enough to warrant a criminal prosecution: things like drunkenness, loutish behaviour, intimidation, graffiti, low-key violence or threats of violence, noise, begging, fly-tipping – and extending to rather more exotic public activities like urban exploring, parkour and dogging. Like all the best authoritarian instruments, the ASBO was open to bizarre interpretation and abuse by those with the power to issue them: leading to absurd cases like that of the 13-year-old who was forbidden to use the word 'grass' to intimidate people, or the shepherd prohibited from grazing his flock of 500 sheep in an intimidating manner. The burgeoning grime scene was to meet the burgeoning New Labour disciplinary regime in the most unfortunate manner.

* * *

Tracking down an antenna is fairly easy for the authorities. Tracking down the studio it is attached to – by an undetectable microwave signal – is much harder. This is where surveillance came in. Having taken over from the DTI in pirate-hunting, Ofcom were escalating their efforts to seize the equipment of stations like Rinse FM, frequently confiscating their rigs and taking the station off air; but as grime reached its peak, the station was doing well financially – according to Geeneus, taking a couple of thousand pounds a week in advertising and subs – and could afford plenty of back-up transmitters. 'They were smashing down walls and parts of buildings, cutting open air vents, they was going completely in to get to us,' says Geeneus, as he and Slimzee went to ever-greater efforts to cover their tracks, and move their kit to harder-to-find spots. Increasingly paranoid, Geeneus took to wearing masks when he set up the rigs; Slim was less bothered. 'I'm on this stealth thing, ninja-ing in and out of everything. I'm on the roof with a balaclava on, and he's like "you've lost your mind",' said Geeneus, who, as the smaller of the two, found himself being lowered down air vents with a torch strapped to his head, or removing pieces of flooring and booby-trapping the route to the transmitter. One local rival station, Rush FM, had hidden their transmitters in bricks, surrounded by CS gas; they got taken off air repeatedly, ran out of money, and eventually gave up the fight. Rinse were determined to avoid the same fate.[3]

It became increasingly like an episode of *MacGyver*. 'We were putting the rigs in lift shafts in the blocks,' Slimzee told me, 'climbing up on top of the lift, then D-locking it, so it was hanging from the thing that holds the lift in place. And they would still somehow get up there and get it out. Or we'd cut open pipes, like cut open the tin, and tie a carjack to the rig and push it out of sight.' The Rinse FM rig had moved two miles south-east from the Roman Road to 28-storey Shearsmith House in Cable Street in Wapping: closer to Canary Wharf, and closer to the centre of London. While Geeneus would be fully masked-up as Rinse's stature grew and grew, Slimzee remained unfazed. 'I knew how to run the block, knew how to walk around it. I was going up there in the daytime, rather than at night – so it weren't really bait [obvious], and people thought I was a workman: all you've got to do is put a little suit on, blue bottoms and stuff. Some people used to take mops with them when they were putting rigs up.'

But Ofcom were preparing a sting of unprecedented sophistication, using all of the London city-state's new technological armoury. They had hidden one CCTV camera in a bottle-bank at street level, across the road from Shearsmith House, and placed another minuscule camera, hidden in an electrical box on the top of the block, where the stairs led out to the rooftop. After some time monitoring and gathering surveillance material, one day they trailed Slimzee from the rooftop, to the studio, and back to his house, just off Roman Road. They raided all three premises, and arrested him, seizing three stations' worth of transmission equipment, all the specialist keys to get into the tower blocks, computer equipment, and even the Rinse FM accounts book.

'When they showed the evidence in court I realised they had put cameras everywhere,' Slimzee said. 'They had one right near my house. They must have got up to my kitchen window somehow, looking in, because there was a photo of my girlfriend and the baby there. I don't know how they got that picture.'

Determined to show that Rinse would not be bowed, and also to undermine the Crown Prosecution Service case that Slimzee was a solo criminal mastermind, Geeneus took an iPod and another transmitter, and put the station back on air immediately, broadcasting mp3s while his friend was still in the police station. Slimzee was given a £500 fine and a five-year ASBO prohibiting him from going above the fourth floor of any building. Slimzee was still only 23, and, in the short-term, the ASBO killed his career, and led to a nervous breakdown and years away from the limelight. 'I was really ill,' he said, recalling a dark time in his life. 'I didn't know what was going on. I was trying to fight it but I couldn't – it overtook me. That's why I've put loads of weight on now, because I'm on loads of medication for it. I was getting pains all over my body, psychosomatic pains: it was weird, my body was telling me there was pain there but there wasn't. So I was trying to sort that out and trying to DJ, but in the end I couldn't do it. And I had a young baby growing up … it was just too much for me.' Later in the 2000s, Slimzee would come out to play the occasional set at FWD, bringing out his old dubs, the ones no one else has or has ever had, but it's only since 2014 that he's been back on radio, and playing live, regularly: a decade since his arrest. It's not unreasonable to see him as a martyr for the whole of the grime scene – not only its greatest DJ, but the one who took incredible risks, and suffered a great deal, so that the rest of the scene could thrive. I hope anyone who appeared on Rinse before 2004 has said thank you to him, at some point.

It's certainly true that there is no one in the latter-day, chart-topping grime scene who underestimates the importance of the pirates. Hearing grime's originators talk about what pirate stations meant to them is to understand – to get a glimpse, at least – of just how transformative they could be: a form of empowerment over the neighbourhood around them, and over the city itself. If you'd come from nothing, here was an opportunity to become local-famous. Joining the pirate world for the first time transformed the horizons as seen from London's margins. Geeneus has said that as a teenager he was an obsessive fan of radio – not of the music they played, even, but of radio, the medium – to the point that he pretty much gave up on school, because he had already decided that pirate radio was all he wanted to do.

'I went on a tower block for the first time, I climbed on the roof, and I was like, what is going on up here – it was like a whole other life. What I imagined as a kid, it was a whole heap more, there was this next level of everything to do with radio. Straight away I was like: this is *amazing*. I'm on a tower block, we've sneaked in a tower block, climbed up on the roof, I'm standing on top of the tower block now, 27 storeys high, looking across the whole of London, figuring out how we're going to switch on the radio station. Generally in life, people say I don't really get excited by much, but I think it's because them things there were amazing, and it's what I spent the majority of my younger life figuring out how I could be involved in. So now when people say, "Do you want to go on the London Eye?" or "This is a good thing to go and look at," I'm like, "I'm not interested." Do you know what I mean? – it's boring.'[4]

The pirate MCs never sounded bored, by contrast. If you're bothering to devote your time to this performance, unpaid – indeed paying for the privilege, if anything, why wouldn't you bring along all the hype and energy built up in you prior to that point? The dedication to radio as a medium in itself is remarkable: even when the scene was in the doldrums, in the late 2000s, stalwart DJ and producer Spooky would travel with his record box across London on three night buses, at midnight on a week-night, to do a set on a low-key station – just to play. You can still hear the frisson of energy in the archived sets from the old days, recorded onto cassette and then ripped – such a violent term, so grimy, so *piratical* – to mp3. The whoops of celebration off mic in the background, as someone drops their killer bars. The screeching halt of a record being pulled up in excitement, overwhelmed by the MC's delivery, buckling under the hype – and sometimes leaving the MC responsible for the reload bars still on the mic, and the others in the background as an echo, still screaming the punchline a cappella, as a kind of celebration of the rewind, a victory lap after the record has stopped, because the hype is still propelling them. It's like the moment when a cartoon character runs off the edge of the cliff, but their legs are still cycling – and every bit as exhilarating.

Most of all, it offered a phenomenal feeling of empowerment, connecting that creativity directly to a network of listeners. 'It felt so special,' Rapid from Ruff Sqwad told me once, slightly dreamily. 'You'd make a beat in your bedroom, go to some tiny room, put it on the decks, and hundreds of people are listening. That energy was just a next feeling, like you were on top of the world.' Ruff Sqwad, as particularly precocious teenagers, became stars in the hood while still at school – there are Rinse FM recordings from 2001 featuring a 14-year-old Tinchy Stryder, when his voice had barely broken. 'When I first started,' Tinchy said to me a decade later, while people from his record label took his lunch order, 'part of what was exciting about it, was you'd go to school the next day and people would have tapes they'd recorded of us from the previous night.' Getting a set on a leading pirate was a big achievement: they had been those kids swapping tapes of Heartless Crew and Pay As You Go, and now, their schoolmates were swapping tapes of their own sets. Even in 2017, P Money will throw in a line where he says, 'I'm so a-m-a-zing/ back in school I was Roll Deep taping'[5] – the cycle, like the cassette, kept turning.

Once you'd built up a reputation – usually rapidly, such is the way with grime – premieres of new material were a huge deal. In a rave you might be more inclined to skew to the classic instrumentals and your most familiar reload bars, to keep the crowd lively – but on the radio, the emphasis was more on sharing the newest sound. The first time Ruff Sqwad played the instrumental version of 'Died In Your Arms' on their Rinse show – a take on the Cutting Crew VH1 eighties rock classic – and the WHOMP of the drum claps come in, whichever MC was holding the mic at that point exclaimed, 'Clap your hands!' Rapid chuckled when I reminded him of this moment a decade later. 'That was what we were imagining, some stadium-rock thing, visualising all these people clap-ping.' They were conducting the choir – leading them like Axl Rose would, and imagining a vast stadium, a world beyond grime, beyond school, beyond Bow – at a point when taking the bus a few miles north to do a guest spot on another pirate felt like the other side of the world. The sense of a connection to the congregation out there, silent except for the missed calls they sent in for the reload, was as expansive as it was intimate. 'Our minds were so wide open at the time,' Dirty Danger suggested: 'so ambitious – that's how we felt. It sounds funny to me now, one of us saying "clap your hands", but it worked, because other people felt the same way we did.'

There was clearly something mind-expanding in the act of broadcasting, but particularly so, when there were sensational views from studios located high up in tower blocks, as Geeneus said. London is not a skyscraper city, compared to many of its peers – although it has become dramatically more so since grime started out, as the skyline is dotted with super-rich mixed-use office, commercial and residential skyscrapers like the Shard – but it is naturally claustrophobic in its topography. There is not a great number of high hills offering expansive views out over the city; and the obvious exceptions – Primrose Hill, Greenwich, Hampstead – are all notably very green, and very posh. A lack of hills and a lack of views means a lack of opportunities to breathe in, to get a sense of the wider city, to physically look beyond your estate, your neighbourhood, your borough. London topography mitigates against the calming influence of perspective, and intensifies the tensions and myopia created by a milieu of poverty, petty crime and narrow education and employment opportunities. It's easy to see how getting involved in pirate radio offered a kind of peace, even as it was generating an almighty racket.

'Ice FM used to come out of Shepherd's Bush,' recalled Matt Mason, 'and the blocks opposite the green, and the view you had from up there was so great; I used to do the morning show, and looking out to London, especially west London around carnival time, and seeing that skyline and being able to talk to it, and the phone's popping … it's one of the highs of DJing.'

Slimzee's first experience of going up on the rooftop to set up a rig was just as exhilarating as Geeneus's. 'At first I wanted to get down! It was windy, raining; I was really scared. But once you've got used to the height, it gives you such a buzz. Being up there makes you feel really good about yourself – that you're doing something with your life, putting that work in so that people can hear you.' I asked him which of the many 'tall blocks' Rinse had used over the years offered the best view. 'The three flats was definitely one of the best; of course now it's all been done up, you could never get up there again. But that was a *really* good view. You could see Dagenham, you could see Newham, you could see Canning Town: you could see the full works. I mean, really good, like.'

I couldn't help but think it significant that the three areas he mentioned were all less glamorous areas further to the east of Bow, and not those standing on the outskirts of 'proper London': not St Paul's, not the City, not the money and storied histories of the city centre. Dagenham, Newham and Canning Town: the full works.

* * *

For all the tensions and clashes with the authorities, the grime pirates offered a way out of petty crime and violence: and like KISS FM before them, one or two went on to become successful, even kosher businesses. They were rarely intended to be money-making operations, and for most of their lives, they were not – but there were exceptions. Rinse FM's revenue had started out very small: they managed to secure £30 for a weekend's worth of adverts for Limehouse Pizza Palace (more recent corporate partners include Nike and the Tate). But pirate-radio adverts were also often an art form in themselves, especially when the ads were for raves put on by the station's management – familiar MCs from the station would voice them, sometimes playing characters, acting out detailed plotlines as part of a convoluted performance designed to hype a forthcoming rave.

In a bizarre bridging of the gulf between these illegal underground channels and the mainstream music industry, the pirates also hosted adverts from major record labels – Warners, Universal, Sony/BMG – who would send through promotional CDs in the same way they would to Radio 1 or KISS FM. Even Operation Trident, the police's black-on-black violent crime division, paid for adverts on London pirates – it seems incredible that they'd be funnelling money to illegal companies that their fellow officers in other departments were trying to shut down, but on another level it makes perfect sense. The record labels and Trident supposed they knew who their audiences really were, and that they wouldn't be reaching them so directly via stations like Capital FM. Indeed in some cases, the authorities were operating an equivalent of the 'Hamsterdam' plotline in *The Wire* – tacitly cooperating with their targets, turning a blind eye, rather than engaging in pointless, circular games of cat-and-mouse.

'We interacted with the police in a very consistent and deliberate way at Ice and Mac,' Matt Mason says of his involvement in the late garage-era pirates in west London. 'The DTI at the time had the station manager's mobile number, and they would call up and say, "Listen, we're going to hit your rig, we're going to shut you off on Sunday – please do us a favour, please stay off air for like three hours, just make it look like we're doing our jobs." We were running club nights like Exposure at Gass Club, so money was coming into the station: we had more money to put on pirate stations than the DTI did to knock us down. And the money was coming from institutions that pay taxes, that funded the DTI. It looks a bit ridiculous when you stand back and look at it, as most complex things are. But it was all allowed, because if you actually look at it, we're creating culture, it's so great for London, for Britain. We're not selling drugs, we're not hurting each other, we're making music and making people happy. I think the reason we got away with it for so long, and so much, was because actually, we were adding value.

'Ever since the 1950s, ever since the government was so petrified of the fact that 95 per cent of people were listening to rock 'n' roll broadcast from boats in the Channel, they didn't know what the fuck to do about it. Radio was the scariest thing, it was like nuclear technology to them: this thing could destroy the nation. But it persisted, and it became seen as positive. People in the US ask me, "Why does that happen in the UK, but it doesn't happen here?" It's not because British kids are smarter or more daring than they are in other parts of the world. It's because British society let pirate radio happen.'

FIVE

THE MAINSTREAM AND THE MANOR

In September 2003, only a few months after his heated tussle with Crazy Titch on the Deja Vu rooftop, and less than two months after he was stabbed in Ayia Napa, Dizzee Rascal won the Mercury Music Prize. Did he deserve to win, asked the BBC, experimenting with a new approach to interactivity with their audience? 'Yes', said 33 per cent, 'no', said 25 per cent, 'who?' said 42 per cent. He collected the Mercury Award from Ms Dynamite at the star-studded ceremony, took it back to Burdett Estate in Bow, and struggled to comprehend the disjunction between the two. *Boy in da Corner* was always intended as a document. Even at the age of 16, during which time most of his debut was written, Dizzee saw himself as an observer, as much as a participant in the stories he told. A detached social commentator on his peer group – a voice from the inside describing the lives of young people either ignored or misunderstood; not so much a spokesperson, as a reporter. 'MCs better start chatting about what's really happening,' he says censoriously over the opening bars of 'Brand New Day'.

A record which described the dichotomy between the lives of the British sovereign and Dylan Mills ('Queen Elizabeth don't know me, so/ How can she control me, when/I live street and she lives neat?'[1]) also

Two east London icons, Dizzee and the Balfron

launched the latter on a course to become as famous as the former, and won the album a gold plaque, a Mercury Prize, and countless laudatory column inches. By the end of the decade it was regularly cited near the top of 'album of the decade' lists, a visionary work that paved the way for so many others, that changed the conversation about the British underclass being left behind by New Labour. Yet even as it was lauded, only a few voices in 2003 suggested that serious attention to *Boy in da Corner*'s themes was needed: Martin Clark wrote in the *Guardian* after the Mercury win that 'its sobering message is at risk of being drowned out by applause … Every MP in Westminster should be forced to hear it.' This is exactly what happened with the 1995 French film *La Haine*; a document of society's ills so powerful, and hitherto so ignored, that the French Prime Minister held a compulsory screening for his cabinet ministers.

Mathieu Kassovitz's film springs to mind during 'Sittin' Here', the opening song on *Boy in da Corner*: they are both contemplative yet volatile, callow yet wise. The track is devastatingly bleak. It is dominated by a haunted and synthetic twanging which repeats while Dizzee intones, 'I'm just sitting here, I ain't saying much, I just think/My eyes don't move left or right, they just blink.'[2] Our world-weary narrator gazes straight ahead without movement, stoned and immobile – taking in everything that he's seen in his young life, fixated by its permanence. He is an unwilling spectator on life in the manor, unable to tear his eyes away, and unable to use his wisdom to distance himself from the consequences. The track recalls one particular scene in *La Haine*, where Hubert, the most thoughtful and mature of the three young protagonists, smokes a spliff in his high-rise bedroom, his Isaac Hayes record bringing a moment of isolation from the estate beneath him, an oasis of solitude in a world with no privacy. Dizzee and Hubert are frozen in their snatched moments of reflection; frozen by the hopelessness of a community riven by systemic and everyday violence. 'Brand New Day', another of *Boy in da Corner*'s poignant snapshots of bleak social realism, draws on the idea of lost innocence, of growing up too soon and too alone ('looks like I'm losing hope/cos I climb this mountain without rope'), of playground scraps somehow escalating to dead bodies: 'Looks like I'm losing mates, there's a lot of hostility near my gates/We used to fight with kids from other estates, now eight millimetres settle debates.'[3] The first time Dizzee played the song to his cousin, Slix from Ruff Sqwad, Slix 'dropped a tear'.[4] It's an understandable reaction.

Once the fall has happened, the innocence is gone forever. Dizzee has spoken in interviews of several teenage friends being stabbed at 14 or 15. On the little-known B-side 'Dean' he zooms in from a generalised atmosphere of urban tragedy to pay tribute to a lost friend. It's a gut-wrenchingly frank letter to a former school friend, who committed suicide by throwing himself from a high-rise tower block ('I heard they found your body in three parts man'). The cathartic kitchen-sink realism of grime is integral to its identity, even if it is only part of its appeal, and only part of its content – dispatches from the other side of London's social divide, where, 'All five man eating off the same plate, all five cars with the same plates,' as Jme spits on 'Keep Moving': 'if that rings bells we're from the same place.'[5] For Dizzee, social exclusion is immutable and self-perpetuating, 'the same story, now and then different actors.' It is, he says on 'Round We Go', 'just one big cycle here' – joy, love, inno-cence, even life itself: all are transient.

At the root of it all is poverty, and its outward signs and fellow riders: petty crime, lost youth, violence, 'bank scams, street robbery/shotters, blotters or H.M.P', and, on the level of personal life, 'pregnant girls who think they love, useless mans with no plans'.[6] It wasn't something main-stream British culture was used to hearing, certainly not often, certainly not from someone this young and emotionally articulate, in a period that was supposed to be suffused with the optimism of a new century and a new start: a modern, classless society. The modernity audible in Dizzee's music came from its sonics, which were abrasive, discombobu-lating and bewilderingly uncategorisable. If he and his peers were 'a problem for Anthony Blair' – the lyric from 'Hold Ya Mouf' the broad-sheets were fond of quoting as shorthand for grime's disreputable energy and lyrics – it was chiefly because they were doing pop-cultural modern-ism entirely the wrong way. This wasn't *inclusive*, and it certainly wasn't the safe populism that had led to the embarrassing scenes around 'cool Britannia' in the late nineties, when Noel Gallagher had been invited to meet Blair at Downing Street.

At times the press acted like colonial reporters who'd just arrived in the orient – having, in most cases, just taken the tube a bit further east than they'd been before – and were astonished by the customs and practices of the natives. Beneath the headlines about this remarkable teenage prodigy, there was a partial recognition that something else was going on beyond Dizzee Rascal's debut in 2003: an underground scene underneath the break-out star. His occasional collaborators, Lethal B's More Fire Crew, had been one of the few crews, along with Pay As U Go, to straddle the garage-into-grime period with a record deal. Their skittish single 'Oi' had been a Top 10 hit in 2002, but their album had failed to touch the charts, and they split. 'As soon as Dizzee won his Mercury, the majors started calling up again,' Bizzle said in *East is East*, a BBC Radio 1 documentary broadcast in July 2004. 'Like, "Yeah yeah Lethal, how's it going?"' Dizzee had succeeded on his own terms, rather than trying to make pop, or hip-hop, and even though 'the east London sound' didn't have a name yet, there was a sense of proprietary pride and confidence emerging from the generation of teenagers, who knew, in spite of their youth, they were making something entirely new, entirely different, and entirely uncompromising: some of them even started to sign record deals. 'We're still gully: the only pop you'll hear from us is "pop pop pop!", then we're out,' Kano spat on his breakthrough single 'P's And Q's' (the trio of pops mimicking a volley of gunfire). Davinche's production on the track, a propulsive and irresistible riff, with scattergun drums underneath, underlined the point beautifully.

Away from the handful of artists who signed deals in 2003 and 2004, an off-the-grid vinyl industry was thriving, entirely separate from the major labels and the established music business. The youngers who were creating what would become grime had formalised the rolling pirate sound into sellable objects, visiting vinyl-pressing plants like Music House in Tottenham, and cutting the beats they were making on home PCs onto white labels, shifting them at record shops on a 'sale or return' principle. Several artists generally better known as MCs started releasing instrumentals on vinyl this way: including Skepta (starting with 'Pulse Eskimo' in 2002) and Dizzee (with 'Go' and 'Ho', both 2003). The process of producing physical music helped bond together the nascent scene: both the cutting houses and the record shops became essential meeting points – the iconic Rhythm Division on Roman Road in Bow, but also Uptown and Blackmarket in Soho, Independence in south-east London and Big Apple in Croydon – in addition to the network of pirate radio stations, which would lead to future collaborations, remixes, guest spots on the radio, and the production of one-off versions of the records being cut, produced specially for the DJ, often with the DJ's name called out over the top, known as 'VIPs' or 'specials'. It all helped to construct an alternative network existing alongside, and apart from, the existing music industry.

Wiley was one of many who quickly realised, that with a profit of about three pounds on each unit, this could be a better way to make instant cash than the small-time (and sometimes not so small-time) drug dealing some of their peers were involved in. It helped that Wiley was phenomenally prolific: most of his peers would have at most two or three records available in the shops; at the peak of his eskibeat period, in 2002 and 2003, Wiley's music would often cover an entire shop wall. 'When the first batches started making money, I bought a car, and became like, a geezer with a van, selling them straight from the boxes,' he recalled. 'I would have gone anywhere. The local shop was Rhythm Division, but I'd sell them to every record shop in inner London, and outside the M25, greater London; any record shop, anywhere. I'd drive up to Birmingham on a certain day, or Manchester. I think I've covered more miles than any MC.' 'Eskimo' itself, released in 2002, sold over 10,000 vinyl copies alone – with no record deal, no manager, no PR, no artwork, no adverts: all sold from the boot of his car.

In these early years, from 2002–04, the nascent scene began channelling the freewheeling live energy of pirate radio and raves, the pairing of beats and bars, into making and recording songs. You could make beats or write bars at home, but recording vocal tracks required something more like professional equipment. They started going to paid-by-the-day recording studios a lot more to record. Wiley in particular, having made a decent packet from all his vinyl sales, and his album deal with XL, decided it was time that grime professionalised somewhat. He wanted Roll Deep to make an album, and paid the rent on a residential studio in Leroy Street in Bermondsey in south London for the whole summer, inviting not just his crew, but pretty much the entire east London scene. 'My attitude was, get everyone in here! Let's have a fucking party,' he said to me in 2016. 'In a way it wasn't good, because it made some people in the crew think, "Fucking hell Wiley, you've got everyone in here! Why's Kano in here? Why's so-and-so in here?"' For the younger MCs, like fellow Bow crew Ruff Sqwad, it was an opportunity too good to turn down, as producer and MC Rapid recalled. 'I'd be in college and get a call from Wiley and he'd be like: "Come to the studio right now."' They went.

The east London scene pretty much lived in that studio during the summer of 2004 – eating, sleeping, smoking weed, playing pool – and Roll Deep made their debut album, *In at the Deep End*. They also finished two Roll Deep 'Creeper' mixtapes and two Ruff Sqwad 'Guns N Roses' mixtapes, and launched numerous careers in the process. It was one of countless times the godfather of grime has, without being asked, volunteered to pay for other artists' studio time – or their international plane tickets, or brought them along as teenagers to a major show, or to Radio 1 – without thoughts to a future debt, or favour: just because he wanted grime to succeed. 'I've realised recently,' Wiley said, 'that that's why I'm the godfather. Because I think about all of us. In a way, your ideal priority would be just yourself, your manager and your team. I can't think that way.'

Roll Deep were, in 2004, 'peaking on the underground', as Target put it to me, but they hadn't even spoken to any labels, before finishing their album in Bermondsey that summer. It was picked up by Relentless, a plucky young independent label that had soared to prominence after putting out the less slinky and 'grown-up' side of UK garage, including Artful Dodger's 'Re-Rewind' and all of So Solid Crew's material, and they had made a chart hit of Lethal Bizzle's underground smash 'Pow! (Forward)' too. The Roll Deep album, *In at the Deep End*, has aged surprisingly well, but at the time it caused some scepticism: there was a lot on it that didn't sound especially grimy – most notably its two singles, 'Avenue' and 'Shake A Leg', which charted at 11 and 24 respectively, and even saw them smiling and jigging around on *Top of the Pops*. There was consternation on the underground that grime's first crew were finally getting recognition with such playful, soft-centred, family-friendly pop. That XL had chosen Wiley's 'Pies' as a single was met with equal derision by the underground – it was built on a proper eskibeat instrumental, but with Wiley in a fatsuit in the music video, and a chorus based on the football terrace chant of 'Who ate all the pies?', the whole thing seemed embarrassing (and the single didn't make the Top 40).

'When people sign to major labels,' Ruff Sqwad's MC Fuda Guy explained sadly in 2006, sitting in his childhood bedroom in Bow, 'it's not like they're doing it their way; they're doing it the way the labels want them to do it.' He offered up local idols and friends Roll Deep, in particular 'Avenue' and 'Shake A Leg', as specific examples. 'Any real grime fan is going to hear those singles and think "HUH? I like 'Eskimo', I like 'Creeper' … What's this?" But I know them personally, and that's what they got made to do.'

At the time, I nodded sympathetically – such are the compromises the industry forces on you: it's sad, but you can't beat the system right? In hindsight, it seems as though Roll Deep were saying one thing back in Bow, to safeguard their reputation as the authentic kings of grime – they had to be able to show their faces at Rinse FM – and saying something altogether different in the label offices. As the crew themselves tell it now, the pop turn had not just been with their consent, but was entirely their idea. 'A lot of people even now still think we were under pressure to do tunes like "Avenue" when we got signed,' Target says now. 'But we just wanted to make tunes like that! They were literally just some fun ideas, something a bit different. We'd made so many songs with a similar kind of sound, and we'd always listened to and been influenced by lots of different sounds, so we thought why don't we mess around and mix it up. Until that point, if you were a grime artist, you only ever made grime. I think it caught people by surprise a bit.'

The desire to spread their wings and fly speculatively beyond the icy-cold margins was too powerful – after years of growing heat on the underground: Roll Deep wanted a bit of chart success, and a decent pay-cheque, and, as Shabs Jobanputra, CEO of Relentless puts it, some legitimacy: not least because Lethal Bizzle, as head of rival east London crew Fire Camp, had secured a Top 10 hit with 'Pow!'. 'Roll Deep wanted to go over the top,' Jobanputra insists now. 'There was the harder stuff on the album as well, but ultimately they wanted to take grime and make it interesting, comic and fun. All these MCs, Wiley and Scratchy, were brilliant wordsmiths, and they had a comedy value; they had a pop sensibility as well.'

Cold, hard reportage is important, but starts to weigh you down after a while – what's more, if you've become the biggest fish in the small pond, it's a standard trajectory to want to reach out beyond it, after a while. Wiley's debut album for XL, *Treddin' on Thin Ice*, released in 2004, was almost a concept album charting his desire to transcend the 'madness' and 'pain' of street violence, drug-dealing and petty crime: 'I've had enough, I can't cope, I just want to make dough with my ni**as,' he blurts on 'Special Girl' – which is ostensibly a song about settling down into a serious relationship, with the woman of the title a cipher for a different kind of stability. So with Wiley at the helm, managing Roll Deep 'like a youth club', as he put it to me, Roll Deep had plotted out an album on a single piece of paper that became like a holy tablet, glossed with tweaks and comments, as a route to the mainstream, and out of the manor. There was a very deliberate focus on the charts, and on mainstream success, reasons Jobanputra – much of it driven by the same competitive impulses that came from clashing on pirate radio:

'They wanted to be bigger, better and stronger than the next crew, that's why they started making hits. I think they deliberately created anthems knowing that if they were more melodic they would get more money.' Relentless, having started as an independent, underground label, did a deal with Virgin/EMI which helped give them a leg-up in terms of promotion. 'Roll Deep were quite reticent to begin with,' Jobanputra recalls. 'Their peers were watching to see if they made money; there was pressure on them. I think it was tough for a lot of those guys to get out from their estates, but the desire to make music, the passion and the drive to do it, was inescapable. And when they started walking into the offices of EMI and Virgin, they were further emboldened, and one step closer to the establishment. It meant they felt more confident, as they deserved to. It was an opportunity to be legitimised, and given a voice – and not just a fringe voice, either.'

Like Roll Deep, Shystie had already created an album's worth of songs when she began attracting major-label interest, following the underground buzz around her 'answer track' to Dizzee's 'I Luv U'. She was signed to Polydor amidst a flurry of media interest, and quickly hailed as 'the first lady of grime'. Shystie went away and finessed the work she already had, re-recording it on proper studio equipment; but she did so without interference or A&R-ing – without, it seems, even much of a view as to how they'd sell her and her 'double-timing, triple-rhyming' lickety-spit MCing to the pop world. 'They didn't ask me to change anything,' she says now. 'They didn't try and push me to make more radio-friendly stuff. I don't feel like I had to compromise.' *Diamond in the Dirt* was released in July 2004, and didn't chart. 'One Wish' just dented the Top 40. The problem, if anything, was that she hadn't compromised enough for the only channels through which hits were made then: a handful of major radio and TV outlets. 'Because grime was nowhere near where it is now, at the time on radio it was all pop songs and indie bands, so when "One Wish" came out, they were like "Jesus, this is way too hard for radio, we can't playlist this. We can't do anything with this."'

The only TV channels that would play the 'One Wish' video were underground cable outlet Channel U, and MTV Base – and in the latter case, only in their dedicated 'homegrown talent' section, tellingly scheduled for late at night, away from primetime. She was competing for resources with – and inevitably, losing out to – label mates who were already massive household names in US rap like 50 Cent and Eminem. Meanwhile it was 'indie season' throughout: 'It was all Arctic Monkeys and Keane and all these flipping other bands dominating the charts,' she laughs. 'We didn't stand a chance.' It was no tragedy: the album still sold well, and Shystie went on to have a flourishing acting career, starring in the semi-autobiographical Channel 4 series *Dubplate Drama* – there's no bitterness about her experience with Polydor. The other obstacle she faced was less about the prevailing winds of what was in fashion at the time, and rather more wearying: Estelle, another young black British female artist, had just released her poppy and amenable single '1980'. 'Obviously that song was more radio friendly and commercial, and I remember Radio 1 had said to our people they could only push one, and they were going with Estelle's. That's when I learned about radio politics. So "1980" got pushed and pushed and pushed, and "One Wish" got slept on. The industry wouldn't take a risk: for them it was like "it's too dark, it's too ghetto"; but nowadays they flipping love it, they can't get enough of it – it's the same sound!'

Only a handful of artists signed album deals in this first flurry of industry interest – it was never quite a full-on gold rush – and they were all strong talents, who put out good albums; but they never made a great impact on the pop mainstream. Kano released *Home Sweet Home* in June 2005 (peaking in the charts at 36), the same month as Roll Deep's *In at the Deep End* (50), and was followed the next month by Lethal Bizzle's *Against All Oddz* (89). More Fire Crew's *CV* and Shystie's *Diamond in the Dirt* had failed to chart; Durrty Goodz and British R&B singer Gemma Fox both signed to Polydor but 'parted ways' before releasing anything. Wiley's solo debut had peaked at 45 the previous year, and even Dizzee's *Boy in da Corner* had only reached as high as 23. The alien sound of the British underground had intrigued the labels, and the press, just enough to give it the time of day, but they were never pushed hard enough to challenge a diet of proven American hip-hop, pop and R&B imports – artists that needed no A&R-ing, no development, and not even that much promotion – and a steady stream of guitar bands. Beyond that handful, no one else on a thriving underground got a look-in. The two *Run the Road* compilation albums released on 679 in early 2005 and 2006 did a lot to foreground the rest of the scene: Riko Dan, No Lay, Durrty Goodz (previously Doogz), D Double E, Crazy Titch, Ghetto, Ears and a range of producers all got a showcase on the same label as The Streets and Kano; as good as the compilations are, they didn't lead anywhere.

One new arrival in this period ought to have given a huge boost to black British underground music in the mainstream. In August 2002 BBC Radio 1Xtra launched, targeting 15–24-year-olds, 'particularly – although not exclusively – those from ethnic minorities'. The press linked this to the growth of pirate radio (the number of stations was estimated to have doubled during the 1990s, with 400 in London alone by 2000[7]), and some of 1Xtra's DJs were poached directly from the pirates. The arrival of 1Xtra coincided with the increasing popularisation of the category of 'urban music' in the UK, but the BBC were careful not to use it themselves: the wording of the BBC licence stipulated that the station would broadcast 'the best in contemporary black music'. There was precedent for the label as an entry point for people of colour into the industry: the market category of 'urban music' had been established in the 1980s in the US, and the MOBO (Music of Black Origin) Awards had been launched in the UK in 1996. There has long been discomfort about the term as a grouping for the myriad divergent styles that come under the heading – just like the constant quibble about the phrase 'music of black origin' (how about basically all popular music?). In Simon Wheatley's photojournalist book about London in the mid-2000s, *Don't Call Me Urban!*, Pay As U Go MC God's Gift specifically rejects the label: 'it's a way of segregating us,' he says – of ghettoising black British music away from the mainstream. 'When that word came around, everything in the "urban" chart was either Asian or black. The person's ethnic background doesn't matter, because we're not singing in an African language or whatever, so why are we being classed as something?'

Although 1Xtra was launched with shows from some credible names from the UK garage scene (Richie Vibe Vee, J Da Flex, Femme Fatale and Heartless Crew), it was a slow start – available only through the very new medium of digital radio – a medium of which the target audience were the least likely to be early adopters. It was an overdue recognition of how painfully slow to adapt to Britain's multicultural youth cultures the BBC had been. 'I was at Radio 1 when dance music passed it by,' said Radio 1's head of specialist music Ian Parkinson, when 1Xtra launched, 'and black music was nowhere to be heard on the network, so I understand the initial suspicions, but I say give it a chance.' At the time, every one of the 18 members of the BBC's Executive Committee were white (as indeed all ten are now at the time of writing, fifteen years later).

Grime and underground UK pirate sounds still didn't get much of a look-in in those early years: 'When I first joined 1Xtra in 2005,' Austin Daboh would tell me in 2011, by that time the station's music manager, 'I was scheduling the music for a show, and I remember being told off for placing two UK tracks back-to-back.' There was no dedicated grime show, even in its early peak in 2005. Indeed it's noteworthy, in the evolution of 'grime' as a genre, that one pivotal 1Xtra set in July 2004, hosted by Wiley and featuring Trim, Crazy Titch, Lady Fury, Riko, Flow Dan and Fire Camp, was still being billed as part of the station's Garage Weekender. Garage really had waned by this point, but the new guard hadn't fully emerged from its parent genre's shadow, even a year after Dizzee's Mercury win. The industry still didn't know where to put these kids, or what to do with them. Ironically, that champion of outsider music on Radio 1, John Peel, had acknowledged the word on his show two months earlier. 'I'm not very happy with the name "grime", but that's what a lot of people seem to call it, so we'll call it that for the time being,' he grumbled, introducing a live guest set from DJs Eastwood, Krafty and Cameo and MCs G Double, Purple, IQ and IE.

There was a prevailing sense that the institutions of the mainstream industry weren't ready for them, as Shystie had found. 'Without the pirates, not one of us would be here now,' Geeneus told Radio 1's *East is East* documentary in 2004. 'There's no way for people to hear us. How would we have been heard? It's impossible. We wouldn't have been able to get a show on Radio 1 or any other station would we? They'd laugh at us if we tried to send a demo tape to one of the legal stations.' In *The Pirate's Dilemma*, Matt Mason cites a Malcolm Gladwell theory, 'the Law of the Few' to point out that the original MC stars on pirate radio thrived in the long run precisely because they were happy to start out small: Dizzee would never have succeeded if he'd started his career by conscientiously mailing demo CDs of weird, wonderful creations like 'Brand New Day' straight to major labels – they would never have opened the envelope, and if they had, they wouldn't have had the faintest clue what they were listening to. Instead, Dizzee spoke to his small but dedicated audience, and that audience 'let the labels know who he was on his behalf'. A track like 'I Luv U' thrived on the underground, in raves, on pirate radio, as a white label – and didn't get a commercial release until much later, when the industry and the wider public were ready for it.

Part of the problem was that there were precious few people working in the music industry and the media who understood the pirate-radio scene. Chantelle Fiddy was a rare exception, a critical supporting voice in the early days of grime, who put on live shows, worked for 679 Recordings, Kano's label, A&R-ing the second of the influential *Run the Road* compilations, and worked as an influential blogger and journalist. She explained the sticking point was often a lack of interest from gatekeepers, who were especially risk-averse and myopic in a period of dwindling print circulations. 'There's a core issue with many editors,' she told me in 2006. 'They simply can't see past their own socio-economic background and class reference points. Pitching Wiley features to *Mixmag* in 2003, they'd say "no one has ever heard of him". Which was true, if you asked the attendees at Cream or Ministry of Sound, but if you walked through Mile End with him, he was a street demigod. It's narrow mindedness, and it perpetuates social division and the underachievement of any act not appealing to middle-class journalists.' Likewise, I was told by the music editor of a national newspaper around this time, by way of explanation for his lack of interest in grime pitches, 'I'm white, middle-class and I like indie rock, and so do my readers.' They changed their tune eventually, just like the record labels did – but it took years.

The result was that the road from the manor to mainstream fame was only traversed by a very few artists. But the underground was slowly building its own networks – without the help of social media or YouTube, at this stage. One particular media arrival would give room to breathe to grime at this critical time, even if it was itself relatively underground and marginal, a kind of TV equivalent of the pirates: Channel U was founded in 2003 to give a visual platform to grime, UK garage, and up-and-coming British R&B and rap – to black British underground music, essentially. It broadcast on cable, and quickly developed a cult following. When founder Darren Platt passed away in 2016, the tributes flooded in from artists: Platt was 'a visionary', wrote Lethal Bizzle in a tribute on Instagram. '[He] helped me when I was at my lowest point, and got me back on top.' He had pushed grime 'when no one else cared', Bizzle wrote.

'Channel U made the man across the street a celebrity – people who spoke the same tongue as you,' said MC Poet, in a subsequent discussion on YouTube chat show *Not For The Radio*. 'It was still a craft that wasn't respected musically, grime.' That craft, and black British MC-led music, was finally presented on TV as a wider scene for the first time, and Channel U revealed that beyond the handful of crossover successes, the likes of Dizzee, Ms Dynamite or So Solid Crew, there was a whole cohort of stars-in-waiting emerging from the manor. It gave them a platform, and helped fans connect a face and personality to the voice. Channel U, along with the DIY DVD publishing scene that would soon begin to flourish alongside it, was bringing the unvarnished energy of the pirates to a visual medium for the first time. 'We called it pirate TV,' said Vis, the host of *The Ill Out Show*, 'because there was really no rules.' They had 50 Cent, Christiana Milian, Ciara – big US stars – sitting on their cheap living-room sofa, along with Crazy Titch and Lethal Bizzle and Devlin. Stars were made there, and it gave a big boost to the process of propelling grime outside of small parts of inner-city London.

Cat Park, the channel manager at the station, said that it was often a fight for Platt to promote the underground scene. 'There'd be fines from

Ofcom for playing videos that they deemed unsuitable, and he'd have to pay the solicitors' bills that went along with them. He'd have pressure from police who would watch the channel carefully. Nobody was investing in our scene then, nobody wanted to know and people certainly didn't want to advertise on the channel.'[8] In broadcasting a thriving underground, against the prevailing winds of US imports, Channel U also put the likes of MTV under pressure to adapt to what their young audience were listening to, in the same way the BBC's hand had been forced by the success of the pirates. MTV Base, an urban iteration of the American TV mega-brand, had launched in the UK in 1999, but like 1Xtra in its early years, it was very light on homegrown talent, relying largely on ready-made successes imported from the world of American R&B, hip-hop and soul.

Channel U became a staple part of the grime scene – and created a broader shared experience of it: one that pirate radio, by its geographically limited nature, had not been capable of. You'll find YouTube comments attesting to popular 'Channel U classics' attached to mid-2000s videos like 'Southside Allstars', 'Pull Up Dat', 'Murkle Man' and 'Brown Bear Picnic' – the more theatrical and wacky videos and tracks did especially well ('Picnic' is a grimy riff on Teddy Bears' Picnic; Jammer's 'Murkle Man' video sees him dressed as the superhero of the title). Tracks featuring multiple MCs thrived in particular. While beef – between individuals, between crews, between areas of London – was still in the air, and diss tracks were common, the symbol of an emerging unity in the scene came in the now legendary 'all-star' or 'link-up' tunes, where five MCs or more from different crews would come together to each do a verse on a hot new instrumental. These moments were crucial in binding together grime's first wave – in 2003 grime was a long way off the united front visible today, where the likes of Wiley, Lethal Bizzle, Boy Better Know, Stormzy, and road-rap stars Giggs and Krept and Konan routinely put in guest turns at each other's concerts. The all-star track is perhaps the closest that grime has managed to get in a studio recording to capturing the frantic, pass-the-mic hype of a live pirate radio or rave set. It also captures grime's 'scenius', Brian Eno's term for the collaborative genius of a scene, the idea that – for all the MC ego – grime's creativity thrived precisely because it was a collective, not a solitary pursuit.

'We created our own stars,' Lethal Bizzle said to me in 2011, reflecting on the united front that all-star tracks like 'Pow!' had presented. 'At that time grime was viewed in a negative light because people from different crews were beefing with each other, and warring, all that bullshit – so when 'Pow!' came around, with ten different stars on, people were like, "Wow, Bizzle's on it, Jamakabi's on it, D Double's on it, Demon's on it ..." Everyone was like, "What the fuck?" That was when grime was thriving the most, sort of 2004–07, when there were so many collaborations going on.' We were speaking when grime was really at a low ebb, when the scene's brightest talents were all making dreadful, watered-down electro-urban pop, just in the name of getting some kind of industry recognition and financial reward for their efforts. Bizzle's reflections on the collective strengths of the early days, messy and hectic as they were, were delivered with more than a few shakes of the head. 'I think we don't even realise how powerful we are. As a unit, we're more powerful than any record company.'

For those not scoring record deals during this period, the underground scene was home to a mixture of vibrant growth, and frustration caused by hitting the industry's ceiling. Beneath the Dizzees, Wileys, Kanos and Shysties there was an ever-growing range of crews, DJs, producers and MCs across London who were hoping and waiting to see if they could follow a musical path out of the manor. The underground's emerging infrastructure was supporting them, and they could reach out beyond the pirates' aerials for the first time. Substantial rave franchises like Sidewinder and Eskimo Dance built up big followings with all-star grime and garage line-ups – although they had to do so outside of the capital, in towns such as Watford, Milton Keynes and Swindon, such was the pressure from the police after the trouble associated – sometimes fairly, sometimes not – with the UK garage scene, in particular So Solid Crew's tabloid-enhanced reputation for attracting violence. Spinning off these raves were the rave tape-packs, recordings of all the DJ and MC sets at nights like Sidewinder. The format had been a staple of nineties club scenes – which presented an opportunity for people beyond London, its pirate-radio stations and the south-east raves to keep in touch with the rapidly evolving underground.

RWD magazine provided a rare outlet for the scene in print journalism: Wiley used to refer to it as 'the book', because it was the only place that documented everything going on in their world. 'Everything about *RWD* was crass,' former editor Matt Mason told me, proudly – it was a magazine aimed at teenagers, and aimed to speak their language, 'text speak' and all. The first issue, in 2001, had featured a bootlegged Versace advert as the back cover – these were still the garage days, and they wanted that aspirational, designer association, even if they weren't getting any money from Versace for it. 'These cottage industries were growing and growing,' Mason recalled of the early 2000s – 'along with the record shops and pirate stations and the clubs: it was a real ecosystem. And you never would have had that culture without that ecosystem around it.'

One major addition to the existing rave infrastructure inherited from the nineties dance underground was the homegrown grime DVD publishing industry. Out of necessity, grime at its inception was a decidedly non-visual genre, in that so much of it was hidden: digital cameras hadn't been widely adopted, smartphones didn't exist, the established media weren't interested in documenting it, and the hubs for all grime activity were pirate radio stations, which by their nature had to be hidden in the shadows. By the mid-2000s, grime DVD series like Troy Miller's *Practice Hours*, Jammer's *Lord of the Mics* and Target's *Aim High* had become a vital part of the scene. Roony Keefe, creator of the seminal *Risky Roadz* DVD series in 2004, and now a music-video director and black-cab driver, was working in Rhythm Division when he had the idea to put some visuals to the thrilling sounds coming out of the nearby pirate stations.

'There weren't really many music videos from grime artists at all back then,' he recalled. 'Because everything was based around pirate radio it was all semi-anonymous. MCs would come into Rhythm Division, and I remember saying quietly to my colleague, "Oh, is that so-and-so?"' Keefe borrowed some money from his nan to buy a camcorder, and used his student loan to pay for the pressing of the DVDs, and *Risky Roadz* was born – he would travel around London to go and meet MCs in their local area, leading to memorable scenes like Kano spitting his lyrics a cappella in the street, late at night, wearing a dressing gown and holding a cup of tea. In the same DVD, God's Gift delivers a freestyle sitting on a wall, while children play on bikes and a London bus goes past in the background. The aesthetic became a key part of grime's identity: naturalistic, honest and unpretentious – MCs spitting about London as it really was, against a backdrop of London as it really was. No champs, no profiling, no beautiful people, just like Wiley described it.

Largely of course this was just for convenience – Keefe would get the train from Bethnal Green to visit MCs across London and just shoot them where he found them, outside their house or block of flats – but it worked stylistically too; lyrically grime isn't escapist music, with an escapist style – it's not about artistic camouflage, or reaching to a far-away galaxy or island in the sun. It's about the places it came from: from Roman Road in Bow to Meridian Walk in Tottenham.

'It's a DIY style,' Keefe said of the *Risky Roadz* approach. 'It was birthed from wanting to get something done, and making it happen, regardless of budgets, or camera quality. We weren't too worried about the glossy style, we just wanted to show what the scene was about, and show London as we know it – not just what people think London is, because there's misconceptions, that it's all china teaware and crumpets, and there's a lot more to it than that. The world finally started to see what London's really about, from music.'

On the first *Risky Roadz* DVD, south London's Essentials stand around in a back garden and speak to Keefe about their hopes, dreams and frustrations. 'We need more support, man, for the scene to evolve; there's not enough support for the scene,' says DJ Bossman, referring to the limits of the music industry's interest in Dizzee Rascal's peers, following the Mercury win. '[They're] scared to sign people … they need to give people a chance.'

'We'll sell units, we'll make you money,' says Remerdee, also known as Captain, to the laughter of the rest of his crew, addressing the industry directly through Keefe's camera, as if there was plausibly a table full of stuffy old white men in suits hiding behind it. 'Come check us, we're doing our music, it's all from the soul – we've got a lot of people who've come from where we come from … They're going to buy our CD, they're going to understand where we come from. Everyone suffers, no matter what you're suffering, everyone goes through different tings, but it's all pain, you understand? And we express pain, happiness and everything.'

They discuss the major labels too, and reflect on the negative consequences of a few mainstream failures. 'When they don't do well, the majors get scared and don't want to sign anyone else.'

Keefe asks what their hopes for the future are. K Dot, an MC who recorded a couple of the most blistering solo MC tracks ever, but never finished a mixtape, never made a music video, and never got signed, responds, 'I'm in this to live good.'

N.E. (Nu Era) flashes a smile and talks about flying around the world, about going to Japan, about being in the *Guinness Book of Records*. A much-loved character on the scene, he sadly passed away in 2009. His distinguishing lyric was dripping with pathos, inverting the whole logic of MC self-aggrandisement with punishing humility: 'I might not be the best, but I'll still merk any man who wants to come test.' Essentials talk about number-one singles, about building up a business off the back of the music, about following up albums with clothing lines – the will was there, but fate was not: after three promising mixtapes, the crew split acrimoniously in 2006.[9]

Speaking to Maxwell D now, there's a sense of regret that there wasn't the investment and infrastructure to run things professionally for themselves from the beginning, that there weren't any Suge Knight figures around in the scene in the early 2000s who understood its potential. 'So many corporate companies have branded themselves off the back of urban underground music, and are making money money off us now,' he says, 'but the thing is, it should have been us! We should have been young entrepreneurs within ourselves – the Pay As U Gos, the Heartless

Crews – we should have been entrepreneurs having our own stations, doing that stuff for ourselves. But corporations will always win. It's like going against Barclays Bank.'

The grime DVD cottage industry in these formative years provides some fascinating records of the world around the music: historical arte-facts of a part of London life mostly never captured – before ubiquitous documentation via digital cameras and smartphones, and before gentri-fication swept away much of the inner city. Groups of teenagers in track-suits and baseball caps hanging out smoking spliffs, swigging from lurid-coloured plastic bottles of fizzy soft drinks, against a backdrop – just like that captured in Simon Wheatley's photos – of a different London, one transformed in barely more than a decade. It looks greyer, more washed-out, damp: a city yet to be colonised by New Labour's kids-play-centre approach to urban regeneration, all crayon colours and aspirational slogans. Young people who were never MCs sit around too – 'this is Scum Dave,' one of Roll Deep says in a *Risky Roadz* interview segment, by way of introduction, and Scum Dave stares straight ahead, presumably stoned and utterly blank, not blinking. (There's a thread on *GrimeForum* from 2011 where people argue about whether Scum Dave was a) an MC, b) a producer, C) 'a lengman on road' and now in prison, or d) none of the above: maybe he's 'just someone who lives around the way, [an] associate'.)

Even the MCs – who by this stage have done scores of performances at major raves, and hours of pirate radio – are a mess of nervous smiles and gentle shakes of the head. Discarda pulls his chewing gum out with his finger. 'Don't play with your food,' Breeze instructs him, slightly embarrassed for them both. The lack of media training, the lack of expe-rience in interviews – above all, the shyness – is profound. MCs avoid looking the camera in the eye, no one really wants to answer even basic questions. 'Come on,' says Keefe, casting the camera around. 'Who's going to tell me … how did Roll Deep come about?' The same thing happens when he asks what's happening with the album they're making: the camera captures only diffident shuffling, heads withdrawn into hoodies, eyes turning down to the spliff being rolled. It's the reaction you'd expect if you approached any group of teenage boys sitting on a wall facing a basketball court, in the middle of a council estate. Which makes it all the more striking that this particular group were about to change the face of British pop culture.

SIX

GRIME WAVES AND THE RESPECT AGENDA

New Labour was never supposed to be a cuddly liberal project – and the censorious approach that had created the ASBO was just the beginning. Blair's government were enthusiastic about policing not just criminality, but behaviour, and attitudes. 'I am not soft,' Home Secretary Charles Clarke told the *Daily Mirror* in 2005, 'I am neither woolly or liberal.' He captured the macho spirit of the party, and sounded a bit like an MC who was on the back-foot in a clash – the *Mirror* helpfully added that he was 'known as one of the government's "big beasts" and a "bruiser"'.

New Labour did not see their authoritarian streak as incompatible with remaining – theoretically – the party of the working classes, far from it. The argument was that it was all very well for middle-class liberals, *Guardian* readers, to cry foul about restricting freedoms, but it wasn't these metropolitan dilettantes, in their million-pound Hampstead mansions, who had to live on estates where feral youths ran riot, and petty crime, drug dealing and delinquency were ubiquitous. New Labour loved a good crackdown, and were more than willing to use state power to try and restore what they saw as lost civility to Britain's poorest areas. Policing the ills of British society spilled over from specific ASBOs into

Get Money Quick Crew respond to the surveillance state, Kilburn, 2006

something more nebulous, via Blair's largely forgotten 'Respect agenda'. Even culture was not safe: including the music, lyrics and clothing of working-class young people. While the creative industries were being lionised as the economic engine of modern, dynamic, regenerated cities, New Labour was quite happy to try and dictate what was being created within them.

The first major flare-up coincided with the birth of grime, and UK garage's Roman Empire-style decline and fall. In the aftermath of a high-profile murder case in Birmingham, where black teenagers Charlene Ellis and Letisha Shakespeare were shot dead in the crossfire between two gangs, on New Year's Day 2003, the temptation for the press, and the political class, to make a connection to black youth culture was too great – especially since members of So Solid Crew had recently been charged with violent assault and gun possession. There was no connection, material or figurative – it hadn't even happened in the same city So Solid were from – but that didn't matter. It wasn't just some of the crew's individual criminal cases that was deemed a problem, but their sometimes violent lyrical content, the references to 'gats' and Glocks. A prolonged echo of the fractious and heated debate about US gangster rap in the nineties ensued – prosecuted largely by people who, like their American peers, did not understand the difference between cause and correlation. 'Record companies behind groups such as So Solid Crew have a lot to answer for,' wrote the prominent black broadcaster and politico Trevor Phillips in the *Daily Mirror*, shortly after the Birmingham murders. 'The marketing of hip-hop and particularly garage is all about what I call: Gold Chain and no brain.' Phillips, a staunch New Labourite, was appointed Chairman of the Commission for Racial Equality two weeks later.

To the *Daily Mirror*'s credit, they subsequently ran an editorial pointing to the more substantive causes of a rise in gun crime on city streets: greater availability and illegal trade routes following wars in the Balkans, and the lack of restrictions on people buying replica guns, which could then be converted. The tabloid also quoted Ice Cube: 'If I'm more of an influence on your son as a rapper than you are as a father, you got to look at yourself as a parent.' But much of this perspective was lost in the rush to condemn black street music. The Labour Party was all over the subject: David Blunkett, Home Secretary, told BBC Radio 2, 'We need to talk to record producers and distributors and those engaged in the music business about what is and isn't acceptable.' That same week, the first of January 2003, Metropolitan Police Assistant Commissioner Tarique Ghaffur blamed a 'backdrop of music' for gun crime, singling out So Solid Crew. Labour Culture Minister, Kim Howells, accused 'idiots like the So Solid Crew' of 'glorifying gun culture and violence. For years I have been very worried about these hateful lyrics that these boasting macho idiot rappers come out with. It is a big cultural problem.'

Parts of the British music scene made a rearguard action. BBC 1Xtra's Wilber Wilberforce pointed out that urban music was 'a lot less danger-ous than people would like to make out', and that the success of the likes of So Solid Crew was rather more likely to make young people get involved in music than in shoot-outs in the street. Say you *are* an impres-sionable youth who copies their cultural idols' every move – so much of this finger-wagging is predicated on the assumption that teenagers don't have minds of their own, and aren't liable to be every bit as judgemental as their elders – which looks more attractive? Making wads of money and appearing in music videos, or bleeding to death? On the occasions where So Solid Crew members had been involved in criminality, or there had been violence at or outside their shows, it was perhaps unsur-prising: 'We were still living in the same grimy estates, seeing exactly the same people – some of who were awful,' one of the crew's biggest MCs, Lisa Maffia, said in 2005. 'What could our management do? Move 30 of us out of the estate?'[1]

Ms Dynamite, who was always held in a much higher level of main-stream esteem than her peers in So Solid, stepped forward to dismiss the 'bullshit' that UK garage was somehow inextricably linked with violence. She also became one of the first of several artists to work with charities or the state to spread what is often described as a 'conscious' or 'positive' message via music – embarking on a ten-date tour along with Lisa Maffia to raise money for a Stop the Violence campaign. It also gave her the opportunity to argue that a slightly deeper approach than wide-spread condemnations of lyrics might be necessary. 'The problem is poverty,' she told the BBC: 'young people have to live in crazy circumstances and people who do not live in those circumstances cannot judge.'

A series of slightly unlikely though well-intentioned collaborations would follow: Roll Deep's 2006 single and video 'Badman', a cautionary tale about gun crime, was produced in aid of Stop the Guns, a campaign organised by Operation Trident (in which the £100,000 video was paid for by the Met), as was Riko Dan's tune 'Phone Call'. A further Trident-funded ad campaign in 2007 was also targeted specifically at teenagers (according to its creators), with ads on Channel U and MTV Base – in addition to the advertising Trident have always done on pirate stations. Another overlooked Roll Deep track from 2007, 'Respect Us', positioned the crew as moral leaders: the 'youth dem don't want to listen' to Blair's speeches, but 'when we say jump they say "how high"', Scratchy spits, rather optimistically. Skepta's verse sounds like something out of *Sesame Street* – 'don't be a fool, go to school, and be cool with the teachers' – but he had form for conscious grime in this period. On 'Blood, Sweat And Tears', from his debut album, he references Rosa Parks, Haile Selassie and Malcolm X, while Jme, with his typical knack for bathos, calls for a return to pogs, marbles and conkers instead of teenage killings.

A more unlikely link-up in conscious grime occurred in 2010, in which MC Ghetts and the Office for National Statistics paired together in a campaign to reach young BAME Britons who had not registered for the 2011 census. 'I don't want to get political, but it's the principle: there aren't enough of us filling in the forms,' he raps on 'Invisible', trying not to look embarrassed – there's no easy way to make a census sound cool, but Ghetts stoically proceeded anyway, touring youth centres and schools in London to 'drive home the census message' to young people. As awkward and obscure as the collaboration was, the track reveals what might be grime's greatest political power: to give a voice to the voiceless – to boost visibility. 'Invisible' was ultimately an attempt to address social exclusion, because state resources and facilities follow the demographic information collected in the census.

Whether these kinds of campaigns have any kind of impact on bringing young people into the arms of the state, or reducing youth violence, is hard to measure – but the will (at the risk of losing street cred) has certainly been there, even while the same crews often continued to spit gun- and knife-related lyrics. On the grime forums (chiefly *RWD*, *VIP2* and *GrimeForum*), fans have been more likely to scoff at MCs for this kind of low-level hypocrisy, than for 'selling out' and fronting anti-violence campaigns in the first place. It wasn't just the musicians who were giving off mixed messages though. In the space of one month in 2006, David Cameron tried to relaunch the notion of compassionate Conservatism in his infamous 'hug a hoodie' speech, while also castigating Radio 1's playing of violent rap music, because it 'encourages people to carry guns and knives'. The latter did at least prompt a Lethal Bizzle op-ed for the *Guardian* in response, given the inspired headline, 'David Cameron is a Donut', in which Bizzle wearily put forward an apparently controversial argument: the social problems and violence are there already, and making music is an escape route from them – so why are you attacking the music, not the social problems?

Cameron's attitude to music and young people was the norm across the political divide: Tony Blair's appointed 'School Behaviour Tsar' Sir Alan Steer had, earlier in 2006, urged parents and schools to ban offensive and violent rap music, because it could lead to 'further aggression'. New Labour's focus on changing not just policy but individual behaviour was crystallised following the 2005 election, when Blair launched what he called, with a typical lack of self-consciousness, 'the Respect agenda'. In practice it was very similar to the American idea of 'zero tolerance' made famous under New York Mayor Rudy Giuliani, in that it focused on a range of relatively humdrum non-criminal or minor criminal transgressions, like swearing, graffiti or public drinking, in an attempt to transform society from the bottom up. Like Giuliani's strategy, it was defiantly illiberal, founded on sweeping prejudices and quite comfortably open to abuse. It was also intimately connected to the plan to regenerate, cleanse and more aggressively police urban public spaces. That it added an extra dose of Blairite officiousness, moralism and bureaucracy – respect my agenda! – gave it the appropriate homegrown twist.

There was, of course, a Respect Tsar. In the name of looking busy and authoritative, New Labour appointed hundreds of 'tsars' – policy chiefs drawn from business, the civil service or academia. 'Tsar' is a patently absurd job title, but one suited to an elitist approach to governance, and it was continued by David Cameron; between 1997–2012, a staggering 260 government policy tsars were appointed. The breakdown of this (by definition unelected) demographic tells a story about how Britain is governed: of the 260, 85 per cent were male, 98 per cent white, and 83 per cent over fifty years old when appointed.[2] How else would you know who to respect, or how to respect them, without someone with the same job title as a pre-revolutionary Russian monarch to instruct you on the matter? Blair's choice for Respect Tsar of Louise Casey attracted controversy when she was appointed in 2005, as she had recently joked in a leaked after-dinner speech to senior police officers about 'decking' her bosses in No 10, and that ministers might do a better job 'if they turn up pissed', since 'doing things sober is no way to get things done'. Respect as I say, not as I do.

The Respect agenda was designed to put the law-abiding majority back in charge of their local communities, said Blair. But poverty was nothing to do with it. 'At its lowest level, it's just about good manners,' said Blair at the launch of the Respect Task Force, and, 'At its worst, it's a complete indifference to anything other than self.' The same leader who had brought Thatcherite individualism into the philosophy of the Labour Party was still content to dictate the importance of solidarity and community-mindedness to others. David Cameron, as leader of the opposition, contended that Blair's respect rhetoric was just hot air, accompanied by 'gimmicks' from the government, and he counter-attacked, bizarrely, with his own launch of a programme for 'Real Respect' in Britain. (Cameron was not wrong in his 'gimmick' criticism: one of Blair's ideas was to march drunk people to cash points for on-the-spot fines.) With the two main political parties desperately trying to out-respect each other, it was Dizzee Rascal who addressed the subject most astutely, on 'Respect Me', from his second album *Showtime*. Linking underground music to criminal behaviour amounted to 'so many claims and no evidence', he spat, before admitting he had 'a few mates that have been convicted, yeah so what? It's the hand life dealt them/We weren't blessed with the system's TLC: government should have tried to help them.'[3] The government website (respect.gov.uk) and logo presented respect as a cycle, with the slogan 'give respect, get respect', and employed a stock photo on its front page displaying a group of four teenagers, each of them wearing tracksuit tops with their hoods up, drinking from cans of beer outside a shuttered shop. It seems safe to assume this was a depiction of insufficient respect in a public space, rather than an exemplar of mutual giving and receiving of respect – a community, sharing convivially in their beer and their conversation – for us all to aspire to. But who knows?

New Labour were keen to connect violence on the streets to a wider culture. This reached a nadir in 2007, when the Prime Minister responded to a succession of knife and gun murders with a landmark speech in which he claimed political correctness was stopping people from speaking honestly. The Callaghan Memorial Lecture was delivered in Cardiff City Hall in April 2007, and swung from issues of urban regeneration to remarks strongly implicating black Britons in their own suffering. 'The black community need to be mobilised in denunciation of this gang culture that is killing innocent young black kids,' Blair said, coming very close to suggesting there was something amiss in black culture itself. The speech caused a substantial backlash, even though Blair ventriloquised its most controversial line: he quoted a black pastor from a London church, who had asked him: 'When are we going to start saying this is a problem amongst a section of the black community and not, for reasons of political correctness, pretend that this is nothing to do with it?'

Blair was criticised for dismissing poverty and social exclusion as a root cause, for implying that not enough had been done by black communities to begin with – and for failing to provide support and resources for (already existing) black-led efforts to tackle the problem.

Even parts of the police thought he was too gung-ho. Keith Jarrett, chair of the National Black Police Association, said: 'Social deprivation and delinquency go hand-in-hand and we need to tackle both. It is curious that the Prime Minister does not mention deprivation in his speech.' Intriguingly, Blair had also said in his Cardiff speech that tackling the problem of street violence would be the 'missing element from the regeneration of our cities' and praised the 'immensely healthy and sensible partnership between the private and public sector' in doing so. In his mind, all these things were connected: urban regeneration programmes and 'the right social engineering' would, he said 'cure' the social problems of Britain's major cities. 'People see no reason why the less tangible but still critical aspect – behaviour towards others – should not also be regenerating.' Regenerate yourself, and the city around you.

Aggression and threats of violence were lyrical hallmarks of grime from its inception; something which titillated the mainstream media, but prompted cries of condemnation as well. None of the politicians using grime to point-score about the moral corruption of inner-city youths ever delved into its specifics, of course, or considered that lyrical war might be an art form in itself. Competitive clashing, perhaps most widely familiar from *8 Mile*-style battle rap, is more rooted in Jamaican dancehall sound-system culture, though the grime generation drew from both. Like any folk art it's full of its own internal logic, tropes and codes. The most basic and fundamental of these, understood by even the most excitable 13-year-old boy posting on a music message board – though rarely his elders and betters – is that 'beefing', 'warring', 'sending', 'duppying', 'merking' or 'clashing' is always a performance. The ultimate performative arena is the live stage show, but, deprived of a thriving live scene for much of its life, and without the rather inorganic and staged context of actual battle rap, live war tracks would often be distributed via radio; Logan Sama even turned this into a regular feature on his KISS show in the mid-2000s, called The War Report, a round-up of who was sending for whom that week. The hierarchy is important – sending for the top MC can raise your profile up, assuming they send back, because it situates you as being worthy of the competition. There's a risk though: fail to match the quality, and the crowd at the virtual amphitheatre will pronounce you killed, deaded, destroyed – and your career might be.

That the top MC in question has usually been Wiley speaks to the fact he can never resist getting involved, and his belief in clashing as integral to grime. Since his high-profile clash with Durrty Doogz in 2001 (before the name change), barely a year has passed without a battle with a rival MC. He revelled in the competition from the outset, in the way it forced him to hone his skills, and attracted attention for the scene, lifting 'the levels' all around. 'I do it so the sound expands,' as he spat on 'WD25'. As Wiley got older, up-and-coming younger MCs kept him on his toes as they sought to clash with him. They kept him relevant – kept him alive.

A well-known and long-running DVD series, *Lord of the Mics*, was built around clashes between MCs: its first iterations arriving at just the time the DVD industry began flourishing. Contests between the likes of Skepta v. Devilman, and Wiley v. Kano, were soon ripped and uploaded to YouTube, which launched in 2005 – these clips became a key entry point into the scene, for new fans who were too young for, or lived too far away from, the key pirate radio stations, record shops and raves. Sometimes MCs' beef would be deliberately staged for publicity, like a fake celebrity relationship, arranged by Hollywood publicists – but even when it was not, it was usually a risk worth taking to help boost your profile. ('I knew I'd get your whole crew saying my name: and now I owe you one, because that's a third of my advertising done,'[4] Skepta spat in 2005, after dispatching SLK.) Most often, it's part of the playful practice of MCing, which is competitive at the best of times – good friends have had lyrical beef for fun, including longtime crew members like Skepta and Wiley – the former's diss track reworked Blur's 1995 single 'Country House', and memorably alleged, 'You need a Tom-Tom just to get around Bow'[5] – so estranged had the godfather of grime become from his roots.

Sometimes what is playful and what is genuine hostility blur: Lethal Bizzle and Wiley's rivalry in the early 2000s, as heads of the two biggest crews in east London, prompted some scathing and sincerely menacing diss tracks, but, as Bizzle has pointed out, immediately prior to the

high-profile 'war', Wiley and Dizzee would come and hang out in More
Fire Crew's studio – because they were part of the same small community. Even at the peak of the beef, Bizzle and Wiley were performing
their war bars – 'your mum's got athlete's foot' was a highlight of Wiley's
many surreal cusses – while standing happily next to each other in the
Deja Vu studio, passing the mic back and forth, grinning broadly, and
doing that jerky, screw-faced, head-shaking dance MCs do when a peer
is *killing it* on the mic, throwing up gunfingers in acclamation of their
opponent. That particular clash, recorded on another DVD, *Young Man
Standing 3*, is far more friendly than even the average formalised battle-
rap clash. Wiley's bizarre stream-of-consciousness approach to war
tracks make them some of the most enjoyable: his 2006 'Nightbus
Dubplate' directed at The Movement (with whom he was collaborating
again soon afterwards) is a glorious six minutes of attacks and non-sequiturs, across which the godfather of grime seems inexhaustible. 'Last
three dubs hit The Movement and crushed it/Saw 'em on the stage and I
rushed it, I've sussed it/Must be the same old kid in the dinner hall,
primary, eating apple crumble and custard/I've got it in me, I'm raging,
fuck it.'[6]

Only occasionally have war tracks strayed from playground
name-calling to something resembling real menace – Trim and Stormin's
clash descended to depths of genuine, if often hilarious discomfort (and
are very much *not safe for work*), while Skepta's multi-purpose diss track
'The End' finished with a slightly chilling, lingering real-world threat
issued over the outro: 'I'll see you man in the rave.' Shystie's 'Murderation',
the final salvo in her clash with Lady Fury, is perhaps the most genuinely
terrifying war track in grime's history – almost seven minutes of
wince-inducing abuse, mixed in with very specific details about Fury's
friends and family (including, memorably, her brother's car number
plate). 'I'm going to end your career in a single hit,' Shystie gloats over
the chorus – and painful though it is, the received wisdom is that she
actually did. It's not the kind of thing that's much fun to listen to, beyond
a hand-over-mouth kind of awe. Like a car crash, you can't look, and
can't look away either.

It's ironic that a scene so dominated by male voices and machismo should see a clash between two female MCs go further than most of their male counterparts, but that doesn't change the fact that grime's gender politics have long been grim, with ubiquitous references to promiscuous 'jezebels' and 'gash', while male MCs' girlfriends and relatives have often, as Wiley's sister Janaya records in *Eskiboy*, been used as pawns in lyrical clashes, which has left them feeling humiliated. (Kano's memorable hyper-local simile, 'your girl's pum pum smells like the Beckton A13 exit',[7] a reference to Europe's largest sewage treatment works, in Newham, was at least not directed at anyone in particular.) No Lay, the west London MC responsible for the early classics 'Unorthodox Daughter' and 'No Help No Handouts', has spoken of 'underlying sexism' from male MCs insecure about being outshone by a female counterpart, and from a media and music industry determined to 'pit women against each other' – just as Shystie had found with Estelle.[8]

Hip-hop academic Richard Bramwell writes that 'many of the themes employed in clashing are characteristic of the carnival grotesque', in that they emphasise 'the material and bodily'.[9] Even while clearly fictional, the explicitly visceral lyrical content helps establish – via shock if necessary – grime's place in the real, physical, material world. There isn't much room for fantastical or magical thinking: grime's storytelling does not abound with LSD-enabled journeys to the farthest reaches of the imagination or outer space – when Wiley spits, 'I push my body in vaginas', it's horrible, and the furthest thing imaginable from erotic. But it is jarring, and striking – like the constant references to stabbing, which can sometimes feel like grime's 'fifty words for snow': you might get splashed, dipped, wetted, shanked, poked, chefed, chinged – either way, it's going to hurt. Grime's highly specific accounts of acts of violence are playfully satirised by the master of the art, Jme, with a litany of deliberatively over-pronounced plosives, on 'AWOH': 'I will dislocate your nose, Furthermore I'll sprain your lip, plain and simp: box you up like you were David Blaine and shit'; or on 'Man Don't Care', where the most humdrum of instruments make for excellent punchlines, 'You'll get a punch in the mouth with my front-door key, punch in the neck with my back-door key, box in the mouth with my X6 key, box in the eye with the fob I use to log in to my H-S-B-C.'[10] D Double E is perhaps the master of the simultaneously gross and playful threat of cartoon violence, promising to 'turn your shirt into a string vest' or that your head will be 'mangled and dangle to the side, just like I wear my Kangol' – and is responsible for one of the greatest opening couplets in grime history, on the classic 'Frontline': 'Think you're a big boy because you've got a beard? Bullets will make your face look weird.'[11] Later in the same track he acknowledges his words are 'right now, joke ting lyrical', but could 'easily turn real ting physical' – it's an explicit expression of what is implicit to all war lyrics: that the MC is dancing around in the grey area between reality and performance. *Don't worry, you know we're just play-fighting, but … what if we weren't?*

The ambiguity of how sincere an MC beef is is part of its appeal, but sometimes the mask drops completely, and the performance is openly acknowledged – sometimes you don't even need to read between the lines. In September 2007, Skepta and Ghetts were invited for a clash on Logan Sama's KISS FM show, as part of a live War Report. As the beats rolled and the lyrical darts flew, Ghetts spontaneously exclaimed: 'This is fun! And they're saying that grime mans can't be in the same building!' before immediately resuming his war lyrics with 'I'll flip my flick knife/shank him six times'. It's strangely poignant that the rival MCs get so carried away with the fun of it all – laughing and cheering throughout – that they end up actually joining in with each other's diss bars, providing a vocal echo to each punchline, with the result that they're giddily chanting along with bars written specifically to attack *themselves*. What better illustration that lyrical war is a performance? It's almost like Punch and Judy.

Demands from the mainstream media that we understand a little less and condemn a little more have held grime back, but the tide has turned, slowly, and writers willing to listen, and look past grime's macho facade have arrived. Jeffrey Boakye's 2016 book *Hold Tight* explores the role of race and machismo in the evolution of the persona of the grime MC:

what had originally been a somewhat nerdy, outsider profile has been ironed out, smartened up and commodified by the music's mainstream success. Generic figures like the hood-wearing, scowling 'roadman' have become part of general British youth parlance, carried by social media and memes outside of working-class black culture. Boakye reminds us of the ludic side of the MC's persona and their innately theatrical instincts as performers: that 'unlike the humourless cool of UK garage, grime was animated, tweaked and gimmicky', even down to the MCs' chosen *noms de guerre*, with their 'cheeky adjectives' and 'eee endings': Crazy Titch, Tinie Tempah, Tinchy Stryder, Flirta D, Footsie – out of context, they sound almost effeminate. You could make a pretty strong counter-argument, too: there are MCs called Armour, (Lady) Fury, Rage and Angry. Perhaps these are still playful character names: it's hard to maintain a veneer of deadly seriousness when you share a name with, say, a henchman from *Bugsy Malone* and Sonic the Hedgehog's sidekick, as Neckle Camp MC Knuckles does. But they're not insincere, either. Rage from Slew Dem had previously called himself Flava, carrying an altogether lighter kind of UK garage connotation, until 'one day it came to me, "Rage" … my whole life, the one thing that was consistent was rage. Rage against the system, rage from not having a father present, rage from being born poor, rage from racism and slavery.'[12]

Even if there was a slightly gawky, oddball sensibility to the MC persona – these were the kids who were too young to get into the garage raves; the ones for whom 'no hats, no hoods' was a deal breaker – the grime scene was always cool, even if that was born more of nerves or defensive hostility than macho confidence. Boakye's contextualising of black cool, in particular black male cool, is essential to understanding grime: 'In historical terms, black cool is an important evolutionary shield,' he writes – amidst a twentieth century of open discrimination, structural racism and National Front marches through the streets of London. 'Being aloof, callous and steel-jawed (i.e.: cool) was an obvious armour against this threat, especially for black men who were viewed with particular suspicion. In those terms, grime's obsession with cool, whilst existing in society's margins, is more than empowerment – it's survival.'[13]

It's worth reiterating that young black men have struggled to be treated with dignity in public space in Britain for as long as they have been in public space in Britain,[14] and that folk memory – and the experience of the immediate ancestors of the twenty-first-century grime MC – attests to an unhappy combination of public suspicion and hostility, police persecution, street violence, and a succession of media-fuelled, racist moral panics. These include not just decades of open police discrimination and racial profiling, 'sus laws' and 'routine checks', but the kind of nasty media hysteria which purported a black mugging 'trend' in the 1970s (compounded by 1980s 'race riots' in several British cities). This kind of toxic innuendo – the implication of a kind of innate black criminality – reared its head again as late as 1995, when Metropolitan Police chief Paul Condon made controversial high-profile comments linking mugging to young black men specifically, suggesting it was a cultural issue, and calling on community leaders to tackle the problem. Black newspaper *The Voice* called him 'an ass' in the ensuing debate, and various criminologists and sociologists effectively backed them up in that description, but it was a further injury inflicted on all black British people. To make matters worse, Condon's police force was at that very moment botching the investigation into the murder of black teenager Stephen Lawrence by neo-Nazis.

This was the backdrop to the grime generation's childhood and early adolescence. Stephen Lawrence's murder had happened in Eltham in south-east London – just over the river from E3, and just a mile or two from grime's south London heartland, Lewisham. In the same year that Lawrence was murdered, 1993, the hard-right British National Party won their first ever election, a council by-election in the Isle of Dogs, just the other side of Canary Wharf from Bow. It caused shockwaves in the national press and political scene, but was less of a surprise to locals: high levels of unemployment and poverty, and the LDDC's prioritisation of luxury flats and transport services for wealthy new arrivals in Canary Wharf, had intensified bitterness and racism. Anyone thought to be not 'local' (i.e. not white), and Tower Hamlets' Bangladeshi immigrants in particular, became scapegoats for the area's isolation, and its abandonment by the authorities. 'Isle of Dogs was rough, and as I got older, it got rougher,' Dizzee Rascal told me in 2016. 'I wouldn't like to say it was a ghetto – no one really likes to hear that, when you're talking about London. It was like Hackney – but how Hackney *was*, not how it is now.'

There is a long history of immigration and multiculturalism in east London, but an accompanying history of racism and animosity too, from sections of the local white population – aimed at French Huguenot refugees in the seventeenth and eighteenth centuries, and Jews in the 1930s; the latter famously culminating in 1936 in the historic Battle of Cable Street (70 years later, home to Rinse FM), where hundreds of thousands of east Londoners of all backgrounds stood up to Oswald Mosley's British Union of Fascists. Less famously, in 1968, 6,000 dockers walked out in sympathy with Enoch Powell's racist 'rivers of blood' speech, protesting with 'Don't Knock Enoch' placards and spooking the unions' left-wing leadership. In the 1970s and 80s east London witnessed racially motivated murders and spates of fire-bomb arson attacks on homes of black and Asian immigrants.

It sounds like a harsh verdict, and is certainly a few decades old, but academic Jocelyn Cornwell wrote in *Hard-Earned Lives* that white working-class east London identity was increasingly defined against change, against 'everything that is new and different'.[15] It is something that neo-Nazis have always tried to capitalise on in areas where changing demographics and poverty go hand-in-hand – and this continues into grime's lifetime as well, in twenty-first-century east London. The BNP made Barking a major target in the mid-2000s, and focused great effort in prising white working-class voters away from Labour by whipping up racial tensions and maximising disillusion with the government. In the 2006 local elections, the BNP focused their Barking and Dagenham campaign on local concern over housing and immigration: among other things they claimed – falsely, of course – that the council had a secret scheme to give African families £50,000 to buy local houses. They won a staggering 15,000 votes and 12 council seats, making them the official opposition in the borough.

As well as the very tangible threat of street violence against young people of colour from the far right, there were other more insidious and deep-rooted forces at work: ones that had always been there, but remained wilfully ignored. Following growing unease over the unsolved Stephen Lawrence murder as the nineties wore on, New Labour commissioned an official investigation, and in 1999 the historic Macpherson Report was published. It looked into the circumstances of Lawrence's death, the Met's catastrophic investigation, and the wider police culture around it, and found a force with an 'alarming inability to see how and why race mattered'. The report also popularised the idea of 'institutional racism', putting forward the still-controversial theory that maybe there were more than a few 'bad apples' in positions of authority persecuting Britain's black and minority-ethnic communities. With the police, rather than young black people finally under scrutiny, right-wing newspapers like the *Daily Mail* and the *Daily Telegraph* finally discovered nuance and rallied to the defence of the boys in blue, denouncing the idea of institutional racism as unhelpful, unfair and sweeping: the whole thing was nonsense, the result of political correctness and the influence of the 'race relations lobby', as the *Telegraph* put it.[16]

The race relations lobby was powerless to prevent the police's heavily disproportionate use of stop and search during the 2000s: by the end of the decade, according to research by the Equality and Human Rights Commission, black people were 37 times more likely to be searched than white people. The police did so under section 60 of the 1994 Public Order Act, which had been introduced primarily to disrupt the illegal rave scene: it gave cops the discretionary right to stop and search if they had 'reasonable suspicion' that someone might be involved in a crime – their unevidenced 'suspicions' are laid bare in these disproportionate figures.

This is the inner London atmosphere that helped form the grime generation's scowl: harassed by dodgy cops, their culture and behaviour decried by politicians, and aware that emboldened neo-Nazis may be lurking in the shadows. It's not exactly controversial to suggest that underneath the energetic bravado of a lyrical clash, and big talk about running things, gangster-style, there was a great deal of vulnerability to the grime generation. Having seen the transition from both sides, Matt Mason from *RWD* is well-placed to describe the distinction between the outgoing UK garage scene, with its mature swagger and serious criminal connections, and the younger, more naive generation that replaced them, and used machismo as a cover for their weaknesses:

'The garage scene never had that vulnerability. The garage scene was a bunch of straight-up fucking crooks, who sold drugs, and ran security firms and some of the biggest hooligan firms in London. Not everybody of course! But there was a lot of people in the scene who were like that; people who'd make you vanish: if you get stabbed on pirate radio, you'd just disappear. But I think with grime, there was actually a lot less ego. Grime sounds violent, and it sounds like there'd be a lot of ego, but actually my experience was, a lot of the guys in the grime scene were just really sweet, really nice guys. And beneath the anger – the thing I'd hear a lot, or just from interviewing these kids – was a lack of confidence. I don't want to name names, but a lot of the MCs, their dads weren't around, they grew up in a rough environment, and grime was a way of expressing bravado. Underneath it all, they wanted to be performers.'

It bears repeating how young grime's originators were: with the exception of veterans in their early twenties like Wiley and D Double E, this was a scene built almost entirely by teenagers. As a result, MC culture in grime is suffused with adolescent male attributes: bluster, paranoia, misanthropy, mood swings and solipsism; as well as, undeniably, a depressing tendency towards casual sexism and homophobia. It's not a grown-up or mature style of music. There are countless Dizzee lyrics that point to his youthful vulnerability, as the *boy* in the corner, poignant indications that the scowl is holding back tears, as well as rage. His words on 'Vexed' are some of the most direct: 'I was raised an only child, not a brother, not a sis, and raised around hate, not a hug, not a kiss/Before this, I was just a failure in the mist.'[17] Such is his pain, kicked out of every class, kicked out of almost every school, he threatens to be submerged into nothing just while standing still – unheard above the din and invisible in the east London mist.

Grime's marginal stance was formed from being on the wrong side of a generational divide. They were the kids who were first alienated and then shut out from UK garage: how were they ever going to afford champagne and designer clothes, and what were lyrics about grown-up relationships, love and romantic betrayal saying to them about their lives? 'Ain't no love ting here,' announced Dizzee on *Boy in da Corner*, as a kind of rejoinder to UK garage's primary fixation. Even his break-out single – really, grime's break-out single – was a song called 'I Luv U', which specifically warned against the reckless, 'life-ending' folly of saying those 'three magic words'. Indeed the more poignant and reflective 'I Luv U Remix', where Dizzee is joined by Sharky Major and Wiley, points to a yearning for that affection ('Can you teach me to share? I don't know how to care, it just wouldn't be fair,'[18] laments Wiley). Grime was never big on romantic love, with a few exceptions, most notably Ruff Sqwad, whose mixtapes were called 'Guns N Roses' because they were in touch with the latter, emotional side too. 'Most of our songs, even though it's grime, were just really heartfelt,' Dirty Danger said to me in 2012, although he wasn't entirely sure where that rush of blood had come from. 'Times must have been really hard I guess,' he speculated. 'Grime was really odd music at the best of times,' reflected DJ and producer Slackk recently, 'but amid hundreds of weird white labels which were blasts of bass and noise, you'd get Ruff Sqwad turning up with two hours of sad spaceship music, and just kill it.'[19] The crew's sledgehammer-subtle version of eighties classic 'Died In Your Arms', and the sublime 'Together', a collaboration with Wiley, were the highlights of their grimy love songs – along with several grandiose orchestral instrumentals, like 'Your Love Feels', 'Functions On Da Low' and 'It's Nuffin'.

The feelings are strong, even if they are formed from a coldness, from a lacking of love, rather than an abundance of it. Grime's principal personality trait is catharsis: it's there in the sonics as well as the lyrics, and whether as furious anger, ebullient energy, hollow bravado or callous nihilism, so much of its emotional range can be seen as a cathartic expression of pain. 'I come from a place where I'm the only one who didn't go to jail,' Geeneus reflected recently. 'I come from an estate, in the manor. Life is hard. It's not like we're having a great life. We're having a terrible life – and for me, doing radio, doing music, is the only thing that managed to keep me out of it.'

A few years ago, Skepta was asked to join the dots between grime and US hip-hop: 'It's all born from poverty,' he said. 'It's all born from pain.'[20] Respect Tsars finger-wagging over violent lyrics, and policy initiatives about street drinking and graffiti could never give victims of social exclusion what they needed; a stake in society, investment in decent social, cultural and housing infrastructure, or the educational and professional opportunities available to peers from more privileged backgrounds. 'Don't receive a lot of love, so I don't show much,'[21] was Dizzee's profound summing up of the situation on 'Do It', *Boy in da Corner*'s heartbreaking final track.

The forms of anger and frustration unique to growing up poor in London have their own modes of expression – and Dizzee's own experience of petty street squabbles and constant trouble at school found the familiar route of music as catharsis: 'I talk a big whole heap of badness/ Because my life's a big whole heap of madness,' he says on 'Do It'. While he may be pensive and sad on the inside – inside his head, inside his mum's council flat – here's Dizzee's mean, angry road persona. He devotes an entire 16 lines of 'Stop Dat' to the 'screwface', his permanently sealed expression to the outside world, born of anger, depression, and the intensity of the manor's claustrophobia (here are the final six):

Screwface means I'm not pleased
Screwface means I'm not amused
Screwface means I just wanna walk not talk
Screwface means I just wanna leave
When I activate my screwface give me space
Screwface means let me breathe[22]

More than just a bit of slang, a screwface is the physical embodiment of the spirit of grime. It's not as simple as a scowl or a frown – for one thing, it's not necessarily negative. Its partner expression is a showerface: the kind you might make if you were a member of Jamaica's Shower Posse gang, as they showered bullets on their enemies. Skepta in his early days was 'a showerface man and I'm going on shower', while he dissed his opponents, '[You] think that you're shower but you can't even jump in the bath.' There is another dimension to it: in the musical context, in the club, your face is contorted not as an act of antisocial toughness, as Dizzee describes, but as the only natural physical response to a decent sound system with a decent sub-bass, or the terminal velocity of an MC's flow on the mic. In the church of grime, when your eyes are half-shut, nose, lips and cheeks screwed up in deference to the adrenaline, velocity and bass weight of the track, this is your moment of physical transcendence.

There is one occasion when grime's war chat has been connected to devastating, real-world violence. In November 2006, Carl 'Crazy Titch' Dobson, still only 23, was convicted (along with his stepfather) of the murder of 21-year-old Richard Holmes and sentenced to 30 years without parole. His half-brother, Dwayne 'Durrty Goodz' Mahorn was acquitted of the same crime, after a year in jail on remand. What distinguished the case in particular – beyond any other senseless tragedy – was the prosecution's case that the murder had been provoked by a grime lyric: Holmes had produced a track on which his friend from their Piff City crew, Shabah 'Shak' Shah, had dissed Goodz, accusing him of having 'lost touch with his roots', and saying 'over the years things change in the 'hood, I used to have a lot of respect for Durrty Goodz … not no more.' The *Guardian* asked, 'Is violence holding grime back?' and purported that 'too often, grime beefs erupt into real bloodshed' – sure, once is too often, so maybe that's true on a technicality (if it is true in this case), but no other examples are forthcoming. Perhaps it was 'something to do with the sound itself', the article continued: 'unlike two-step garage, its sexy predecessor, grime is intrinsically claustrophobic and furious.'[23]

The question too few stopped to ask was whether this was a 'grime beef', or a beef involving two people who sometimes made grime. If you read between the lines of innuendo from 'people who know', and from a reliable-sounding source in John Heale's book *One Blood: Inside Britain's Gang Culture*, it seems a lot more complicated than the press had made out. 'It wasn't about the lyrics. Maybe at first, but in the end it was about people not respecting their positions,' says 'Alex', explaining to Heale that the rhyme had been 'nothing heavy', but what had followed was escalating threats and demands for respect, allegedly involving a visit to Goodz's mother's house, and ultimately, an act of horrific and tragic violence.[24] Had a grime lyric loaded the gun, or fired the trigger? Evidently not. Apart from anything else, as an editorial in *Vice* commented at the time, the lines quoted by the prosecution, and in the subsequent media coverage, were 'the most inoffensive diss lyrics I have ever seen'[25] – but it's easier to echo the idea that music generates these problems, rather than tackling them at their roots.

The tragedy of Britain in the 2000s was the government's ideological fixation on ignoring the root causes of social problems. It dismissed the effects of poverty and social exclusion in favour of dogma about individual responsibility, and a focus on cosmetic fixes: of blocks of flats, of boisterous music genres, of attitudes. British cities, black youth culture, and the behaviour of young people all faced the prospect of New Labour regeneration, and the quintessential moral panic of the period was an appropriately ludicrous exemplar of the Blair era: the terrifying social menace that was the hooded sweatshirt.

Attached to this moral panic was a new social stereotype, a new folk devil: the 'hoodie' became not just the noun for the item of clothing, but its wearer. An urban equivalent of the other greatly maligned whipping child of the age, 'the chav', and just as pejorative: each with their own distinct dress codes, but both of them young, working-class, and understood to be outsiders who deserved to be outsiders – feral youth who not just created, but celebrated their own social exclusion, and thus deserved it. It is an often forgotten dimension to the milieu of the period, but the mid-2000s was open season on the exact demographic who were most likely to make and listen to grime. In 2002 the novelist and critic Tim Lott wrote a revealing op-ed in the *Evening Standard*, positioned as a thoughtful exploration of prejudice and social exclusion in London, apparently under the impression that his self-awareness was somehow mitigating what he was saying:

'My chief prejudice seems to focus on young black men, whom I presume to be West Indian – specifically those who wear hooded tops in hot weather, ride very small bikes much too fast, and hang around in large groups on the streets. My bias against this section of the "black community" – I apologise for the meaningless phrase – is not very defined. It mainly arises from the unprovable and vague suspicion that they are inconsolably grumpy, somewhat misogynist and contemptuous of the law and of white society in general. I feel no hatred towards them, but I do feel fear and a degree of anger at what I perceive as their hostility.'[26]

Extraordinary though the piece was, Lott was clearly not alone in his prejudices: in his instinctive sense that there was a malignant personality underneath the hoods, and that the blame for marginality lay with the marginalised. Little consideration of the causes of social exclusion of young people was given by commentators or the political classes; academic experts and youth charities generally had their analysis ignored. Criminologists suggested that despite New Labour's investment in some areas, a pre-existing lack of opportunities for young people from poor backgrounds was being made worse: legislation like the 1998 Criminal Justice Act had marginalised them further by pushing state support out of reach, and pushing them out of public space.[27] But this wasn't what the government wanted to hear: individual responsibility and discipline were the keys to tackling the criminality and thuggery flourishing among this lost generation.

Tony Blair used his first press conference upon re-election in 2005 to outflank the Conservatives to the right and announce a crackdown on 'disrespect and yobbish behaviour', blaming, among other things, poor parenting – glossing over the fact his own son, Euan, had been arrested for being drunk and incapable in Leicester Square, a few years earlier. There was a flagrant class dimension to the crusade. 'People are tired of street-corner and shopping-centre thugs,' Blair told the assembled media, backing the Bluewater Shopping Centre in Kent, who had just banned hooded tops and baseball caps from the premises in a blaze of press coverage, along with the Trafford Centre in Manchester, and the Elephant and Castle Shopping Centre in south London. The manager of Bluewater told the press that business had soared amidst the publicity, with shoppers happy there were no longer 'gangs of youths simply hanging around'.

The mania reached a new level of absurdity in 2006, when a 58-year-old teaching assistant from Wooton Bassett had a confrontation with a Tesco security guard, after the latter had insisted she remove her hooded top, in line with store policy. Mrs Parncutt had refused, insisting that her hair was a mess: 'I couldn't believe he was talking to me. I'm supposed to look like a nasty thug?' One young offender from Manchester was given an ASBO banning him from wearing a hoodie for five years. Some youth charities gamely tried to defend the basic freedom to wear a hooded sweatshirt, against the demonisation of the press and political class, but went unheard. 'It's very easy to create the stereotype of the young thug as emblematic of society's problems, rather than seek out the root of the problems,' Rachel Harrington from the British Youth Council told the *Guardian*. Even NGOs set up specifically to advocate for children weren't all onside. The director of youth charity Kidscape, Michele Elliott, joined in the calls for a hoodie ban, after she was pushed to the ground by a group of children in a shopping centre, after telling them off for messing around. 'Hoodies have become associated with gangs and gang-type activity,' she told the BBC. 'I don't hate youths, I don't think you should lock them up in cages, but when I see a gang coming towards me now I will cross to the other side of the street.'

While he was frequently mocked for it, in and of itself, David Cameron's 'hug a hoodie' speech that summer was a genuinely compassionate and thoughtful response to the media frenzy, and to New Labour's aggressive response to alienated young people. 'The hoodie is a response to a problem, not a problem in itself,' Cameron said. 'We – the people in suits – often see hoodies as aggressive, the uniform of a rebel army of young gangsters. But hoodies are more defensive than offensive. They're a way to stay invisible in the street. In a dangerous environment the best thing to do is keep your head down, blend in. For some the hoodie represents all that's wrong about youth culture in Britain today. For me, adult society's response to the hoodie shows how far we are from finding the long-term answers to put things right.' Given these insights, it was a shame that as Prime Minister a few years later, Cameron did far more to deepen the alienation of working-class young people than even Blair had managed.

While the class component to the hoodie mania was clear, an implicit association with black youth culture hung heavily in the air around the entire 'hoodie' debate, but was rarely specifically named. It also intersected very neatly with New Labour's obsession with CCTV – it was said that one of the primary problems of the hoodie, beyond it being 'intimidating', was that it was a direct response to the ubiquitous cameras, and undermined their efficacy. How are we supposed to watch your every move if we can't see your face? 'If you've nothing to hide you've nothing to fear' is the catchphrase of the authoritarian, and it was very popular with Blair's government.

The *Daily Mail* ran headlines about a 'new brand of evil hoodies' made by streetwear brand Criminal Damage, which had left 'members of the public intimidated and scared' – because they zipped up to obscure the wearer's face completely. The hoodie was the perfect villain for the post-9/11 clampdown: a period when Labour were planning a £5-billion programme to introduce ID cards to Britain, in support of their blanket application of CCTV to urban areas. Professor Angela McRobbie from Goldsmiths University told the *Guardian* the hooded top was 'one in a long line of garments chosen by young people, usually boys, and inscribed with meanings suggesting that they are "up to no good"' – just like leather jackets or bondage trousers had been in their day.[28]

The grime scene stoically kept their hoods up. Lady Sovereign responded to the media brouhaha with a well-timed piece of zeitgeist surfing: releasing a single called 'Hoodie', a shameless link-up between her label Def Jam and Adidas, in which the chorus ran, 'Fling on an Adidas hoodie and just boogie-woogie with me.'[29] As part of this light-hearted corporate pushback they launched a 'Save the Hoodie' campaign, producing a Lady Sovereign Adidas hoodie, and a website charting the history of famous rebel hood-wearers throughout history, from Robin Hood to Superman. The video for the Hoodie Remix featured Sovereign, along with Jme, Skepta, Jammer, Ears and Baby Blue, delivering their verses broadcast across a pile of stacked CCTV screens. Grime label No Hats No Hoods launched in 2007, an acknowledgement of the rule which adorned a lot of shop fronts, as well as many of the aspirational, grown-up UK garage raves that had shut out the sportswear-clad teenagers who had invented grime.

The hoodie was the perfect symbol for the grime generation, and a society that was determined to demonise them: blamed for gun violence and the moral corruption of British youth, intimidating, disrespectful and feckless. It was also a functional response to the emergent surveillance society, and to urban spaces increasingly crowded with CCTV. The privatisation of previously public space in areas like Canary Wharf gave the guardians of that space all the legal authority they needed to say 'remove that item of clothing or leave the premises', which they never would have been able to in a public park or square. The margins of the poorer parts of inner London were becoming ever smaller, more watched, and more claustrophobic – and even the clothes young people were wearing in them were being policed, from the Prime Minister downwards. Is it any wonder the 2000s produced music as migraine-tense as grime?

SEVEN

NEIGHBOURHOOD NATIONALISM

Since the millennium, urban space in London has become a battle-field on which young people keep on losing. More and more chunks of outdoor public space were privatised as the Docklands had been, and became subject to the whims of their landlords and their private security patrols, while the rest of the city was surveilled and policed ever more intrusively. CCTV watched Londoners' every move, and ASBOs and the Respect agenda helped to turn hanging out into a quasi-criminal activity. In the late 2000s, permanent signs went up on lampposts in parts of east London with the sinister instruction that you were in a 'Good Behaviour Zone', featuring a picture of a CCTV camera, the logos of the Metropolitan Police and Tower Hamlets council, and the advice that 'additional powers to disperse people' had been granted to the cops – along with their barely trained volunteer corps, the Police community support officers (PCSOs) – under the 2003 Anti-Social Behaviour Act.

Amid all the debate about ASBOs themselves, these 'dispersal orders' were a widely overlooked part of the legislation – in part, because the people they were used against were almost all poor, young, and did not have newspaper columns, and also because, unlike ASBOs themselves,

Nasty Crew relax in the manor

149

the cases never ended up in court, and so were never reported on. Dispersal orders allowed police forces to spontaneously, without court involvement or oversight, force 'groups of two or more people' to leave a designated 'dispersal zone' and not return to the area for at least 24 hours, if they were of the opinion that antisocial behaviour was either happening, or likely to happen – adding a nice dystopian flavour of 'pre-crime' to an already arbitrary process. Local councils could designate particular areas 'dispersal zones' for up to six months at a time (and then renew them when that six months had run out), essentially prohibiting groups of two or more from hanging out in public: hundreds of these zones have been applied since 2003, almost always in the kinds of urban spaces where young people congregate: on the streets, in public squares, around shopping centres, next to transport hubs. Additionally, any under-16s found in a dispersal zone between 9 p.m. and 6 a.m., unaccompanied by a parent or 'responsible adult', can be marched home and effectively put under curfew. Breach of a dispersal order is a criminal offence.

At the whims of the local police force, public gathering and socialising in cities could be de facto criminalised by New Labour. Its greatest impact would be on young people growing up in the most crowded urban areas, and in the most overcrowded home environments. If your parental home is a six-bedroom detached house in Dulwich with a huge garden, or in a village in the home counties, rather than a tiny council flat in Bow, where you share your bedroom with one or more siblings, the legislation would be less likely to affect you. Young people from poor backgrounds were having their freedom restricted from several different angles, even while senior police officers and the press happily labelled them 'feral'. Even those bits of state support that were offered came with a catch: while New Labour invested in youth services and youth centres after coming to power, they also focused youth work on individualised, short-term 'solutions' to problems, and like everything else, it became increasingly driven by targets and outcomes, and organised along business lines.[1] Other avenues of public social activity, or even – god forbid – festivity, like under-18s raves, which had been a critical and popular part of the late garage and early grime scene, started to disappear after 2004. Another overlooked aspect of London's development, securitisation and gentrification during the 2000s had the effect of limiting the mobility of young people from poor backgrounds: more comprehensive installation of ticket gates at tube and railway stations in London from the nineties, and the introduction of the Oyster card system in 2003, as well as consistently above-inflation fare rises, prevented affordable or free travel around the city for young adults (albeit services were half-price for under-18s). London's public transport was ranked the most expensive of any city in the world by 2015.

When the wider city is less accessible, more dangerous and more heavily policed, 'the manor' is rendered even more important. Grime's strength was always in its intense localism, more than its expression of universal truths: crews from different London neighbourhoods described their ends with glowing pride, in part because they continued to be excluded from grander national or civic identities. The result is something reminiscent of what the sociologist Les Back called 'neighbourhood nationalism': a positive identification with the local area and the people in it, one that often transcended racial divisions, sharing slang and culture, to create a sense of civic harmony, even while racism and hostility remained commonplace in the city and the nation at large – the idea that 'if you're local, you're all right'.[2]

The cosmopolitan hybridity intrinsic to scenes like two-tone ska, jungle, UK garage, grime and dubstep lead to some fun cultural collisions, layers of different identities, where cockney rhyming slang, Jamaican patois and twenty-first-century London slang overlap and cross-pollinate. White MC Nikki S's bars on 'Legendary' boasts of the ease of his multiculturalism, even while supporting a team with a reputation for racist thuggery: 'I'm a Millwall man, not West Ham/To my white mates I'm like "OI OI", to my black bredrins I'm like "bless fam".'[3] Skepta's track 'Man' reflects the same kind of harmony, with a subtle swap of two key nouns: 'Came a long way from when whites never used to mix with blacks/Now all my white ni**as and my black mates, we got the game on smash.'[4]

Conviviality in the local community often came as a product of the danger that lay outside it, however. The grime scene 'felt more like a community' in the early days, says D Double E: 'it felt a bit closer: we had to work our way out of certain conditions – it used to be quite racist back in the day in east London.' Academic Anthony Gunter has shown that the growth of black and Asian youth 'localism' in recent decades was partly a response to the threat of racist violence in the wider city. All of his young east London subjects can give examples of other less safe neighbourhoods nearby: they mention specific National Front-run pubs that are known and discussed in the community, and carefully avoided.[5] Similarly, Les Back writes that coming up against the barriers of institutional racism for some of his black interviewees – especially in employment, after leaving formal education – would provide a certain amount of shock, contrasted with the multicultural sociability of the local neighbourhood.

While there are precedents in parts of the UK hip-hop, reggae, jungle and UK garage scenes of the eighties and nineties (including a rich vein of reggae tracks about the Brixton riots), grime, more than any genre in its ancestry, makes a huge priority of neighbourhood pride. If you're from the ends, then you know, if you aren't, then you don't. This is a genre for which a pivotal track, released in January 2003 in that crucial late-garage-into-grime period, was called 'Are You Really From The Ends?' – beginning with the dramatised, accusatory speech 'Yo bro, where you from? You're not from the borough, you're not from the area, you're not from the ends ...' Too many boy dem want to pretend, you see.[6] Grime's 'rep your ends' lyrics and anthems are not just countless, but integral to its entire identity. 'Don't chat shit if you ain't from the ends, if you ain't from the bits, if you ain't from the block,'[7] Dot Rotten growls on his desperately bleak mixtape-masterpiece, *This Is the Beginning*. Grime's local fixation even gave rise to the coinage 'endzish' – i.e. being concerned with, and loyal to, the ends.

The south London anthems alone are legion: positioned against the east hierarchy, crews like South Agents and South Soldiers wore their allegiance prominently in their names. The most prominent of south London crews in the first wave, Essentials, made a track called 'Doin It Now' as a direct challenge to the rest of the city: 'You don't want to play with boys from south London,' spits Remerdee, before the chorus 'New Cross Gate, Brockley, Catford, Brixton way, Deptford, Peckham, Lewisham, 'llow [forget] Stonebridge, Tottenham, Slough: look who's doing it now.'[8] This south pride – particularly in the grime heartland and 'blue borough' of Lewisham – continued up to The Square's 2015 tribute to 'Lewisham McDeez', a track calling on MCs to meet in the local McDonald's for a clash. From SLK's anthem 'North Weezy' ('the north west city, where tings are gritty') to Elf Kid declaring he is 'Deptford Market's local rep' or Ipswich's long-forgotten Hectic Squad asking, 'What You Know About Ips?', the grime canon is full of key lines and tracks in which the MCs' identities are so wrapped up in the local area's identity that separating them is impossible.

Grime's king of local obsessions is, ironically, the MC who has lived mostly either in Kent or Cyprus (or Canada, or Jamaica, or Liverpool) for the last decade: the godfather. Wiley's references to Bow litter numerous bars in numerous songs, the glaringly obvious one being his 2007 single 'Bow E3', in which he namechecks the local sights: Tredegar (Road), Monteith Estate (the home of his tower block, Clare House), Malmesbury (Primary School), Vicky (Victoria) Park and Moon Lee (Chinese takeaway). These reference points are far too obscure to call iconic in any city-wide sense, let alone beyond London or the UK: they're all minor residential streets and amenities, all within a mile radius of each other, in an unfashionable and little-known part of east London, all walking distance from Wiley's childhood home. Contrast it, in terms of the breadth of its horizons, to Jay-Z and Alicia Keys' New York anthem, 'Empire State of Mind', with its bombastic, five-boroughs-spanning references to globally recognised places like Broadway, Harlem and Yankee Stadium. It might seem a mildly hyperbolic comparison, but both are anthemic singles by MCs widely recognised as being at (or near) the top of their respective genres – for Jay-Z, the song is there to rep that 'Afrika Bambaataa shit, home of the hip-hop', for Wiley, 'we made the genre everybody's onto, it's all come from Bow E3'. The tracks serve the same purpose, but one is playing to the world gallery, against a backdrop of sweeping strings, with the bombast of a Hollywood film-score; the other, equally sincere, shouts out a tiny, dowdy local takeaway which currently has a rating of 2.2/5 on Google Reviews.

Though its horizons may have broadened a little over time, grime is in its essence not just local, but microscopically local. To make another hyperbolic comparison: US rappers like Lil Jon have a tendency to shout out the entire American South in their tunes – an area home to approximately 100 million people; Tinchy Stryder made a track called 'One Of Those Days' narrating one hectic day in his teenage life, with trouble brewing in the ends, the police circling, weed in the air, Wiley summoning him to the studio: all of it centred around grime's single most iconic location: Roman Road in Bow. Is it any wonder people like to describe grime's sonics as 'claustrophobic', when this is the world it inhabits? 'As you get older,' Tinchy reasoned, when I brought the song up with him a few years later, 'your brain becomes more open to painting pictures that everyone's in tune with. But back then, if you weren't around Bow, you might not understand.' That single road and its street market, locally known as 'the Roman', is mentioned in tracks by Kano, Ghetts, Dizzee and Merky Ace and (on several different occasions) Wiley, whose childhood home was a two-minute walk away. 'Roman Road was so lively,' Wiley once said to me, 'because it had that street market culture, every Tuesday, Thursday and Saturday – even walking around the local area, you could see Roman Road was the nurturer. It all has something to do with the Dizzees and Wileys coming through. It nurtures people to strive.'

Grime's neighbourhood nationalist tendency is a response to urban claustrophobia, and a reflection of the need to confidently declare a positive identity: to stand up and be counted as a representative of your area; especially if it's a re-branded, comic-book grime version of it. (Roll Deep's Limehouse is known as Wilehouse, OT Crew repped Barking and Dogenham, The Square's T-shirts name the blue borough Slewisham, while SN1's Peckham is Pecknaam.) Perhaps these identities are all the more tempting if you're a person of colour for whom diasporic identities feel precarious or contingent – if owning one or more of 'British', 'English', 'Jamaican' or 'Ghanaian' feels complex or out of reach, or has been denied to you. 'Repping' is an interesting verb, in how generalised its meaning becomes: you might hear an MC just say casually while hosting a set, 'Yeah, we're repping': one of those broad, generic bits of slang that says, even in the most generic sense, we're here, we're representing: ourselves, our peers, our area, something. It's wrapped up in grime's tendency to write self-help pep talks ostensibly directed to its listeners, but maybe really, subconsciously, directed inwards. You're lacking confidence, but you shouldn't be: 'Stand Up Tall', 'Pick Yourself Up'. 'I stand tall in the Deptford flats,' spits Remerdee on Essentials' 'Headquarters', capturing the spirit of grime's hyper-localism – it is designed to uplift yourself, via pride in your ends. It's something So Solid Crew's Asher D sums up in his bars on 'Southside Allstars' too: 'I just want to stand correct for my block.'

'Southside Allstars' and 'Headquarters' were two prime examples of the locally-orientated all-star tracks which dominated the pirate airwaves and Channel U in grime's formative years. The latter – subsequently renamed 'State Your Name' upon its release – required each MC to present themselves as if in a military line-up: Remerdee, aka the Captain, asks of each MC in turn: 'what's your name soldier? State your location. Who are you repping?' And after they've answered that, they're ordered to 'drop and give me 16' – bars, rather than press-ups, of course. 'You're messing with the New Cross blue boss,' spits Essentials' K Dot in his 16, 'it's K Dot, Kidman, bad man from Brockley.' The implication of militancy is a recurring theme – from Newham Generals to South Soldiers – not only because it suggestions violence and machismo, but also the idea of repping your area, and even wearing a uniform indicating your allegiance. 'If you're from dirty south, salute, and you've got a bandana to match your tracksuit ...' Young Dot spits on 'Dirty South Salute' – this is grime at its most gangsterish, where the (gang) colour of your bandana is enough to mark your territory.

Nikki S and Nyke's 'Southside Allstars' is perhaps the most ostentatious example of neighbourhood pride, a legendary Channel U-era all-star track featuring a staggering fifteen different MCs from across south London, each repping their crew, their neighbourhood, their postcode, or all three. It was, Nikki S said to me from the back seat of his cab, 'a statement, rather than a club tune'. It was a response to, and intensified, the south v. east tensions of the early 2000s. So Solid Crew had dominated the MC-driven side of UK garage so completely that, according to Nyke, all the east London top dogs (Geeneus from Rinse FM, Diesle from Deja Vu FM) had a 'secret meeting' in which they plotted to build up an alternative power base. 'They basically said, "We're going to build a fence up around east now, and start burrowing in, and making our own sound."' Alias, the respected early grime producer who made the 'Southside Riddim' instrumental for them, deliberately neglected to stamp his 'Alias' audio-logo on the track, as he usually would. 'He was worried that his tunes would get shut down by Slimzee and Geeneus,' Nyke recalled – the association might be too controversial. 'I remember the east London artists were ringing up our manager, Sponge, because he would be orchestrating raves still in south, and they were like, "What, is it cool to come south? Is it beef Sponge?"' The very last line of 'Southside Allstars', after almost six exhausting minutes of chest-beating and relentless hype, is the devastating mic-drop of, 'You can roll deep but not around here.' Did they mean 'roll deep' or 'Roll Deep'? Almost certainly both.

The consequence of this intensifying neighbourhood nationalism, of outward pride and inward claustrophobia, was that anything beyond the boundaries of the neighbourhood felt at best like an alien landscape, and at worst like enemy territory. For Geeneus, a teenage fixation on getting onto legendary jungle station Kool FM presented a huge obstacle: everyone on Kool FM was from Hackney, and he was in Bow. Back then, it felt like those areas were worlds apart, 'Like the difference between London and Manchester,' rather than being about 15 minutes down the road. 'Don't worry about what's going on across the water,' K Dot from Essentials says on the first *Risky Roadz* DVD, when he's asked how his south London crew will cope with east London's dominance of the scene. He makes it sound like another country, but the body of water he's referring to is the Thames, not the Atlantic Ocean or the English Channel. Almost every MC I've ever interviewed has talked about their first experience going to perform at a pirate station or a rave outside their immediate neighbourhood, and the anxiety associated with the expedition. 'I remember going to Eskimo Dance in Watford, and it felt like the furthest place in the world,' Tinchy Stryder told me in 2010, confused by the myopia that had once been the norm. 'It was weird, I didn't ever look at the bigger picture.'

It was a weird disjunction for a crew like Ruff Sqwad, with their expansive musical horizons, making epic-sounding 'stadium rock' grime like 'Died In Your Arms' or 'Together', but still nervous about their music taking them more than a few miles from their front door. It was no small thing for a group of black east London teenagers to travel to parts of north London or Essex ('even Dagenham!' Dirty Danger exclaimed) to do guest shows on other pirates, or visit vinyl-cutting houses or recording studios. 'In a sense you're risking your life,' Rapid told me, earnestly, 'because we used to come out of our area where we're comfortable, taking buses and trains to Tottenham, or walking deep into areas in Hackney from the bus stop: we'd have people asking, "Where are you from? What are you doing here?" seeing people pulling out guns at the radio stations, dogs, whatever – it was a harsh time.'

This is the more perilous side of the intense, claustrophobic atmosphere the grime generation grew up in: 'slipping', or being caught alone or outnumbered, outside of your area – it relates to the meaning of the phrase roll deep, in fact: when you move, move in numbers. 'No whip, out the manor linking chicks: that's slipping,'[9] Kano helpfully explains on 'P's And Q's'. Wiley was not the only grime MC to be stabbed (14 times, on two separate occasions) while out of his area – he also wrote a specific song about getting caught 'slipping in south west London … wrong place, wrong time'. The evolution of this kind of nihilistic territorialism, the negative side of the convivial neighbourhood nationalism, became increasingly hyped by the media as 'postcode wars' during the 2000s – though it was, inevitably, more complicated than that suggests.

Location-specific criminal gangs have a long history in London prior to this point, going back decades, if not centuries – at my school in south London in the mid-nineties, the playground chat was all about the 28s (in Brixton), and Wo Shing Wo, a triad gang (all over) – but the received wisdom is that inter-area hostility has greatly intensified in the last 20 years: it correlates, in fact, with the increasing gentrification of the inner city. The relationship between music and these conflicts was tenuous in grime's heyday, but it still affected young black musicians, insofar as their safety when they roamed outside of the neighbourhood was under threat in a way that was both unique, and generally overlooked by the powers that be. By the end of the 2000s the connection was becoming less tenuous, reflected in the overlap between 'road rap' music videos and (albeit hype-driven) 'gang-related' videos on YouTube, becoming a surreal public forum for inter-area conflict in London. Depressingly, it is even less tenuous now, with respect to drill music, in particular, where performative lyrics about riding to 'opp blocks' to attack or humiliate opponents seem to correspond more and more with the reality.

'It's mad,' mused DJ and MC Complex in Simon Wheatley's *Don't Call Me Urban!*, summing up the futility and absurdity of the conflict between Lewisham and Peckham, located just over the borough bound-ary in Southwark: 'It's all south east London really, but they have blue bins and we have green ones, and if it was just one area there'd be no problem.' He also suggested the problem had intensified in the short space of a decade, in grime's lifetime: 'I live in Peckham, but no area is great enough for me to put my life on the line. I'm not putting my life on the line for a postcode! I try to explain this to my cousins but their generation's different. I left school in 1999 and now it's 2008 and a lot has changed.'

To insert myself into the story momentarily, as a marker of how race and class privilege can determine the way you move around the city, I remember being momentarily surprised by a black workmate saying to me, in 2006, that her little brother was about to turn 17, and she was determined he would learn to drive and get a car immediately. We were both lifelong south Londoners, both in our mid-twenties. I'd never learned to drive, and she hadn't either – there never seemed any point, in a city with a public transport network as comprehensive as London's – but her little brother was a black teenager, in London, in 2006, and thus, she reasoned, needed the safety of being able to move around the city without risking trouble. The point is, you don't have to be involved in any kind of trouble, let alone a known gangster, to warrant an attack – you just have to be *not* known to local young people with gang pretensions, and thus assumed to be an enemy, and fair game. This is what Rapid means by 'in a sense, you're risking your life'.

Without the safety or money to travel, you're restricted to a small bit of turf, watched from all sides, back to the wall, justifiably paranoid and tense. 'Imagine if we never grew up on a council estate, and was country manor raised with a spoon in our mouth: would we still be making fuss about the east and the south?' Dizzee asks on 'Imagine', a poignant track off *Showtime* about class, privilege and 'selling out'. He concludes that 'we don't know who the real enemy is … instead we defend a couple square metres of pavement.'[10] Territorialism intensifies as the space you are allowed access to gets smaller. This same futile postcode-warrior mentality was lamented more than a decade later by teenage south London rapper Dave (partial to the odd grime crossover tune); on 'JKYL+HYD' he squeezes in an extra dose of tragicomic pathos – the madness of defending an area with your life which you could never hope to own a home in, to have a proper stake in – and under grey London skies, to boot: 'Man are still beefing over ends, but we don't own this land, and we don't even like this weather.'[11]

On the 2004 Radio 1 documentary, *East is East*, still only 19, Dizzee was asked to explain his references to a 'ghetto mentality' – similar to what the rapper Skinnyman called, on his thematically grimy album from the same year, a *Council Estate of Mind*. 'Our ghettos aren't necessarily massive projects,' Dizzee said, comparing them to American mega-estates, 'but they're council estates [where] people have a ghetto frame of mind: you've got a small perspective on things, you see it a certain way, from the corner.' This explanation of the myopia of the ends casts significant light on the title of his debut: Dizzee was not just *the boy in the corner* because of a personal loner sensibility, or because he'd been sent there by an exasperated teacher – his whole outlook, and that of many of his peers, had been shaped by life on the margins. It's hard not to feel like you're in a corner, when you've been backed into it. In a sense, the creation of grime was not just a collective act of identity formation, but the creation of a space – one positioned in between dominant American pop culture, the alienation and hopelessness of British society (especially as jobs-for-life and the welfare state disappeared), and inherited second- or third-generation immigrant cultures that felt less relevant to the young lives of those touching the mic.

Given the intensity of the manor, it's no wonder that the possibility music offered for escape was tantalising. Playing abroad for the first time, or even reaching new audiences beyond the youth club or the local pirate station was mind-expanding. The location didn't even have to be glamorous, to begin with. For Skepta, going to St Albans, north of London, to do Manic FM, or to Stevenage, Hitchin or Hatfield – exurbs and small towns circling the north of London – to play a rave, or on a pirate station, was part of building up his first non-local fanbase, and realising that the music's popularity could travel beyond the manor. But it was also an escape from the claustrophobia of the ends, its drama and road beefs. 'In the early days,' he laughed, 'going to Stevenage was like going on holiday.'

Being on the margins of urban living does not mean living in the furthest outskirts of the city, necessarily – it's not about how close you are to the centre in miles; to the citadels of power, to the tourist attractions, to Westminster or to Buckingham Palace. What matters is your economic distance, your social distance, your psychic distance, and your ability to move freely around the city, unharmed. As grime helped some of its crossover stars to get out of the ends for the first time, interaction with the 'official' parts of London recognisable from a postcard marked a kind of graduation, from the manor to the parts of the city already open to those with class, wealth and race privileges. On BBC London radio in 2010 Dizzee recalled his fond memories, in the early days, of coasting over the bridges over the Thames at dawn, on the way home from a rave in south London: 'that's proper,' he said – that 'feels like a movie.' The host, Robert Elms, asked if he felt a sense of inclusion in his home city. 'More so now,' Dizzee replied, 'now I've come up in the business world.' Money delimits, and poverty constrains.

'I was born in this little bit of rock, in the East End,' he said in an interview with the *Independent* back in 2003. 'But I'm in the world now.' It's startling to think that people he grew up with were not 'in' the world, as far as Dizzee was concerned, so tightly bound was the geography.

There is also another side to grime's neighbourhood nationalism: a forgiving and expansive sense that anyone who has chosen to be in the in-group of this maligned form of underground music, anyone who is listening – on the radio, in the rave – is all right by the MC. All the more so, in those early years, when the idea that anyone beyond the postcode might care was dazzling and flattering. 'How did they even hear of us?' London MCs have said to me several times of their first interactions with random fans in Scotland, or beyond the UK. You can hear expressions of a kind of community solidarity in MCs' asides and ad-libs to an audience on radio and rave tapes from over the years: 'big up the north London crew … south London crew … east London crew … west London crew'. And it goes outside the M25, too, to a sense of a nationwide or global community; Dizzee's 'Stand Up Tall' may start out with the assertion that he's 'London city forever', but also that he is 'ghetto wherever', until he's shouting 'Big up my Midlands, up north troops', and then, beyond England, 'Big up my Ireland, Scotland types' and finally 'Europe, USA troops'. He does it on 'Get By', too, muttering the sermon's opening incantation: 'London ghetto, Birmingham ghetto, Manchester ghetto, Luton ghetto … each area council estate.'

There's a sense of solidarity with the troops and ghettos in other cities, in other ends of London, or in other countries: on a banal level, the troops being shouted out might just be fans: anyone who 'gets it', anyone who supports the music. But it's also perhaps a kind of testament to the way cities are evolving: divisions deepen and the wealthy centre becomes estranged from the urban margins. It's a pattern repeated the world over:

economic globalisation, increasingly complex migration patterns, and cultural globalisation mean that the super-rich living in gated communities or helicoptering into their penthouses in London or New York share more with their fellow elites in Johannesburg, Moscow or Rio, than they do with the poor people living two miles down the road, and vice versa.[12] In this respect, Dizzee's 'troops' in Bow have more in common with their peers in council estates in south-east London, or Paris, or Atlanta, than they do with fellow Londoners who are lucky enough to grow up with a decent amount of economic, housing and health security, who aren't harangued by the police on a daily basis, and so on. 'Ghetto wherever' is a shout-out, a testament to the fact that moving around the world won't change him, but it's also a description of the global thread connecting the urban margins across the world.

Sometimes, grime has taken on a grander civic identity, and the mantle of speaking to or for London as a whole – on Kano's 'London Town', Ruff Sqwad's 'London' or Devlin's 'London City'. The latter is a starry-eyed, twinkly paean to the capital, and literally charts a journey from the margins, the Dagenham where Devlin grew up, into the West End for a lads' night out: 'I'm on the A13 on the way to the city,'[13] it begins, a tribute to the trunk road linking the city centre to the Essex borders, the same road that divides Bow from Canary Wharf. It's fairly rare for grime MCs to romanticise the capital like Devlin and Ruff Sqwad do on these tracks – 'the best city in the world when everyone's not shanking and blasting' is Devlin's qualified compliment – but the desire to do so is clearly there, even if it's almost impossible to overlook the hardships they've grown up with. 'Right about now man have got nothing but nish/east London where it smells like fish,'[14] runs one of the verses on the Ruff Sqwad track.

Wiley's three-minute letter to his grandma, 'Nan I Am London', is a glorious personification of the city from the MC who spits bars about the capital incessantly. 'Ask anybody, anytime, anywhere, if Eskiboy represents London? I *am* London.'[15] It's tempting to compare his sense of belonging and identification with London to the attitude of his forebears. Could a 1970s reggae artist, or 1950s calypso artist, have transcended a sense of unease and alienation in the city to write a song pronouncing, 'I Am London'? Lord Kitchener's 'London Is the Place for Me', written upon his arrival from Trinidad on the *Empire Windrush* in 1948, is a celebration of the city: but it's a giddy tale of arrival at a 'mother country', not one of direct identification or recognition. For all the grime generation's manifold types of exclusion, they were embedded, and justifiably defiant about their right to the city. Dizzee Rascal was asked a few years ago on BBC Radio London whether he thought, in fifty years time, people would still be listening to his music. Of course they would, he laughed: 'I'm here – I'm in the fabric.'

You hate me don't you? You hate my people, your plan is to terminate my culture, you're fucking evil. I want you to recognize that I'm a proud monkey. You vandalize my perception but can't take style from me.

THE BLACKER THE BERRY

NO ~~BLACKS~~ BASHMENT

NO ~~DOGS~~ GRIME

NO ~~IRISH~~ DUBSTEP

THE SWEETER THE JUICE

Ⓝ

If you make any of this banned music and you are from croydon, please contact. If you have an opinion on this, take a picture and/or hashtag   . If you want to support, buy a t-shirt and wear it in croydon this summer
There is a secret signature to prove you didn't do this so give credit where credit is due. Thanks to Croydon Council,Police and the concept of Gentrification!!

EIGHT

SHUTDOWN

It is 2011, I'm sitting in a Soho basement office with Lethal Bizzle – who is managed by a rock and metal management company, with *Kerrang!* posters up in the lobby. Grime has long since hit upon hard times – it's been years since the radio-rave-riddims heyday of the scene. Most crews have split, a lot of MCs have given up, and a lot of producers and DJs have done the same, or switched their attention to funky house, because there's actually a club scene to speak of, and DJs can get regular bookings. The few MCs who've managed to cross the floor from the underground to the charts are restricted to making passionless, formulaic electro-pop, and it's making them money, but it's not really making them happy. Lethal has been skewing towards an indie-rock crossover crowd, playing rock festivals and collaborating with Babyshambles. We're talking about his plans to re-release 'Pow! (Forward)': the original grime anthem that was so raucous it was banned from clubs across London and the south-east – he has fond memories, but there's a wistful tone to the whole discussion, a clear sense that something fundamental has gone missing.

'In all honesty, what's held grime back a bit, is that – as much as it's very dominated by MCs, and the lyrical side – we've lost the fact that this

Posters in Croydon call out institutional racism

is supposed to be dance music. That is the whole reason we are here. The dance and enjoyment side, the club side, that hype, that crazy energy, has been taken away. No one's saying because you do grime, you can't do other stuff, but I just think it's important for everyone to remember why we're here. A lot of the beats that are being made now, they're cool, but … when we first started to create this thing, it was about going along to clubs, people singing along to the songs, singing along to bars, going crazy to the beats, seeing *girls* skanking out to hard, bouncey, grimy beats. But the music just got so YouTube-y, iPod-y, in-your-house listening, rather than in the club … and the whole dance element just got taken away. This sound, this whole grime thing, is dance music.'

'Pow!' had developed a fearsome reputation the first time around, becoming a novel dancefloor phenomenon, a grenade thrown into the middle of the refined and sexy 2-step shuffle. 'A lot of these urban clubs had never seen anything like it before, it was just insane,' Bizzle says, likening the response to a mosh pit, and an atmosphere of punk-like rebellion against their elders and betters in the garage scene. 'It was so *exciting* at that time, because that club hype, that energy, it was such a big "fuck you" to people who didn't want to give us a look in.' He adopts the tone of a surly teenager. 'Like, "Fuck it, we'll just do our own thing anyway." When you see "Pow!" in a dance, and you see the reaction, you're sold straight away: the impact, the energy is like no other. DJs used to say to me, "I don't know what to play after that record, I've got problems, there's nothing else I can really play … it's too much."'

Tim Westwood once complained, 'You can't play a hip-hop tune after "Pow!" It's like a volcano erupting.' When it played on Notting Hill Carnival's Rampage sound-system, it led to trees snapping, as revellers who had positioned themselves in their branches responded to its energy. But the urban club owners were not into it – it wasn't *banned by the police*, as tantalising as that legend is – so they started putting up signs in their DJ booths warning against playing the track. 'All Lethal B tracks are banned from this venue (including instrumentals),' read one such sign, a testament to the power of Dexplicit's creation: even the instrumental alone was too incendiary, too liable to start a riot. 'Before we even touch the mic, when people hear those opening beats, they're going crazy,' said Bizzle's fellow Firecamp MC, Fumin, in 2005.

The dancefloor devastation wreaked by the 'Forward Riddim' may be an extreme example, but it points to grime's riotous power – 'we are,' as Wiley once spat, 'extravagant in the bashment, blazing fire in the bashment.' As well as its heritage in the hectic energy and low-end skanking of jungle (and the MC-led side of UK garage), grime as a club music form owes a great deal to its forebears in nineties dancehall: legendary artists like Ninjaman and Shabba Ranks, or Beenie Man and Bounty Killer, going head-to-head in a mic clash at infamous Jamaican stage-show Sting. The idea that pirate radio constitutes 'practice hours' or 'warmsing' (up) for the performance of the stage show, where you draw for your most aggy, most well-known 'reload bars' to get that intense crowd reaction, and a rewind, is sketched out in a sports metaphor: you train for match day, then you perform at the best of your ability when the big day comes. And even while it is a performance, an 'MC Cup Final', as Logan Sama once described Eskimo Dance, the point is that you stay true to the music as it is supposed to be: raw, honest, stripped back – no pyrotechnics, no video backdrops, no planning or structure at all really, just straight rollage from the DJs and concentrated hype from the MCs, each clamouring to mark themselves out from their peers and getting the biggest crowd reaction. 'We're bringing the streets to the stage,' as a 17-year-old Dizzee says in between bars at one of the epochal Sidewinder nights in 2002 – and that's exactly what it was.

The journey from youth-club mic battles to Boy Better Know headlining their own sold-out festival takeover at the 20,000-capacity O2 was a long one, but the role of the actual physical stage itself is critical to how grime turned MCs from hosts into superstars – and distinguished grime from the low-lit, eyes-down, DJ-booth-hidden-away-in-the-corner topography of a lot of club genres.[1] Sidewinder, which had started in 1999 as a UK garage night, played a significant part in the popularisation of the format of the grime stage show – along with Wiley's Eskimo Dance, which ran from 2002 to 2005 in its first incarnation, as well as the under-18s series Young Man Standing, and nights like Rumble and Stampede at 'endzish' venues like Palace Pavilion and Stratford Rex. 'It started with a little stage invasion,' Paul Spruce from Sidewinder recalled.[2] 'We always had a massive stage; that came from the old era of acid raves, because they always had their friends, family, everyone involved on stage.' The tendency among the grimier UK garage crews – So Solid and Pay As U Go especially – to bring their mates and youngers along to MC marked a break from the standard garage performance aesthetic: a single MC delivering their relaxed, mostly inconsequential bars as an accompaniment, hosting rather than dominating the attention, or singers performing short PAs of a few of their singles. 'Then there was this whole other thing going on in the youth clubs,' Spruce continued, 'with kids spraying bars together on a set and getting reloads. That crossed over into the raves heavily in 2001 ... It was our version of Jamaican soundsystem culture.'

Grime doesn't exactly encourage dancing in any formalised or recognisable sense – there are no steps to learn, or novelty dance crazes – but it does lend itself to a more spasmodic version of a reggae skank: 'shocking out' or 'brucking out' perfectly describes the kind of violently electrified flurry of limbs that a grime beat invokes in the dancer. I remember seeing Dizzee's 'Stop Dat' played in a Chock-A-Block rave at the Egg in 2009 by DJ Spyro, to an explosion of unadulterated, cathartic glee which sums up the grime club experience. Sonically, 'Stop Dat' is a bit like striding confidently up to the edge of a tower block rooftop in *Blade Runner*, spreading your arms wide and surveying your domain, before swallow-diving happily off the top. It's the future, and it's a dystopian one: a buzz of robot helicopters whirring, a snatch of a national anthem for an alien planet, a shudder, and then the drop – not so much a drop as a trap-door opening beneath you into the jarring punk assault of beats and bars: three hundred people giddily having a massive fight with the space in front of them, thrashing about like Jaws is trying to drag them under. It's grime as transcendent aggression, and its reception on the dancefloor (and the inevitable rewinds) reiterates what any grime fan knows – as metal, hardcore or punk fans boisterously pogoing do too – that in the right context, a showerface and a beaming grin are the same thing.

The irrepressible hype in early grime raves led to some seminal moments. The clamour of air horns, whistles and a teenage riot almost breaking out as Jammer performed 'Murkle Man' for the first time at Young Man Standing, his dreads flying everywhere, prompting rewind after rewind. Wiley bringing out the young titan Dizzee and the even younger Tinchy Stryder to perform at Eskimo Dance, Tinchy still only 15, sending the crowd into apoplexy with his reload bars, 'let me see the gunfingers.' And then, another foundation-stone moment, the seminal on-stage battle between Pay As U Go and Heartless Crew in 2001. As the heat rises between the two garage crews on stage, a young Wiley inter-venes to tell the MCs to simmer down: 'Lyrics for lyrics, calm. CALM.' You want to swing at this guy? Here's the mic. It's almost an equivalent to Bob Dylan going electric and being booed by folk fans at the 1965 Newport Folk Festival: a moment of high tension and live drama that becomes part of music folklore: a turning point in the way people think about the genre and its culture. The Pay As U Go v. Heartless clash was referenced in tunes by MIK and P Money, and even more prominently, on Skepta's more overt tribute and grime history lesson, 'Lyrics', which sampled Wiley's intervention, and featured the young MC Novelist: a track recorded 15 years later, showing the enduring power of mucky bass and a skippy flow – Novelist was just four years old when the original clash happened.

These ephemeral moments, freed from the strictures of studio record-ings, are vital to the evolution of any genre of music as a living, breathing thing: mutable, unpredictable and communal, where the fans' presence and reaction helps shape the music's development. Sound-system culture belongs to the dancers, too, and the music wouldn't exist without them – every producer-DJ knows about the idea of 'road-testing' a new dubplate in the club, on a proper system; because how else would you know? Beneath the larger stage-show raves like Sidewinder, you have the incubatory role of influential smaller clubs, like the legendary FWD>> at Plastic People, where evolution and cross-pollination happen *inside* the dance. In 2005–06, it was dubstep bleeding in and out of grime: DJs like Plastician and Kode9 and Tubby would play a mixture of both genres, and MCs like Riko Dan, Newham Generals, Skepta, Wiley and Jammer would spit over the top – or the MCs would come down with a grime DJ, like Maximum or Karnage, and stick around to spit over dubstep sets from Hatcha or Skream. Spotting Wiley standing alone in the corner imbibing the sub-bass during this period was a common occurrence, as was seeing him or Skepta spitting over Skream's dubstep wrecking-ball 'Midnight Request Line'. (This even led to a terrific collaborative track between Plastician and Skepta paying tribute to the FWD>> experience, the lighters held aloft and the juddering 'bassline in your nostril', which he called 'Intensive Snare'.) Smaller raves like this help scenes to breathe and evolve and mutate in real time. I saw the same thing happen again a few years later, in 2009, when Boy Better Know's DJ Maximum was booked to play a grime set at FWD>>, but stuck around to fill in for an AWOL peer and play some zeitgeisty UK funky: he pitched up beats by D Malice, Lil Silva and Crazy Cousinz, and MCs Jammer, Badness and D Double seemed to be having the time of their lives attempting to adapt their flows, experiment with something new, and spit over such unusually upbeat and percussive instrumentals.

Unfortunately, grime's live vitality was choked off before it could even begin to flourish, especially in the capital itself. The Metropolitan Police's use of a 'live music risk-assessment form', Form 696, under the 2003 Licensing Act, gave them the power to determine whether an event might be a risk to public safety, and if it was, they required licence holders to provide the full names, addresses, telephone numbers, and dates of birth for all of the artists and promoters on the line-up, often with very little notice. If that wasn't possible, they would take passports instead. Form 696's motives were barely concealed: one question on the eight-page version made clear it was used for racial profiling: 'Is there a particular ethnic group attending? If "yes", please state group.' Another section outlined the specific attention to black music: 'Music style to be played/performed (e.g. bashment, R&B, garage)', while another gave examples of types of musical artists as 'DJs, MCs, etc' – there was no mention of flautists or alto-sopranos.

At the exact moment grime began to take off, the Met began systematically monitoring, targeting and shutting down black music nights, with participation from Operation Trident, the specialist unit targeting black-on-black gang crime. The Met were comfortable with being independent arbiters of which artists or genres presented a risk, and sometimes would just bypass Form 696 altogether to directly shut out grime: 'I was supposed to be playing in the grime room at the Music For You Festival,' Logan Sama told me in 2007, 'and the police actually said, "You can't have a grime room."' These instructions were always given straight to the licence holders, the venue owners or management, rather than to the promoters – partly because they weren't interested in a meaningful discussion about the possibility of trouble with people closer to the music, and partly because this way, the instruction is accompanied by a threat, either implied or explicit: 'If you don't comply, we could take away your licence.' The Met became self-appointed experts in British urban music, happily reeling off lists of 'risky' genres, according to David Moynihan, a grime promoter in the mid-2000s: '[I was at] a meeting with council officials and the Met, when I was involved in putting on a community festival on the Hackney/Tower Hamlets border. The police told us categorically that we weren't allowed to put on music that was "grime, garage, rap, reggae or R&B". Funny that they knew what grime was when some of my friends don't.'

The problem was not risk management in itself, but the blanket approach to entire genres, and the Met's wilful lack of dialogue with promoters: the people booking the musicians, and the people who best know their crowd. Moynihan, who put on Dirty Canvas for two years in some unlikely venues – including the Whitechapel Art Gallery and the ICA – did not once hear from the police directly.

'I'm surprised that they've been left out of the dialogue,' Operation Trident's Steve Tyler admitted to me at the time. They were left out of the dialogue again in 2007, when their 'No Hats No Hoods' label launch at Rich Mix was surreptitiously visited by plain-clothes police: Jammer, along with several of the other MCs performing on the night, was covertly followed out of the venue, and then stopped and searched.

'We just thought, "These people came down for free, for our label launch," and felt quite shit about it,' Pete Todd from No Hats No Hoods said. 'Especially since we've done this night for two years, and done about 20 shows, and we've got a complete clean bill of health. I don't think many nights in any genre could say that! We should win some kind of fair-play award, but instead we're being singled out.'

Jammer, an artist with a history of positive community work, and a mentor to young aspiring musicians, was equally unimpressed by this unwarranted intrusion: 'When I came out of the venue after performing they stopped and searched me. It's a piss-take – I went there that night to *work*. They've basically stopped and searched me in my workplace! They do seem to think artists are carrying weapons, which is mad – we're there to prevent all of that. This kind of thing just puts negative energy into the music, which itself is supposed to be a positive thing.'

Perhaps the most instructive collision of police prejudice and frustrating stupidity was the short, fun life and shorter demise of Straight Outta Bethnal, journalist Chantelle Fiddy's grime night which ran in Shoreditch in 2005–06. When Leon Johnson, the young man also known as MC Slinger, was murdered in March that year, the police investigation started a chain of events that reverberated on the scene in which Johnson occasionally participated. Fiddy posted the following statement on her blog charting the chain of events:

Following the unfortunate murder of YGC's MC Slinger (also on 24 March but of no relation to the event), the Met phoned 333 [the venue] asking for my number, in turn requesting information from myself and the performing acts. Being the only grime night and one that also happened the night of the crime, we seemed an obvious port of call to them because this was a 'grime murder'. Tell me, if someone into rock music is murdered, does it then become a rock murder? I'm baffled as to why it only seems to be crime related to black music or music of a more street form that gets tagged in this way. With the police sniffing round, you can't blame 333 for wanting out, likewise I understand they have a job to do and want to find the killer, if you're hitting a brick wall then you need to tap up info wherever you think possible. So despite hordes of press support, six months of trouble free parties and a growing reputation, we're homeless.[3]

By the mid-2000s, people in the scene had already become pessimistic about grime's live potential in London. They were getting bookings in English towns outside, but not in the home of the music. The problem was, for all the Met's wild swatting at grime, they were actually basing their policing on *something* – even if that was arguably, at least some of the time, a generalised racist folk memory, rather than actual intelligence. Serious trouble at or near raves in the late days of UK garage had been common, and had taken a serious toll on the scene's reputation. A man was stabbed to death outside a So Solid Crew show in Luton in March 2001; two people were shot at a party for So Solid's Romeo at the Astoria in November that year; shots were fired again, leaving one man dead, when gunmen burst into a Lisa Maffia single launch in Turnmills in 2003; and then in 2004, three men were involved in a shoot-out outside the Urban Music Awards at the Barbican.

'The police were shutting down a lot of raves because of crews, because there was a lot of trouble,' says Maxwell D of these latter days of UK garage, blaming 'the level of violence on the street, and the way things were on the street, and the mentality of the gangsters in them days. People used to see each other in the dances, they had beef from all different areas – they all loved the music too, and they were gonna follow where the girls go. Because all the girls were going to these raves, so man weren't staying at home, you know? They wanted to see Pay As U Go and Heartless.'

It was just wildly unfair on the remaining 99 per cent of the crowd, apart from anything else. Dizzee Rascal's 2017 track 'Make It Last' tackles violence in that period head-on, and is positioned, he's said in interviews, as a corrective to latter-day grime hipsters who want to deify the late UK garage days, without realising how dodgy the atmosphere could often be. The track references a gang-related shooting on the steps of Palace Pavilion in Hackney in 2006, Dizzee witnessing beef between Brixton and Peckham guys at Imperial Gardens (closed in 2003), and a double murder at the Tudor Rose nightclub in Southall in late 2002: 'All I saw was G's, bredders on their knees, screaming "Why d'you take my boy away? God help him, please!"'[4] The night in question was called Unarmed 2, and was dedicated to stopping gun crime among young black people, the *Evening Standard* reported at the time.

While the police have tended to overstate the scale of the problem, Dizzee was right that others have underplayed it. Actual grime musicians were not in any such denial: they just understood the context, and the unfairness of it all – that there was serious trouble in the world outside the dance, and sometimes it was brought into the dance; that, of course, is not a rational or fair justification for collective punishment, or for shutting down an entire genre. When I spoke to Ruff Sqwad's Fuda Guy in 2006 he sighed deeply about 'road people causing a fracas in the dance', and the fact that that legacy of trouble from an earlier generation, and the police's overreaction to it, had meant the majority of their bookings were away from where most of their fans were, outside London. The de facto grime ban significantly stifled the careers of Ruff Sqwad and their peers: the live circuit is the best way to consolidate and build a fanbase – not to mention inspiring the next generation of DJs and MCs – and to get paid for your efforts, especially in an era when Napster, Limewire and Kazaa had snuffed out most record sales. 'It's so frustrating, raves getting locked off, especially in our city,' continued Fuda Guy, 'because at the end of the day, I like to perform! Forget the money for a second: this is what I do, it's my skill, I enjoy this – I like to see people scream and shout for me.'

Sometimes, it wasn't gangsters from outside the music world, but beef between crews that developed into physical confrontations. The launch party for SLK's classic 2005 single 'Hype Hype' was a bit too close to its title, and turned into a brawl; while the north-west London crew's clashes with east London's Nasty Crew at raves led to people on both sides getting physically hurt, they told Simon Wheatley in *Don't Call Me Urban!* 'Man's older now,' MC Mighty from SLK told Wheatley a few years later, 'and looking back, it was fucking pathetic.' The serious gangsterism that had affected UK garage was absent, though grime was affected by trouble too: the final Eskimo Dance in London, in late 2003, witnessed scuffles, bottles flying, and crowds stampeding for the exits. The question becomes: is that enough to shut down an entire scene, in an entire city? I've seen a scuffle at a major grime night once, at a Sidewinder rave in 2006: it was in the hotbed of urban gang violence that is Swindon, Wiltshire – it was, likewise, pretty pathetic, but it was at the very end of the night, didn't seem to affect anyone but the people involved, and no one was seriously hurt. 'I haven't ever seen a serious violent incident in a grime rave,' DJ Logan Sama said in 2006. 'I've seen them at house raves, I've seen them at hip-hop raves, I haven't at a grime rave. I've seen fist fights, but I see that in the Red Lion pub.'

Sama saw a number of grime nights he was booked for cancelled during this period, closed down without explanation, other than references to 'intelligence about an incident'. This wasn't good enough, he said:

'If they do have reliable information that they think there's going to be an incident, then closing it down indicates they don't feel they can prevent that incident. They need to admit that, and then look into why – because if they are *the police* then they need to be able to actually *police* things. They can't keep saying. "Oh no, we can't handle this," because that's not good enough, that means they're not doing their job properly. Closure is not a realistic option – you can't just stop things happening because there's an implied threat there. It's very draconian, and it's not actually solving any problems at all. You're not solving any problems with gun crime, or drug vendettas, or road beefs, by cancelling parties. It's just not effective policing. Just because there's a social problem, it's not acceptable to close down positive musical events aimed at that demographic.'

I first wrote about Form 696 and the Metropolitan Police's targeting of grime nights in 2006; two years later, a petition, along with a campaign supported by UK Music, the musicians' rights body, finally helped me to get the story into the *Guardian*, and elsewhere in the mainstream press: the form was overly bureaucratic, racist, and stifling the live-music industry. A judicial review was sought, and in December 2008, with the campaign taking shape, the form disappeared from the Met's website, to be replaced a week later with a version half the length. The 'which ethnic group' question was suddenly absent, replaced by one asking: 'Who is the target audience? (Include here if Birthday Party.)' It's hard not to conclude that the Met's response to accusations of racial profiling and prejudicial policing was some particularly gnarly sarcasm. It was good, as ever, to know they were taking complaints about institutional racism seriously.

Breaking ranks somewhat from the Met's normal position of silence and obfuscation on the matter, David Isles, a Detective Superintendent with the Clubs and Vice unit, insisted in 2008 that critics of Form 696 were 'naive', and admitted the form had been introduced because of concerns about black-on-black shootings around nightclubs. 'This is about black kids being shot and stabbed and being targeted ... you have particular gangs aligned to particular types of music and that obviously created an environment where rival gangs would target them. It wasn't about the music, it wasn't about the venue, it wasn't about the promotion – it was because gangs were associated with those particular events.'

It's a confusing defence, and a misleading one: if it wasn't about the music, why did they need a list of (black) music genres due to be played? If it wasn't about the music, why did they need incredibly detailed information about the performers? The campaign against Form 696 had an effect, nonetheless, and parliamentary scrutiny of the Licensing Act in May 2009 by the House of Commons' Culture, Media and Sport Committee led them to conclude that the 'government [should] relax restrictions in this area, which in some cases are unnecessarily draconian, and in others simply absurd'. The committee recommended that the form be scrapped altogether. The Met did nothing of the sort, and instead, simply changed the wording around its usage again, this time narrowing it so that a Form 696 was necessary only for an event which 'predominantly features DJs or MCs performing to a recorded backing track', which 'runs anytime between the hours of 10 p.m. and 4 a.m.'. So, a grime night then.

It was a bureaucratic tool being wielded as a weapon: bluntly and without nuance. In the same month that parliament dismissed the Met's 'authoritarian' behaviour, Project Urban, a major event planned for the indigO2 on 3 May, was deemed a 'high risk' event by the authorities and cancelled with only weeks to go. The promoters had booked an all-star cast of performers, headlined by Wiley and Tinchy Stryder, and had already spent tens of thousands on a cross-media advertising campaign, when the Met pronounced the event 'high risk', due to some missing data on their 696 form: they had failed to supply the date of birth for two artists performing. There was still plenty of time for the promoters to re-submit the form with the full information, and to further assuage the Met's concerns, they offered to put on £4,500 worth of airport-style security. But the venue, part of the O2 complex, had already taken the decision upon themselves to cancel, and inform all ticket-holders. There's something similar to the Straight Outta Bethnal story: nothing untoward had happened, nothing untoward was about to happen, but some dumb bureaucracy and the police steaming in with a figurative siren blaring, combined with a music industry at best unsure about black music and at worst actively prejudiced against it, was enough to shut down a rave, with all the ruinous knock-on financial consequences. Why even bother trying?

Obfuscation remained the name of the game for venues and the police alike: especially when promoters tried to push into terra incognita and put on grime nights more ambitious than small, 300-capacity basement clubs in Shoreditch and Dalston. In February 2014, City of London Police leaned on the Barbican to cancel a major Just Jam event featuring Jme and Big Narstie (and Omar Souleyman, Mount Kimbie and various other alt-hipster favourites beyond the grime world). On the record, the Barbican didn't want to say why, muttering something vague about 'grounds of public safety following dialogue with the City of London police'; but there were rumours about 'intelligence about an incident', pressure regarding the Barbican's licence, and so on. The City of London police then issued a statement saying they were concerned about 'overcrowding' and under-18s possibly having access to the Barbican's bars: absurd on both counts, since the same could be said to apply to literally any one of the non-cancelled events – theatre, classical music, ballet – happening all year round at the venue. But then the regular Barbican crowd is about 40 years older and considerably whiter than the average grime crowd; what seems more likely is City police had projected backwards an entire decade, to the shoot-out outside the 2004 Urban Music Awards at the same venue, and decided that was reason enough to shut down Just Jam.

Giggs, the first and biggest star to cross over from London's 'road rap' scene – adjacent to grime, but slower, more trad, more nihilistic – faced years of Met blacklisting and blocked shows, to the point that police interference has become an ongoing part of his story. In 2010, his entire ten-date national tour was cancelled after intervention from the Met started a domino effect. In October 2013, during promo for his third album *When Will It Stop*, having already had the London date of his tour pulled by the Met due to 'intelligence about a major public order incident', Giggs had arranged a series of old-school CD signings to promote the album, at branches of HMV in shopping centres around the UK. Out of the blue, with a couple of days to go, they were cancelled too – as ever, without an explanation. From a series of about 20 phone calls at the time, I divined the process ran like this: the Met called HMV to pressure them to cancel, HMV declined (because having an iconic rapper turn up in your shop is pretty good for business), so the Met called the shopping centres, i.e. HMV's landlords, and put the frighteners on them. Westfield Stratford, by the Olympic site, The Bentall Centre in south-west London, and Reading all cancelled the events happening on their premises, without explanation. The shopping centre PR teams either refused to answer questions about why, or muttered something about cancellations being the result of a lack of proper paperwork (just an outright lie, but such is the world of PR).

What makes reporting on these police interventions so tough is the walls of silence erected by anyone who actually knows what's going on. The Met throw their hands up and profess to know nothing about cancellations, making it harder to raise objections, or ensure a modicum of accountability or journalistic scrutiny. Venues usually decline to comment, wary of upsetting the people with the power to nix their licence, and promoters and artists tend to keep schtum because they don't want a reputation for being trouble-makers. Eventually, an HMV Live Event Manager confirmed to me that Westfield and Bentall operations management teams had told them that Giggs would 'bring a bad crowd' – and that their shopping centre landlords had come to this decision quite suddenly, as if someone had put in a phone call. The shopping centres wouldn't say who. No one would. Giggs, sensing the possibility of flipping the bad publicity on its head, announced on social media he would turn up on the street outside The Bentall Centre to sign CDs anyway. Several hundred excitable teenage fans showed up, took selfies with their hero, got their CDs signed, and – miraculously – left with all their limbs intact.

Sometimes, it is the local authority that takes it upon itself to lead the way in shutting down black music: Croydon – home of Stormzy, Krept and Konan, Section Boyz and most of the creators of dubstep, among others – became notorious in 2016 after the local police force placed extraordinary pressure on the Dice Bar not to play Jamaican dancehall. Minutes of a meeting between council licensing officers, the police and Dice Bar referred to an agreement that they would not play 'bashman' (bashment) or 'John Paul' (Sean Paul) – the Dice Bar were, officers said, 'not adhering to the music policy'. Licensing officers had told owner Roy Seda that dancehall, i.e. 'what this borough finds unacceptable forms of music', should be off-limits because it 'attracts a certain type of person'. Really, the main thing that marked out the outrageous interference in Croydon was that the officers were foolish enough to leave a paper trail of their 'guidance'. Insidious, behind-the-scenes pressure normally stays behind the scenes. In 2010, Shoreditch's 650-capacity Cargo warned Scotland's musically wide-ranging Lucky Me collective not to play any grime – but we only know about that because they tweeted their disgruntlement. Generally, these conversations go unreported: promoters and DJs don't want to lose future bookings in a cut-throat business, so they grumble quietly and keep their heads down.

Too little is understood about the costs of Form 696 beyond a general sense of its unfairness. For one thing, cancellations or not, there is a huge data protection and privacy issue for black artists – the details are so hard to get hold of in the first place, that in practice, they're just circulated all over the place, between promoters, venues and bookers: home addresses, dates of birth, the lot. Another is what happens after the police have run checks, and made their (entirely unaccountable and unexplained) decision about the risk level of the event. On the occasions when the police aren't demanding a total cancellation, there is still a negative chain of consequences. If a promotion is deemed medium or high risk by the police, it can still go ahead, in theory at least: but there is the burden of hiring extra security personnel, ID scanners, knife arches or policing, all at great financial costs – and this news always arrives at a time when promoters have already budgeted, made advance payments, paid for publicity and so on. The result is that, whether they choose to cancel, or to go ahead, they lose out to the tune of hundreds, often thousands of pounds.

Another quirk is that if an overseas artist is on the bill, the police, being as they are British police, can't run a background check – so if a Form 696 is requested, the event is automatically graded medium as a minimum, with all the associated costs. This isn't, of course, a problem that touring overseas rock bands have – rock music, of course, has a proud history of abstinence, obsequious law-abidance and general zen-like behaviour – only rappers or R&B stars. (Likewise, numerous satanic-metal and white-power bands have managed to perform in London in the last decade without Met interference.) There's also just punitive levels of bureaucracy: if the form is not submitted on time, you're automatically graded higher – so if it was a low, it becomes a medium, if it was a medium, it becomes high. The final sting is the exemptions given to big live music corporations, the kind that own large gig venues, like Live Nation, the Academy Group and AEG – they have their own arrangements with the police, and don't have to do risk assessments. The result is the same artist can appear at a venue like Brixton Academy unhindered (and, shock horror, without an accompanying bloodbath), but sink a small club promotion company the moment they get 696-ed.

'Our financial officer has been doing some forward planning and sincerely thinks even though we've been doing this for a decade, we should be looking at getting into another business,' one small promoter of urban music nights told me in 2017 – all because of the extra costs burdened by Form 696. 'It feels unfair because if you go to a commercial club night on any high street on a Friday or Saturday night, the amount of violence you'll see from just drunken behaviour is almost guaranteed. We literally never have any trouble at our nights, but we're the ones whose business is suffering to the point we might have to close.'

With gentrification and soaring rents also rapidly closing down the number of small- and medium-sized venues in the capital – to the point that Boris Johnson, as Mayor, commissioned a report into London's declining nightlife – the possibilities for the next generation of grime MCs to perform live has been attacked from all sides, to the point that it has often been impossible.

'The problem ultimately is the people making the decisions are old and out-of-touch – using their memories of trouble from over a decade ago to tar everything with the same brush,' one major grime promoter told me. And he's right: when the Metropolitan Police Authority reviewed the form in 2009, they cited So Solid Crew in 2001, Turnmills in 2003, and others in 2004 and 2005. Of course, the Met's Clubs and Vice Unit maintain that the form has prevented further such incidents, by enabling police to work together with promoters and venue owners. (The grime promoters I've spoken to, who never hear from the Met, do not see it this way.)

In 2017 the story flared up again, following grime's mainstream resurgence and pressure to scrap Form 696 from the media and a young Conservative Culture Minister, Matt Hancock, keen to a make a name for himself. In the ensuing press coverage in autumn 2017, the Met maintained on all fronts that not a single event had been cancelled that year due to a Form 696. This was just a flat-out lie. To pick one instructive example, which shows how police 'intelligence' is used: Kojo Funds, a hotly tipped young east London MC and singer, making a mixture of trap, R&B and Afrobeats, was due to play a show at the Borderline on 26 March. The Borderline is not an endzish club, it's a small but famous venue in Soho often used for industry showcases of new 'buzz' artists. The Form 696 review came back from the police with only two days to go until the show, with the information that they had been 'keeping an eye on Kojo Funds', and that he was connected to gun crime and the Custom House gang (located just to the east of Canary Wharf in the heart of Newham Council's ongoing 'regeneration supernova'). But don't worry, because they had the kind of weighty supporting evidence you would expect to corroborate such an allegation: they sent the Borderline two paragraphs copied and pasted from music websites *Noisey* and *UK Rap.TV* about the beef between Kojo Funds and J Hus. The show was cancelled.

What is sometimes forgotten, amidst the frustration and anger about black music being targeted in recent decades, is the history of persecution of black culture that precedes it. Black Londoners had long been excluded from white nightlife spots, pubs and entertainment venues by what was known as 'the colour bar': essentially, landlords would just refuse to serve black customers. The result was that black social life in London was forced by necessity to find its own spaces, initially the illicit, off-the-radar 'shebeens' in areas like Notting Hill and Brixton, often soundtracked by live jazz. Even these private spaces were attacked by the authorities, usually local councils and the police working together, with support from local white residents. In 1961, the chief of Brixton police initiated a familiar-sounding campaign entitled Operation Shut Down, using surveillance, undercover policing and raids to close numerous black clubs and social spaces. It was not just the authorities, but British newspapers who tried to whip up moral panics around shebeens, claiming that they were dens of vice and iniquity, where drugs, gambling and violence were commonplace. Racism was integral to the picture, both institutionally, and in that the colour bar was sometimes enforced by local fascist groups like the Mosleyites in the 1950s and 60s. The 1965 Race Relations Act gave black Britons a legal avenue to challenge discrimination in pubs and clubs, but it didn't stop it happening – shebeens remained persecuted spaces by those outside them, and therefore liberatory spaces for those inside.[5] Fighting for the right to party might sound like a relatively glib thing to care about when so many life-and-death injustices remain unresolved, but they're all interlinked: the right to a social life is fundamental, to enjoy culture, free and unmolested, and it's no surprise that it has been so often pushed out of reach of young black Britons.

Grime is often described as a kind of outsider art – uncompromising, difficult, non-conformist. There are many reasons why that's the case, but chief among them is the marginal status forced on grime's creators. The genre's treatment by the Met left them unable to perform in their home city, indeed in the genre's home city, and left a generation of young musicians out in the cold, lacking in confidence, and barely able to make any money at all from their music – to the point that making it became entirely unsustainable. Panicked police overreaction to youth culture movements goes back to Teddy Boys in the 1950s and beyond – it has as long a history as the racist intervention in black social spaces such as shebeens. But few youth sub-cultures can ever have been so consistently hammered by the authorities as grime: almost to the point that it killed the scene altogether – it certainly changed the sound, as Bizzle says. It was *supposed* to be dance music – but how could it be, if no one ever got the chance to dance to it? In their blanket overreactions to violent incidents in a UK garage scene that the grime kids had already been excluded from, the Metropolitan Police not only shut down the main platform for reaching new fans, and the main way of making a legal living from music, but effectively silenced the voices of the exact same young people they were harassing on the street every day.

NINE

DIY AND
REDEMPTION SONGS

In May 2007, Logan Sama wrote an article for *RWD* magazine to address the received wisdom that grime's moment had passed. Most of the handful of MCs and crews that had been signed had been dropped by their labels. The three that remained had taken to collaborating with Arctic Monkeys and Lily Allen (Dizzee Rascal), Babyshambles and Kate Nash (Lethal Bizzle) and Craig David and Damon Albarn (Kano), making altogether more insipid music that 'sounds like grime but a little slower', as Kano put it on 'London Town'. A lot of underground MCs gave up the hobby and got real jobs, and some of those who remained switched their flow down a gear, to spit over more familiar American-style rap beats. Sama's piece was typically forthright in its argument:

'Grime is dead. Didn't you know? I have heard it said in a couple of interviews by non-grime artists. I've read it on a couple blogs. Heard it from DJs that used to play Grime … Yeah man, I agree. It is dead. If you don't love it, don't try and make it. Don't try and get into it. There's no money for you here. Piss off. We'll keep it our secret until such time that we are ready to bring it to the wider world on our own terms. When it will get played on daytime radio as it is, without having to sample eighties pop records or bring in someone else to give it credibility to middle-

Skepta in his 'King of Grime' and wearer-of-hats phase, 2007

of-the-road, out-of-touch playlist execs. In fact, I might even put that on a T-shirt. Grime is dead. Fuck off and leave it alone. There's nothing here for you to exploit. Bye.'

I first interviewed Skepta that same spring for a modest 'zine called *Woofah*, standing outside a rare London grime night in Shoreditch at two in the morning. In the preceding years, Skepta and his brother Jme had been touted as two of the most likely MCs to cross over from the underground. ('Jme and Skepta have both completed albums, so A&Rs feel free to dust off the cheque books,' Sama wrote in 2005.) Skepta and Jme were charismatic and witty, with clear-voiced flows and strong reload bars. But it never happened – and they both seemed focused on pursuing their own agendas anyway. While finishing his degree, Jme had slowly, without much fanfare, turned his first independently released mixtape, *Boy Better Know*, into a label of the same name, releasing mixtapes for other MCs, as well as a range of BBK T-shirts, and taking care of every last detail himself: the design, printing, distribution and marketing. He kept the CDs and T-shirts in boxes in his parents' garage, and sold them in the same way everyone had sold their vinyl a few years before: driving them around to record shops in the boot of a car, or queuing up in the local post office and posting them out to fans.

That night in Shoreditch, Skepta talked about 'Stageshow Riddim', his new dancehall-inspired release, complete with air horns, crowd noises and rewinds built into the instrumental, and, in dancehall style, 11 different vocal versions buzzing with frantic levels of adrenaline. It was an especially tragic irony that this riotous homage to grime's live energy had arrived when the real thing had been all but eradicated. We discussed the state of the scene: all told, it didn't look good. By this point, even the underground was struggling; the previously thriving DVD publishing scene was being undermined by a new website called YouTube, and vinyl production had dwindled to almost nothing, so record shops were closing. DJs were using CD decks, and illegal downloading was now so easy and routine that fans were rarely paying for the artists' mixtapes. The more cutting-edge pirate stations had mostly switched to focus on dubstep and the UK garage-like club hedonism of funky house; and several grime DJs had followed, since they could actually get bookings that way, without their event being 696-ed. The result was far fewer grime shows on the radio, and fewer crews operating in general. Even if you did want to follow Logan Sama's 'true believer' path and keep making grime, there was no way to make even a subsistence living from it. Journalists blithely pronounced grime dead. It had been fun while it lasted.

Skepta was fully aware of the new realities – no one's getting record deals worth £150,000 anymore like Wiley and Dizzee had done, he said – instead 'it's a hard-working thing', and BBK would 'treat it like a business'. He gestured to 93 Feet East's clientele of new ravers, indie kids, grime stans, industry types, and assorted Friday night drinkers – overall, a much whiter and more hipster crowd than a typical Sidewinder or Eskimo Dance. Even then, he seemed to have a sense of the plain-speaking, mass-appeal ethic that would, against all the odds, eventually lead him to superstardom, even if no one else saw it coming. 'I try and be clear with everything I say, that's my style. Obviously, we live in a very multicultural country, and I try and speak to everyone if possible, which is the reason we play to crowds like this. A lot of the other grime MCs play to normal thugged-out crowds, but we play to a lot of different kinds of people. It's all about communicating, man! I see all these people around me, if I want to walk up to them and say something to them I can say it, so why shouldn't I be able to do that in music?'

It really felt like the industry's brief window of interest had permanently closed. Skepta had been tantalised with the possibility of releasing his debut album on Mike Skinner's Warner Brothers/679 subsidiary label The Beats – but Skinner had signed rap duo the Mitchell Brothers 'instead'. It was cool though, Skepta said, because Skinner and he were going to re-record and re-release his underground hit 'Single' as a collaboration, so he'd still get some mainstream shine out of the relationship. (This didn't happen either.) Given the way the prevailing winds were blowing, and the fact he was being interviewed at 2 a.m. in a beer garden, by a novice journalist, for a 'zine, and not sitting in swanky major-label offices being tended to by a management team and a PR agency and doing a cover story for a glossy monthly, he was bizarrely confident. Is there still a place in the mainstream for MCs like you and Jme? I asked. 'I believe that we don't have to change grime to make anyone buy it,' he insisted. 'People are running away from grime thinking it's not working, but they're sell-outs, man. That's why Boy Better Know is easily going to be the best thing in grime.' At the time, I thought it was empty bravado.

Elsewhere, things weren't looking good. Having signed a deal with Ministry of Sound off the back of the success of their raucous single 'Hype Hype' (which transcended the underground to reach number 21 in the charts), and with a view to an album deal, north-west London crew SLK were dropped as well. 'We were young kids off the road, got a break, and didn't know how to deal with it,' Mighty from SLK said later. 'We'd be going to do PAs and getting into fights with other crews – all the time – and the record label would be hearing about this, and there's only so much they can take.'[1]

Relentless had stuck by So Solid Crew through their many transgressions, lyrical, trivial or serious, but not all labels were prepared to do the same. Jme covered some of these growing pains on his first major underground hit, 'Serious': 'Just cause we come from the gutter, and we know about scraping the bottom of the butter/Don't mean we have to be sinners: major labels don't want killers.'[2] It was clear already by 2006 that grime was not going to become a widespread commercial success, an equivalent to US rap in cultural dominance or record sales. Indie rock was still all over the charts and the radio stations, and ready-proven, market-tested, A&R-ed American urban imports required little to no effort to turn them into successes in the UK as well. The gold rush had barely started before it lost its shine.

'The working relationship between urban music acts and the major labels has become very dysfunctional over the last two years,' Chantelle Fiddy told me in 2006, as we tried to pick over what had gone wrong. There was, she said, blame on both sides. 'A lot of grime MCs don't understand the work ethic, or aren't willing to agree to the kind of relationship you need with a manager – someone you need to consistently take orders from for about two years – or a major, to break into the mainstream music industry. Those urban acts that have succeeded (Ms Dynamite, Kano, Lady Sovereign, Dizzee Rascal and to a lesser extent Lethal B and Shystie) have signed up with big managers and got to work. But equally, the majors have neither any idea how to, nor the will to try and consistently make urban acts big in the UK. And sure, grime's aggression is a hindrance, but don't tell me that 60,000 metal fans at Donington Monsters of Rock don't like aggressive music?'

The received wisdom emerging was that the chart success of 'Pow!' had been a one-off, and a fluke; that the ferocity of grime at its purest was too much (and quite specifically, too fast) for radio play; and that listeners weren't ready for grime's sheer newness, its alien sensibilities and esoteric language. Race was an issue too, thought Chantelle Fiddy. 'Acts like Mike Skinner, Plan B and Lady Sov (none of whom proved themselves within grassroots urban music) clearly have an advantage, or are perceived by the music industry to have an advantage, because they're white. And sure Mike Skinner sold more copies of his album than Wiley did, because Skinner's subject matter appealed to a white mass market: but the US majors have no problems selling black rap stars' subject matter to a white mass market, either in the US or over here. So something must be lacking in the UK majors' marketing departments.' Wiley even turned a lack of saleability into a diss, in a line on his 'Nightbus Dubplate' war track for The Movement – also from 2006: 'We all know that *you* are harder to market than *me*,'[3] he scoffed. Pete Todd from independent grime label No Hats No Hoods speculated at the time that first-wave grime was just too alien, too avant garde, to be understood by a music business far removed from its origins. 'When grime first came out there were no journalists who understood it, apart from a select few, and no radio people understood it. No one got it: "Is it hip-hop? Is it dance? What do we call it?" For me that's what makes grime so exciting – but it makes it really hard in terms of marketing.'

For the select few who had hung onto their record deals, like Kano, there was almost a hint of agoraphobia – here he was, standing alone, on the open plains of the mainstream. Nasty Crew had disintegrated into squabbles behind him after he left: and to a large extent, so had the collective spirit of the underground as a whole; the raves and the pirates, and several of the other most promising crews had disappeared. The whole thing had been thrilling, but also a kind of permanent headache, where the underground MC got little for their efforts except the respect of their peers. The future was uncertain and disconcerting. On his debut album, Kano had written a delicately poignant and introspective track, 'Sometimes', about being 'the next one to blow', signing a deal and 'moving on', and the chasm he was about to try and leap across: 'Sometimes you'll see me in a daydream, thinking "Can the underground go mainstream?"'[4] He was still only a teenager when he wrote it, in 2005, and it would be another decade before he got the answer he wanted.

In June 2007 I met Kano in the basement of the BBC studios near Oxford Circus before a 1Xtra performance; he was in a dressing room, curled up on a sofa asleep, while two of his friends played computer games. As he came around, he talked about the obstacles he was coming up against: 'We're already in a box being from the UK, and being a black artist from the UK puts you in another box, and to be characterised as a black "grime" artist from the UK puts you inside another box'. On his recent mixtape – he was making mixtapes for the manor, and albums for the mainstream, living a double life – he'd rapped on 'Layer Cake', in a resigned tone of voice, 'I'm in an industry man, in Eng-er-land, where I'll never sell more than an indie band.'

There were existential questions for those that had a sniff of crossover success – Kano referred to himself as 'Kano the artist' in the third person, as if it was someone else: the guy who wrote songs in a plush studio and took naps backstage at the BBC, rather than spat bars in a grubby pirate radio box-room. 'You do have to be two people,' he said. 'I think it's important to keep one foot in each camp though.' He wasn't the only one who prized the rarefied identity of 'artist'. It's a common trope to hear from a rising MC: I can do more than this, I'm versatile, good music is good music, genres are irrelevant ... I'm not just a mic-man. Lethal Bizzle had even put this distinction into a diss track for Wiley, the hilarious 'Kylie Riddim', where he vocalled the backing track for Kylie Minogue's 'Can't Get You Out of My Head' ('Let me merk him on his *own* riddim', he began – Wiley's middle name is Kylea), and chided him with the punchline: 'I'm an artist, you're just a rave MC.' Deadening.

For some MCs, becoming an artist meant maturity and versatility; for others, it meant watering down your sound for people who didn't respect you to begin with. After being cleared of the murder Crazy Titch had been sent down for, Durrty Goodz returned in 2007 with a blistering ten-track mixtape, *Axiom*, which addressed, among other things: his incarcerated half-brother, Roll Deep working with Trident, being dropped by Polydor, and the music industry's contempt for black music. 'They've got Lemar singing like Frank Sinatra, so we forget about Afrika Bambaataa,' he spat on 'License To Skill'; the chorus promised he was 'on a mission like James Bond, to expose what the majors have been on'.[5] While his new music was inspired, in person he was as jaded as you'd expect someone to be after having their album dropped and spending a year in Belmarsh on remand. 'The major record companies are supposed to help guys like me be heard,' he told me. 'But they're lazy. Their hearts are not in the music. If the corporates want to talk, our ears are open, and they can come and talk business. But we're not going to be pressured this time. This is not Polydor here, we don't just talk and get nothing done for ten or 11 months.' As burdened as he was by what had passed, he was determined to make independence work; to embrace artistic freedom and actual freedom in the same motion. 'The reason the grime scene has had to cut out from the majors [is] because we're not about waiting around for ages just to do something simple like put out a CD. Major labels are like big ships, they take too long to turn around.'

Mixtape culture spread like bindweed in 2006 and 2007, which saw grime's distributional problem become unexpectedly inverted: from there being a dearth of finished grime vocal tunes available to buy a few years earlier, there were suddenly too many. Every part-time MC in the country suddenly seemed to be putting out 20-track CDs, with artwork which looked like it had been designed on Microsoft Paint, containing an average of three or four absolute bangers, a few guest tracks by their mates, a few vocals of random non-grime beats (usually major US rap beats), and then ten or so 'freestyles' (less thematically focused, less thoughtfully structured, less song-y) over whatever grime instrumentals were doing the rounds at that moment.

Skepta was determined that his debut, which he had given the inspired (if not exactly subtle) title *Greatest Hits*, was *an album, not a mixtape*: he kept saying those exact words on every pirate set he appeared on – as if there was a kind of poverty of ambition to talking down your work like that, under-selling it, making it sound cheap and unfinished. Not everyone felt that way. For an oddball auteur MC like Trim – aka Taliban Trim, Trimothy, Trimble, Trim Van Helsing, Shankvan, Badboy Trim, Osama Trim Laden, Trimski, Trim Trim Charoo – mixtapes offered exactly the room to breathe he had been lacking when he had been in Roll Deep. 'You see Flow Dan and dem? I'm on a different programme to them,' he spat, departing from his crew in 2007. Always one of the most creative and difficult-to-read, with a beguiling, lackadaisical flow, Trim used mixtapes to experiment. 'I treat them as training,' he said in 2008.[6] 'I'm not trying to make the best record in the world. What I'm doing is pushing myself, being different and seeing where that takes me.' It took him to all sorts of new places: not least to extensive collaborations with electronic producers from outside the grime scene like James Blake, and 15 mixtapes in the last decade.

The self-released mixtape offered a lot of MCs who'd come through the pirate radio scene the opportunity to put out a finished product stamped with their own name for the first time. It allowed them to explore independence from their crews, from the scene's collectivity, and (by force of necessity) from the industry. It offered a DIY simulacrum of an artistic legacy, something finite and unbreakable, a departure from the spectral and transient role of the rave-and-radio MC in the jungle and garage eras. Riko Dan, another MC with a strong personality and unique flow, had been through the label experience with Roll Deep, and, like several others, was clear to frame grime's DIY turn as a positive decision by people who wanted control of their own destiny. 'The big labels don't understand that people want to hear you for what you really are,' he told the *Guardian*. 'The scene is realising now that if you want to do something, you have to do it yourself. The fans don't want you to be watered down, and selling out isn't going to make you happy, either.'[7]

There's a hint of sadness underpinning some of the best tracks from this period: an implicit poignancy because they were always going to be overlooked, sell little, and miss out on the mass market they might have received if they'd been released a decade later. Pathos also sprouts up in the chinks emerging in the MCs' youthful armour: they've seen a few of their peers cross into the mainstream, leaving them behind – and if you were really the best MC, as you claim, why would that happen? Nasty Jack's 2007 underground single 'Oh Yes' is a terrific upbeat grime tune, perfect Channel U fodder with a pop hook from Motown classic 'Please Mr Postman' (the idea shamelessly nicked by producer Blackjack from US rap star Juelz Santana's tune of the same name), but some of the MC's chest beating is dripping with unintentional pathos: 'Now they wanna know: "Didn't he used to hang with Kano?" and now they're like, "Jack, you're the star of the show."'[8] But he's not – the song is great, and it deserves to be a hit, but the video is filmed in a dowdy yellow underpass at night, and no one from the industry is even pretending to watch anymore. Another telling line, 'I be getting money like if I was signed', inadvertently sums up the spirit of the period. (Not to spoil the illusion and pull back the curtain on the great and powerful Oz, but they definitely weren't.)

Hubris is poignant when your words suddenly ring hollow. In the early days, East Connection's Jookie Mundo's catchphrase was that he was 'ready to blow', and of course it set him up for a fall – by 2005, Skepta was puncturing these words in a diss track: 'Jookie Mundo don't earn no wages, Jookie Mundo's been "ready to blow" for *ages*'. There's only so long you can keep saying 'I'm about to blow' before you stop believing it – and occasionally MCs took off the mask and gave voice to their anxieties. Trim's 2008 mixtape track 'Inside Looking Out' is barely known beyond the cult MC's small but vocal cohort of cheerleaders, but it's up there with the most beautiful and introspective moments in grime's history – using a startling instrumental by Geeneus's younger brother Jerzey, a tragic synthesised violin, alternately picked and bowed, that builds and builds until the dam bursts and the sonic tears all flood out. Spitting his bars at confessional, conversation-level volume, Trim acknowledges the wearying challenges that would drag numerous MCs away from their creative aspirations, and issued an ultimatum to the world at large: 'I'm willing to stand on my own and face the scene, run my mouth until the cows come home, and make tea. But if *Monkey Features* ain't me, by volume six, I'm out: I've got yutes to feed. And if one day you see Trim, let me know how the scene's getting on.'[9] It was an ultimatum that sounded like a farewell; Trim's subsequent mixtape *Monkey Features*, his fifth in the space of two years, did not lead to world domination any more than the previous four had, but fortunately he reneged and kept making music anyway.

The scene *was* getting on, and trying to build more of its own infra-structure, with almost no interest from gatekeepers in the established music industry. In 2008 young fans got together to create the non-profit organisation Grime Digital, comprising a GrimeForum, Grimepedia, podcasts and an online store. Logan Sama's show on KISS FM was getting big listening figures, but it was the only mainstream broadcast outlet for grime – there still wasn't a dedicated show on 1Xtra. As he wrote in his *RWD* editorial, he thought the only way to succeed was playing the long game. 'I think we should be realistic,' he told me in 2006: 'just try and get albums out, on a budget, to make a profit – and then move on to the next album, building and building. You can't expect a scene that's got hardly any infrastructure to be massive overnight. But I think naturally it will evolve – look at the Boy Better Know [mixtape] series: Jme started off doing just one CD because he had a bunch of tracks lying around, and now it's like a big thing where he's sold 3,000 units on the first day of release; it was in HMV straight away, they're putting big orders in for it.'

As a label and a business model, Boy Better Know was integral to grime's evolution as a self-sufficient scene beyond its years in the doldrums. Jme's design skills helped make the merchandise an immedi-ate success: other crews and labels were quickly on the phone calling up

Jme, asking where he got his T-shirts printed: so he'd take Chipmunk, or Tinchy Stryder down to the T-shirt printing place. 'It's just like back in the day when you'd see your bredrins' music videos on Channel U and didn't know how to even start – we all help each other out,' said his BBK crew mate Shorty recently. Before long there were knock-off BBK T-shirts and hats being sold on market stalls in grime's inner-city heart-lands – pirating the pirates.

A decade later, as the crew filmed a music video to mark a major collaboration with Nike – the crew had designed a Nike x BBK football shirt – Jme explained that nothing had fundamentally changed in their DIY approach: there was no warehouse, no deployment centre, no employees, and no office. 'All my merch, all BBK merch, all Skeppy's merch used to just go in my garage at my mum's house, like the rooms was just fucking IKEA boxes, and it's the same now. When we take orders, we put them in bags, print out the labels on a little printer from Staples, stick them on, take them to the Post Office and drop them off. Even today, the record label's not like a company, where you have every-one in the offices, with a secretary sitting at a desk – it's just a group of friends, and a PC. The company is just a PC, and a web page. For Tinchy Stryder, back in the day, he came to my house, I had two mixtapes out, he said, "Ah, could you do the artwork for me?" Ruff Sqwad, BBK: what-ever, it's all just a family – so I gave him all the designs, he can press whatever he wants to press, sell it however he wants to sell it, with the label name, without it – that's how it is with everybody.'

Other bold DIY projects sprouted up in the aftermath of grime's first golden age. Ghetts' 'Fuck Radio' project was created as a well, fuck you, to a slowly dying pirate scene that had become a victim of its own success: too many MCs were turning up at studios unbooked, and too much attention was being drawn to the secret locations (especially when there was trouble between MCs, as happened occasionally). So the management at key stations like Rinse and Deja limited the number of grime shows, and the number of people allowed on each set: at Rinse there was a 'no guests' rule, meaning MCs couldn't bring through their youngers and give the next generation experience and exposure, which had always been vital. Shut out even from the world that had given birth to grime, 'we had to take it back to bedroom sets', Ghetts explained on the subsequent *Fuck Radio* DVD – their podcasted live sets gave a platform to a mostly younger generation who would grow in prominence considerably in the late 2000s, MCs like Scorcher, Wretch 32, Ghetts, Devlin, Dot Rotten, P Money, Little Dee, Griminal and Little Nasty.

The Fuck Radio sets had the same wild energy and collective power as the best early pirate shows – MCs joining in to help finish each other's punchlines, cacophonies of hype and cathartic rewinds – but with the benefit of having prepared more conscientiously for the occasion: they would bring their books along and spit new bars from the page, rather than memory. It's no coincidence that the first four MCs in that list, who released a rap-leaning mixtape collectively as The Movement in 2006, became known for a more 'technical' lyricism, something closer to the kind of dense wordplay of some American rap, with more internal puns and allusions. They also tended to use Dipset-style rap beats: at a slower pace and usually built around big vocal or orchestral samples.

This led to a small-scale culture war within grime in the late 2000s, as some MCs continued to 'turn UK hip-hop, scared their debut album will flop', as Jme spat on 'Serious'. Wiley was more scathing on the 'Nightbus Dubplate', accusing The Movement of ripping off their style from American rap icons, via the *Smack* DVD series and the D-Block label: 'Please don't watch *Smack* DVD cos it clouds your judgement. You can't hear me, you're still watching *Smack* DVD. About "the Movement's like D-Block", why are you like D-Block? You're from England, you batty! Who are these pricks meant to be, really though? D-Block? What is all this Biggie and Pac business?'[10]

Butterz label owner, DJ and scene stalwart Elijah wrote a blog post on the same theme in 2008, despairing about the burgeoning obsession with the American rap notion of 'swagger' or being 'fly', 'the new default topic for an MC to talk about'. He speculated that MCs had realised violent lyrics would prevent them getting daytime 1Xtra play, and so were reaching across the Atlantic. It was cringeworthy, especially when grime had so decisively established its own voice, independent of US rap. Like many fans, Elijah wasn't impressed: the adopting of American slang 'dilutes the authenticity' of the MCs' bars, he wrote. 'When I hear terms like "getting my guap" and "trapping" or "dawg" it just screams Dipset imitation to me.'[11]

As the second half of the 2000s wore on, other parts of the grime scene were splintering in the direction of funky house, or UK funky, something that has to be understood in the context of the Form 696 shutdowns. Funky house had been around in some form for years, but was thriving from 2006 in particular among people from the UK garage-grime continuum, because it offered something of the rave spirit that had been missing in grime's aggy years: firstly, actual raves that went ahead, and weren't shut down by the police, and secondly, something closer to gender balance in the dance. 'It's great,' said SLK's Van Damage: 'how garage used to be before all the violence.'

Titans of the early grime scene like Jon E Cash, seminal producer of 'sublow' with Black Ops, had got into hosting funky house raves. Essentials' DJ Bossman, a Rinse FM mainstay, changed his name to Perempay, and continued on the same station, playing UK funky and making some house bangers himself; Davinche released UK funky tunes as Dee; Maxwell D relaunched his career as a funky MC with Blackberry Hype; former UK garage and grime producer-vocalist Donae'o released a whole album of percussive, African house-influenced funky. Jme's largely instrumental *Tropical* albums, meanwhile, remain some of Boy Better Know's best releases – a series of instrumental grime motifs spread out on a beach in Napa, given a sugary cocktail, and then taken to a house rave for the evening. Bassline was thriving in the midlands and the north, dubstep and UK funky were thriving all over the place, and the internet was joining all the dots between them: grime's fellow travellers and sibling genres were occupying the very clubs and pirate stations that grime had effectively been banned from entering.

As 2007 ticked over into 2008, another handbrake turn from 140bpm hardcore grime made pop stars out of a generation of MCs who had all but given up on the idea. At the forefront was Ruff Sqwad's diminutive

Tinchy Stryder, the sweet kid, the girls' favourite, who had brought the house down at Sidewinder and Eskimo Dance aged just 15, squeaking out 'let me see the gunfingers' to several rewinds. He was the only MC to get signed during grime's doldrums: by two white Norfolk teenagers, Jack Foster and Archie Lamb, who had dropped out of sixth-form college to start a record label, Takeover Entertainment, with a £10,000 loan from Archie's dad, Liberal Democrat MP Norman Lamb. They released Tinchy's first proper studio album, *Star in the Hood*, an underrated grime record with pop sensibilities, and a strong pointer of what was to come. The video for the single 'Mainstream Money' cut between the origin and the destination of the journey he was embarking on – posing with Ruff Sqwad in front of the three flats, and laying down vocals in a high-end recording studio. 'This ain't the days of run up on the ends,' he spat, 'nah that's dem man, that's the old E3.' It was time to leave childish things, and the manor, behind.

They kept trying to refine a workable pop-grime formula, but in the end it was a completely unexpected single by the godfather of grime which changed everything. When Wiley released 'Wearing My Rolex' in May 2008 – a bubbly, summery electro-pop song made by grime producer Bless Beats – it accidentally created a new paradigm that would overwhelm the pop charts. Within two years there were 12 number-one singles in this vein from grime MCs. After years of being ignored, patronised or misunderstood, black British youth culture, grime culture – watered down and souped up, with a cocktail umbrella and a plasticky Ibizan backdrop – was suddenly the most popular show in town.

It helped that the industry infrastructure has been infiltrated somewhat, with former pirate-radio grime DJs like Target on legal radio stations, former MC Faction G working at Atlantic, and former Deja Vu DJ Benny Scarrs at Island. It was Scarrs who signed Tinchy Stryder to Island Records, when still just a junior in the A&R department. His boss asked him who Island could sign that would give them a hit like 'Wearing My Rolex', and in response Scarrs quoted Wiley – 'the best A&R this scene's ever had' – specifically his 2003 pirate-era lyric: 'if you know about Rascal watch out for Stryder.' Shortly after that conversation, in a moment of serendipity, Scarrs answered his boss's phone to find one of Tinchy Stryder's management duo on the line, nervously asking for a meeting. 'They came in suited and booted, these 18-year-old white boys from Norwich, with Tinchy who I knew from my Deja days. My boss gave me some advice, like *Star in the Hood* is good for 1Xtra, but it's not going to cross over.' So they summoned producer Fraser T Smith, who had worked with Kano, and would later work with Stormzy, and came back with an electro-rap tune called 'Stryderman'. 'Every day I was going to my boss, "Stryderman, Stryderman – sign this tune, sign this tune!" I wanted to get an act under my belt, and I wanted to push something I believe in and understand, and just not be doing photocopies anymore.'

'Stryderman', Tinchy told me, 'felt like the last throw of the dice in the mainstream' – and the studio time to make it had been funded directly out of selling *Star in the Hood* T-shirts (a clothing line that would soon occupy window displays in JD Sports around the country, selling hundreds of thousands of units). Scarrs' bosses obliged and signed Tinchy to a singles deal; 'Stryderman' came out in July 2008 and went straight on the Radio 1 playlist, when Dizzee's own unapologetic, Calvin Harris-augmented electro-pop single 'Dance Wiv Me' was number one and 'Wearing My Rolex' was still in the Top 40.

By the time I met Scarrs towards the end of 2009, Stryder's first album with Island had gone gold and he'd had two number-one singles and another at number three, in the space of a year. Scarrs had been catapulted up the hierarchy and was Head of A&R. 'It's been a phenomenal year,' he told me. 'It's been like the spread of an epidemic.' Scarrs described an industry looking to the London underground for the first time since UK garage. 'There is a feeling of a gold rush now – in both directions. Labels are looking for the next Dizzee, Stryder and Chipmunk, and a lot of MCs that were disheartened with the scene have resurfaced and are looking to cross over.' Chipmunk had scored four Top 10 singles in 2009 (and one number one), and Dizzee another two number ones, 'Bonkers' and 'Holiday', to go with 'Dance Wiv Me' – the titles alone tell the story of how he got there. That year, Tinie Tempah had his first number one with 'Pass Out', and the following year five more number ones followed for Tinie, Dizzee and Roll Deep.

They had finally made stars out of grime MCs; but with music that barely resembled grime. Dizzee's version of 'why the music changed' is pretty persuasive; he says it was primarily defined by his new audience and lifestyle – he was supporting Justin Timberlake on tour, 'shouting a load of bars' at 50,000 people who wanted a singalong, and it just didn't feel right. The winning formula was simple: towering Ibiza electro-house synths, slower rapping and simple lyrics about cars and girls and holidays, and schmaltzy, sung (and often autotuned) choruses. Benny Scarrs thought it had been an accident. 'I don't think it was actually planned. I don't think anyone sat down and said, "You know what, we're going to make 120–130bpm four-to-the-floor tracks with house influences." Obviously grime runs at 140, but 140 might be a bit much for daytime radio, so people slowed it down, but kept the grime flavour, and tried to bring in more melodic moments.'

Following the first wave, many established underground MCs had their own electro-house pop-crossover efforts signed for a label release – Scorcher, Devlin, Griminal, Dot Rotten, Skepta, Mz Bratt – and *X Factor* singer Cher Lloyd even brought Dot Rotten and Ghetts onto her album as guest MCs. The jump to pop made more sense for some than others. Tinchy was always going to work as a teen girls' pop favourite – short and sweet, pop-rapping alongside a former Sugababes singer – while former Channel U urban all-rounder crew N-Dubz were a good fit for a pop transition too: because it simply wasn't as great a distance to travel, musically. But MCs like Griminal, Ghetts and Dot Rotten had been responsible for some of the most bleak, hardcore grime ever made. Dot Rotten's *This Is the Beginning* mixtape remains one of the greatest ever, but he sounds sincerely on the verge of a breakdown ('I've been feeding myself since I was 14 years old,'[12] he cries on 'Broke For So Long'). At last there was a commercial vehicle for grime MCs that could rival American hip-hop imports – in part, Tinchy told me, because the transatlantic zeitgeist was leaning in their direction: 'In the past people have felt like they've had to imitate America to get in the charts, and if the Americans are making the most successful and popular sound in the world, and everyone's relating to it, then fair enough. But now it feels like a lot of American acts are making this sort of sound, like Lady Gaga: the songs that are topping their charts at the moment is more of a European sound.' It's an argument that Skepta put to me too, in 2015: that there was a rational explanation and a British connection to the Balearics that made the formula work. 'When I made tunes like "Amnesia", and I was going to Ibiza and smashing it, to me that's like an English thing – that's something I would do if I wasn't a rapper.'

The divide between grime's mainstream and what was left of grime's underground was widening. Chipmunk infuriated grime fans and musicians in 2009 when he called the scene 'wack' and 'ambitionless', by way of 'explanation for my elevation'. Underground MC Big H, former ally of Skepta and Jme from their original crew Meridian, became a favourite among the hardcore refuseniks for a while, by staunchly rejecting the idea of crossing over and 'prostituting' himself: 'MCs these days are despicable,' he said. 'I see people like Stryder going to number one, and he's got some good bars – but the bars he went to number one with are not his number-one bars.'

But in general there was little bitterness towards those shimmying off to the Mediterranean: 'they deserve to get paid at last' about summed up the response of most fans, many of whom in any case had long since moved on to listening to UK funky or road-rap MCs such as Giggs. Who could begrudge the MCs a chart hit and a decent pay cheque – even if they were not being paid for their number-one bars? Purists getting mad at their favourite 'greazy' MC making songs about girls and sunshine and parties were just haters: it was 'like being angry with David Beckham for leaving the youth team', said Dizzee. It shouldn't have been a surprise, either: injunctions to get out of the ends are stretched across the early lyrics of those who finally did. 'If you know you from the slums, keep reppin' no doubt/Stay ghetto if you must, just remember to get out'[13] spat Dizzee on 'Get By', from 2004; Roll Deep's 'Let It Out', from their first album, carried the same message: 'I've seen the road to success, I'm getting out of here/If we're patient, we can all get out of here.'[14] Dot Rotten laid the issue (and his soul) bare on the desperate, self-explanatory track 'Get Out Of The Hood'. The 2008–12 cavalry charge for the charts did not come out of nowhere, it was just the first time the attempt had worked. Jamie Collinson, label manager at independent hip-hop label Big Dada (who have released albums by Wiley and Jammer, along with their regular UK hip-hop fare), told me that Wiley had been sending him reworkings of 'Overload' by the Sugababes and Roisin Murphy's 'Dear Miami' years before recording 'Wearing My Rolex'.

With the pendulum finally swinging away from indie rock, 'urban' music was suddenly in the ascendancy – the former grime kids were joined by British rappers and R&B singers like Example, Labrinth, Taio Cruz, Mz Bratt, Ironik, Professor Green, Plan B and N-Dubz. In 2010 I sat in on the normally arcane and secretive BBC Radio 1 playlist meeting, to see how technology and changing tastes were transforming the way they went about making hits: in order to keep up, they were doing a lot less leading, and a lot more following. A comprehensive market-research system was in place, with weekly polling of four hundred 12–30-year-olds about the station's playlist choices, as well as turning keen eyes towards internet and social-media buzz. Pluggers – the people employed by major labels to push their new releases on radio producers – had seen their power wane considerably. 'There are just so many other sources of information out there these days,' Radio 1 head of music, George Ergatoudis, told me, casually mentioning that he'd just been chatting to his opposite number in the pirate world, Geeneus, about the new Katy B single that Rinse were releasing.

BBC 1Xtra had always been institutionally tied to Radio 1 in a way that, say, BBC Asian Network was not: the station was in the same chain of command, and located in the same building. Before the Radio 1 playlist meeting began, the music manager at 1Xtra, Austin Daboh, gave a Powerpoint presentation to the selection of kingmakers – mostly twenty-something producers from various different Radio 1 shows. He explained that it was 'the year of urban'; there was no disagreement with this analysis. Guitar music was deep in the doldrums, and none of them were in a rush for it to come back. 'Wearing My Rolex' had been the 'seminal record that opened the floodgates', Daboh told me that day. 'Before, on the Radio 1 playlist it used to be almost a one-in-one-out policy in terms of urban records ... maybe one would go on, and if it charted well, great, we could get another one on. But now, you can see the playlist, there are six, seven, eight urban records on the playlist, and there are a good four or five others the committee are considering.

'Urban music is here to stay in the charts,' Daboh concluded: a rubicon had been crossed. He reasoned that earlier infiltrations, such as the UK garage period, had proved to be short-lived because they were limited to one specific genre. But by 2010, different types of British R&B, hip-hop, grime and dubstep artists were simultaneously making their way into the charts, and the need to rely on American imports had diminished – this time, it would be sustainable. Slow-moving cultural changes were finally having an effect, too, he said. 'There are finally more senior people in British society who are black, or Asian or mixed race, or are from a council estate background, and it's not a token gesture anymore. And young British people from different backgrounds are into council estate culture: whether you're from middle England, or from Luton, or from a gritty part of Manchester or Liverpool: street culture, Foot Locker culture, is a part of what you are now.'

The music industry had fallen in love with urban, and the effects were being reflected elsewhere, galvanised by the success of films like *Kidulthood* and *Adulthood*, and TV series like *Dubplate Drama* and *Top Boy* – all of which featured grime MCs either in starring roles, or on the soundtrack. The wider millennial black British youth culture and its argot (Multicultural London English, or MLE, as linguists designate it) was leaking out of the estates and into popular culture at large. Grime slang infiltrated the mainstream vernacular, and even the *Daily Telegraph*, the newspaper of sleepy retired army generals everywhere, published a glossary explaining what words like 'nang' and 'peng' meant – with the clear implication that 'you're probably wondering about all these funny words your children or grandchildren are using'. In 2009 the

Sun's infamous entertainment section, Bizarre, sensing where the next generation of readers would be coming from, established a running feature on the 'Brrap Pack' generation of urban stars, even going so far as to sponsor a national Brrap Pack tour, with Chipmunk, Tinie Tempah, Ironik and Mz Bratt.

'I understand that the Brrap Pack thing was meant to be flattering,' Tinie Tempah later told the *Daily Star*, tiptoeing a little, 'but it's pigeon-holing in a way and I want to break through that. I'm friends with Kylie, Damon Albarn and Chris Martin, and one day I want to just be in the same category as them.' While Tinie had never been part of the grime scene's collectivity – 'the underground scene where I came from was very cliquey,' he has complained – he was right; there was a clear attempt to create a new ghetto inside the world of British pop, rather than let the musicians exist on their own terms. There was also – though he refrained from saying this – a condescending, almost smirking tone to a lot of the coverage of these funny-talking young people of colour taking over the charts.

At times, the embrace offered by parts of the British establishment to grime's first generation of pop stars was conditional on their humiliation: it was visible in the tone-deaf Radio 4 comedies mimicking 'youth' speak, or news reports that Prince Harry had met Dizzee Rascal backstage at a music festival and engaged him in what onlookers described as 'an excruciating display of shadow boxing and "street" handshakes'. The entire British establishment's relationship with black British youth culture had been marked by ignorance and contempt throughout the 2000s: going back to the start of the millennium, with the public disavowals of 'macho idiot rappers', and the elevation of Ali G, played by a white public schoolboy and Cambridge graduate, as a kind of minstrel avatar for that idiocy, clowning for a mass gallery of sniggering white Britons. Shortly after her death, it was revealed that the Queen Mother had enjoyed performing Ali G impressions with Princes William and Harry; William was such a fan of the character, in fact, that Poet Laureate Andrew Motion marked his twenty-first birthday in 2003 with a 'rap poem' recognising him as a 'new kind of royal figure'. Motion's bars featured the staggering refrain: 'Better stand back/Here's an age attack/ But the second in line/Is dealing with it fine.'[15]

An uneasy duality was operating during the ascension of the Brrap Pack. The music industry and media were falling over themselves to celebrate 'urban', but there was no trickle-down effect for the underground – its artists or its infrastructure – any more than the Canary Wharf hedge-fund billionaires were improving the lives of their neighbours in the Crossways Estate. Which is how you get a situation where, in September 2009, as the decade drew to a close, the Radio 1 playlist could be chock full of Brrap Pack dilutions taken straight from 1Xtra, and simultaneously the GrimeForum could host a nine-page thread entitled 'Fuck 1Xtra', who had just announced their new schedule and a series of new DJ additions. Amid the objections to all the electro shows, the primary issue was that 'they're completely neglecting proper underground black music' – with not even a monthly grime show on the roster.

A pyrrhic victory had been achieved, and it seemed to have a sort of finality to it: 'Pow!' had been a fluke, *Boy in da Corner* had been a one-off, and – having tried several different approaches – faintly urban Ibiza dance-pop was evidently the only way the grime scene would ever get within reach of mainstream acceptance, or sustain careers in music. Meanwhile, 140bpm beats built out of sheet metal, sub-bass and sci-fi lasers, fizzing with double-time, lickety-spit lyrical sparks, had had their day. All genres die. Why even be upset about it? It's natural, it's necessary: it's meant to be. Get past the denial, anger and bargaining, and get on with acceptance. Pundits queued up to bust a little skank on its grave. 'No matter what anyone might say, grime – the London-bred bastard child of hip-hop, ragga and garage – is a stylistic dead end', began the *Guardian*'s review of a Kano live show in late 2007, calling the genre 'insular' and 'pacing impotently around its own self-made prison cell'.

A few brave voices on the underground remained confident, even when things were at their bleakest. 'It could take a decade before they accept grime like hip-hop, rock and reggae – but check this, I'm blowing up today,'[16] Ghetts was spitting in 2007 on 'Fuck Radio Volume 5', defiant while the once-thriving infrastructure of radio, raves and riddims was collapsing around him. That same year I went to interview Wiley for the first time. He was still living in a small council flat in the Isle of Dogs, still making mixtapes. I put to him the consensus view that after the major-label flops and the unfulfilled potential of the first wave, grime was over. 'Nah,' Wiley said, relaxed. 'It takes time! It takes ten, 15, 20 years to build a scene. Don't worry, grime ain't dead. It's got ages.'

TEN

WE RUN THE STREETS TODAY

If it seemed like the grime kids had been welcomed into the bosom of the establishment at last, it soon proved to be a loveless embrace. In the cold winter of 2010, following the announcement of swingeing cuts to public services, David Cameron's new Tory-Liberal Democrat coalition pushed through a tuition-fees bill which would triple the ceiling on annual university fees to £9,000 a year. They also announced the scrapping of a New Labour scheme called the Education Maintenance Allowance (EMA): a means-tested incentive scheme encouraging working-class 16–18-year-olds to stay in education, worth £10–30 pounds a week to teenagers from poor backgrounds. In November, a student uprising exploded from nowhere that immediately eclipsed even the epochal protests of 1968 – tens of thousands of university students took to the streets, broke off from sanctioned protest routes to play cat-and-mouse with the police across the centre of London, and stormed the Conservative party headquarters at Millbank. Along with the more organised university students, thousands of younger teenagers, school and sixth-form students from the same London council estates that produced grime, turned out – to protest against the cuts to their EMA, and the coalition's apparent determination to make university the preserve of the elite once again.

The 2011 riots in London

These events were, on the whole, either under-reported or mis-reported, and their significance was consequently almost entirely overlooked: it was perhaps the biggest political mobilisation of working-class teenagers in modern British history. Over the course of five weeks, they repeatedly clashed with riot police in central London, overtook the Tory HQ at Millbank, and used a battering ram to try and storm Her Majesty's Treasury, as fires burned and Lethal Bizzle's 'Pow!' resounded in Parliament Square behind them. Not for the first time, the vast majority of the media didn't even notice the grime kids were there – the overwhelming tone to the coverage was to dismiss it as a self-indulgent middle-class student rebellion, 'rich kids on the Cenotaph', as *New Statesman* political correspondent James McIntyre lamented, petulantly rioting in the name of lower fees for themselves. This was a myth, as any journalist who abandoned the warmth of their offices would have discovered.

On the morning of 30 November, as snow fell across the city, I joined the students from Westminster Kingsway College, a Further Education college with over 60 per cent black and minority ethnic students, and the same proportion in receipt of the EMA. They needed the EMA for books, travel to college, even to buy food to help feed their families, they said: and now a degree seemed more far-fetched than ever. 'The people that are telling us we have to pay,' complained one, 'are the people that went to university for free.'[1] Some of them were excited to be out of the ends: marching down the middle of the road in Bloomsbury, or dodging riot-police kettling lines, in posh and alien areas like Westminster. It was a political act in itself, an empowering piece of trespassing beyond the invisible boundaries of the familiar city, and an incursion into parts of London where they would always be eyed more suspiciously, by cops or otherwise.

'These are our streets today, we run the streets today,' one of the Westminster Kingsway students said, smiling broadly as he and his peers marched down the middle of the road: 'David Cameron we're coming for you bruv, we're coming for you!' Alongside righteous anger and excitement, they took the framework of traditional protest chants and modified them with a distinctly grimy irreverence:

'When I say Nick Clegg, you say dickhead/Nick Clegg! Dickhead!/ Nick Clegg! Dickhead!'

'No ifs, no buts, no education cuts!/No ifs, no buts, Cameron has no nuts!'

'I don't wanna pay no p/I just wanna go uni for free.'

The scansion, grammar and vernacular was straight out of a grime lyric – playful, offensive, slangy and hilarious. 'Nick Clegg you are top pussyole, allow the cuts,' read one placard. They danced, chanted, and some fought to push back the lines of riot police, standing side-by-side with the undergrads, anti-cuts activists and Black Bloc anarchists – they even shared an unofficial uniform with the latter, bound together as enemies of the government, the *Daily Mail*, of scandalised grown-ups everywhere: black hoodie wearers of the world, unite!

When one of the teenage EMA protesters got a chance to talk to BBC *Newsnight*, he spoke with the same desperation and nihilism you hear in grime. With a black bandana over his face and a dark grey beanie, accompanied by his mates jostling into the edge of the frame like lesser MCs in a grime video, his voice straining with anger, he exclaimed, 'We're from the slums of London – how do they expect us to pay £9,000 for uni fees? And EMA's the only thing keeping us in college. What's to stop us doing drug deals on the streets anymore? Nothing!' Research by the Association of Colleges found that 70 per cent of EMA recipients said they would drop out of education if the grant was abolished.

The final of four major demonstrations in a matter of weeks took place on 9 December 2010, the day of the tuition fees vote in the House of Commons. Around 40,000 people joined the demo, the vast majority 21 and under, and this time there was a feverish air of climax about it. Wishing to avoid the iconography of a showdown in front of parliament, the Met had cordoned off Parliament Square with metal fencing; but the march arrived there anyway. At around one in the afternoon, the fences were ripped down, and the square was occupied. Surrounded by the august institutions of the Palace of Westminster, Westminster Cathedral, the Supreme Court and the Treasury, and overseen by statues of

Mandela, Churchill and Lincoln, several thousand protesters were soon victims of the Met's favourite new tactical ploy, 'kettling' (or as they euphemistically called it, 'containment'[2]), in which no one is allowed to enter or leave the designated area. All exits were hemmed in by riot police, specifically the Met's stormtroopers – black snoods up and thick plastic visors down – the Territorial Support Group. There is a strong argument that kettling breaches the European Convention on Human Rights:[3] since it is essentially collective punishment, and depriving individuals of their right to liberty, detaining them without arrest or charge. Its deployment as tactic of choice at this point in London's history, used alongside extensive monitoring and filming by police FITs (Forward Intelligence Teams), makes perfect sense. The city was more securitised and surveilled than ever before, and public space less free and public than ever before. With no prospect of being able to leave the Parliament Square kettle, the young protesters had little else to do but try and breach the police lines – testing their new environment and feeling its barbed-wire edges, like caged animals – and to make their own entertainment: chanting, making new friends, passing around hip flasks.

Early in the afternoon, beneath an imposing statue of Edward Smith-Stanley, the 14th Earl of Derby, the music arrived. A battered portable sound-system, no more than a speaker in a trolley, was wheeled up alongside us by a squatter-punk type in his forties, a wizened veteran compared to the vast majority in the square. He initially played what he described as 'politically right-on reggae'; it was rootsy, 'conscious' (i.e. directly, earnestly political), and relaxed; people milled about chatting, seeming to enjoy the music, but not really engaging with it. You hear a lot of this kind of music at protests, and have done for decades; the baby-boomer canon of sixties protest rock has created a bogus assumption that political music has to brand its politics in capital letters across its forehead – or across its acoustic guitar. 'It's not about the content, it's about the energy and aura,' as Slew Dem MC Tempz put it, when I told him later one of his songs, the gleefully violent 'Next Hype', had been played by the young protesters.

If grime was the soundtrack to a 'post-political' generation, that didn't mean political music had disappeared, just that the nature of political expression had been changed, muffled by two decades of post-Cold War intellectual degradation and neoliberalism. 'The post-political is the most political,' claimed one poster from the young propagandists in the Deterritorial Support Group. It was an epochal moment, a kind of changing of the guard, when the conscious reggae was replaced. A teen-ager asked politely if he could play a few tunes, and was duly handed control of the jack into the amplifier, which he connected into his BlackBerry. In that moment, a new political consciousness was fed through the speakers and, facing south from the north side of the square, resounded towards the House of Commons. A generation often said to be too narcissistic and apathetic to ever leave their bedrooms simulta-neously found their voice, and their soundtrack. Within minutes there was a spontaneous rave going on in Parliament Square, a tightly packed dancefloor-cum-moshpit of over a hundred young protesters.

It was a breathtaking and iconoclastic setting for the same music banned from clubs and shut out by the music business: underneath 'the mother of parliaments', and overlooked by dead white men carved in stone (including Jan Smuts, the racist pre-war leader of South Africa), London's teenagers moshed, danced around, and threw their hands up to dancehall, R&B, hip-hop, UK funky, dubstep and grime. No one had expected them to protest; just as no one had planned this playlist – instead requests were called out, the jack swapped from one teen's mp3 player to another: Elephant Man's 'Bun Bad Mind', Vybz Kartel's 'Ramping Shop', Rihanna's 'Rude Boy', Sean Paul's 'Like Glue', and from London, road rap and grime: Tempz's 'Next Hype', Jme's 'Serious', and, getting the most raucous reaction of all, Lethal Bizzle's 'Pow!' – the song banned from clubs seven years earlier because it was just *too much.*

For a while at least, the kettle's edges were blunted, as Parliament Square was turned into a celebratory, rebellious occupied space. But this close to the winter solstice it gets dark by 4 p.m., and as the afternoon wore on, and the temperature plummeted to zero, the need to escape grew more urgent: the protesters wanted to go home to eat, to drink, to use toilets, to sit on sofas. To reduce the risk of hypothermia. Several protesters were hospitalised by police truncheons, one needed brain surgery and was lucky to escape with his life. There was a horse charge. A portacabin was set on fire, letting off huge clouds of noxious black smoke. Just before 6 p.m. the news came through that, with the support of most of the Lib Dems (who had made opposing rises in tuition fees a key election pledge earlier that year), the bill had passed, by 323 votes to 302. At around 7 p.m. a few protesters gave up on trying to escape the lines of riot police on Whitehall, and started throwing rocks through the windows of the Supreme Court. Others climbed up onto window ledges and were close to breaking into the building, before the riot police stormed into the kettle to chase them away with truncheons and riot shields. The same happened with the Treasury, riot police desperately trying to keep the double doors shut from the inside, as teenagers chanting 'We want our money back!' used metal fences as battering rams.

Outside the Supreme Court, another mobile sound-system – no more than a speaker in a trolley – pulled up, a trail of young protesters following it like the Pied Piper. One teenager climbed on top of a dustbin to dance, ripping his shirt off despite the freezing temperatures; another did the same, facing him, ten feet away – 'Dance off!' a few kids chanted. As the tuition fees bill was being passed in parliament, darkness fell over the Palace of Westminster, and hundreds of young people danced around these figures, silhouetted against the blue-black dusk, lit only by burning placards, and the night lights on Big Ben. The most tumultuous response, again, was for Lethal Bizzle's 'Pow!'. 'How you gonna buss if there's no room?' MC Fumin asks on the track's opening bars; 'buss' as in buss [fire] a gunshot, buss a move, or just metaphorically, strike out, and express yourself: find space – and freedom. The thrilling cacophony of Dexplicit's production channels the high-rise tension of city life, but just like any claustrophobia, it seeks freedom, and space. Just like an angry young person trapped in a police kettle, having their future – indeed, their present – cut to shreds by cadres of old Etonians and Lib

Dem hypocrites. 'Gimme room gimme space,' begins one of Skepta's trademark early bars.

'Don't dismiss us,' Bizzle said to me a few weeks later in response, addressing David Cameron. 'We've got more power than you have on the youth. You're a millionaire guy in a suit, your life is good – you can't relate. These kids can relate to people like myself, Wiley, Dizzee, Tinie Tempah, Tinchy: we're from the council estates, we lived in these places where they live, we know what it's like. We're the real Prime Ministers of this country.' From the EMA kids in Parliament Square he had picked up the anger at the government's austerity regime, too. 'It's a big "fuck you" to those sods, and to the cuts. David Cameron is still a donut. I told him six years ago what's going on, and he tried to neglect it; now it's on his front doorstep. He should really be scared. I've got more power than he has, when it comes to those kids: they're singing my song, in his front garden.'

A couple of days after we met, I sent Bizzle a link to video footage of the kids dancing to 'Pow!' under the shadow of Big Ben. He called back immediately: 'Fucking hell, I got goosebumps watching that. When you're on stage it's a different kind of feeling, but that video, with nothing pre-arranged, just seeing it from the outside looking in, you're actually seeing how they really feel about your music. Singing along word-for-word, rewinding it – it's inspirational. We don't even realise how powerful we are.'

As it approached midnight on 6 December, to clear Parliament Square, rather than simply let people go, we were force-marched onto a much tighter and more dangerous kettle on Westminster Bridge, and crushed into such a tight space that some protesters suffered respiratory problems, chest pains and the symptoms of severe crushing. It felt 'like I'd been in a car accident', one female student said. A Hillsborough-like panic and crowd surges had been avoided only by luck, rather than judgement. With the walls on either side of Westminster Bridge barely waist-high, it was tremendously fortunate no one was pushed out into the still, icy depths of the Thames below, where death would have been inevitable. Watched over by parliament, angry, scared and exhausted, the teenagers strained their voices in a call-and-response chant: 'Whose streets? Our streets!/Whose bridge? Our bridge!/Whose city? Our fucking city!'

Some of the protesters had been kettled for almost nine hours, many of them children – but all the media attention was on the broken windows, and the fact someone had half-heartedly tried to poke a stick at Prince Charles in another part of central London. In the eyes of almost the entire press, merely by engaging politically, the EMA kids had forfeited their right to be treated with respect – or even granted habeas corpus. For the twenty-something middle-class radicals among the kettled protesters, especially the white ones, the protest had been a shocking realisation of what police brutality and media contempt actually looked and felt like up close, rather than in the abstract. For the EMA kids, it was much less of a surprise. One of the Westminster Kingsway students was interviewed again a few weeks later.

'Everyone's talking about Charles and Camilla. It's a big fuss over nothing, they weren't even hurt. They should be asking why these students are angry.' He looked into the camera and posed the vital question: 'Why are we angry?' Lethal Bizzle knew the answer; David Cameron, if he did, chose to ignore it. Nine months later, England's cities were on fire.

The demands over maintaining EMA and affordable higher education were hugely important, but were just the most immediate issue stoking anger and frustration: the experience of growing up in London as a teenager in the 2000s, especially as a poor teenager of colour on a council estate, had not been an easy one. Triangulated machismo was the watchword of the political classes throughout grime's lifetime: from Blair's 'compassion with a hard edge' in 1997 to Cameron's advocacy of 'active, muscular liberalism' in February 2011 – for every gesture of support from the state, there had to be a whack around the back of the head with a stick. Ultimately, things had not got better. New Labour had tweaked around the edges of poverty in various ways, but inequality in London's poorest boroughs remained a chronic problem. Child poverty in Tower

Hamlets in August 2011, a year after Labour left office, was still 46.1 per cent (it would rise further under the coalition), compared to a national average of 20.1 per cent – and the worst in London by some distance. Their tough stance on an underclass guilty of 'welfare dependency' – Blair suggested the state should offer 'a hand-up, not a hand-out' – actively contributed to a shift in public opinion against people on benefits, the scrounger underclass on their sink estates: New Labour led rather than merely followed public opinion.[4]

The coalition's cuts were rapidly making things much worse for young people from poor backgrounds. Cameron's Big Society concept required charities to pick up the slack left by his slashing of welfare provision and local council budgets. It was a nineteenth-century model: charity and volunteer groups helping the poor and needy in the place of the state – and the charities knew they couldn't cover this growing deficit even if they wanted to. In June 2011, Geraldine Blake from Community Links in east London was asked about the legacy of Cameron's 'hug a hoodie' speech: she responded that their local council, Newham, had already suffered £50 million in cuts because of Coalition austerity: 'That inevitably translates into less funding for youth services, for family support, for play, for advice – for the whole range of things that support young people who are facing enormous pressures.' Those pressures went unnoticed by many Londoners – middle-class adults sipping wine on Broadway Market wouldn't have realised anything was any different. But as the summer of 2011 warmed up across the capital, murmurs grew about consequences to these mounting tensions. At the end of July, the *Guardian* sent a video team to speak to teenagers in Haringey in northeast London, where the council's youth funding had been cut by a staggering 75 per cent, and eight out of 13 youth clubs across the borough had been closed.

The young people talked about gangs, about youth violence, knife crime and gun crime, postcode wars – but most of all, they talked about the absence of ways out: paid work, places to hang out, anything. The walls were closing in. The words of one black teenager, Chavez Campbell, would resonate far beyond that week.

'It's rough. When youth clubs are shut down, it cuts kids' routes off, and links – they don't really have anywhere to go. I think [the summer's] going to be swarming, people are going to want things to do, people are going to want jobs, and that's going to be frustrating. There's more crime on the road, because there's nothing to do,' he said. His conclusion was chilling. 'There'll be riots.'

Accompanying the boredom, idleness and poverty Campbell described was a long-standing source of antagonism and injustice, a spark that had ignited frustration into anger and violence before: the relationship with the Metropolitan Police. Despite numerous attempts to 'rebuild' relationships with the black community, to learn lessons and reform practices following the riots in Brixton in 1981, in Brixton and Tottenham in 1985, and Brixton again in 1995, and following the Macpherson Report into institutional racism, the disproportional treatment meted out to London's black population remained a chronic problem. Routine harassment, mysterious deaths in custody or 'following contact' with the police, and the refusal to take reform seriously meant trust had barely improved. Between 2008 and 2011, the Met were 11 times more likely to stop and search a black person than a white person. It was a fact of life that young black men in particular had come to assume would never change.

MC Rage from Slew Dem accounted for the casual police racism and aggression with which he had grown up. 'The way some officers would treat us would let me know it was personal for some of them. Back then being called a black cunt by a police officer was so normal you wouldn't even think to press charges – that's why for me police brutality isn't just physical it can be verbal and mental as well.' He was, he admitted, often 'getting up to no good' when he was younger. 'But it's a systematic problem. Crime and poverty go together like rice and peas.'

The casual, everyday discrimination experienced by young black men comes through in Jme's extensive, always polite, always exasperated filming of the Met's regular use of stop-and-search against him while driving, which he turned into a YouTube series he called 'Chatty Policeman'. 'Frequently I get stopped by the gammon,' he lamented on his 2012 single '96 Fuckries', 'coz my whip looks like it should be owned by Jeremy Clarkson or Richard Hammond/Feds pull me like I'm a drug baron, chatting bare shit, can't understand 'em.'[5]

It seems appropriate that I was initially directed to Tottenham High Street on the evening of Saturday 6 August by a tweet from a local MC. Wretch 32 had enigmatically written 'Wish I was there. If you know u know.' It didn't take long to work out where, and what, he was referring to. Peaceful protests outside Tottenham Police Station had been called by the local community to demand answers about the police's killing of 29-year-old Mark Duggan, just around the corner. He had been shot while driving his car two days earlier, in broad daylight, and the Met had still offered no explanation. His friends and family's pleas for answers went unheeded – no one from the police would come out to meet them. By the time I arrived an hour later it was getting dark, and the peaceful protests were transforming into an increasingly tense stand-off outside the police station, with several lines of riot cops blocking the main road.

Reporting from Tottenham High Street that night, I saw Molotov cocktails and fireworks hurled at the police lines, retaliatory horse charges at the watching crowd, shop windows smashed open, and a red London double-decker bus – that iconic image of the capital – burned to a cinder. Over the next five days, 30,000 people across England's towns and cities took part in riots, arson and looting.

Mark Duggan was known to people from the local grime scene: Skepta, Chipmunk and Wretch 32, all from Tottenham, had already posted RIP messages before the trouble broke out – two years before his death, Duggan had even appeared in the background of a Skepta music video. Another leading Tottenham MC, Scorcher, had an even more profound personal connection to the local history of police violence and mass unrest. He tweeted on that first night of the riots: '25 years ago police killed my grandma in her house in Tottenham and the whole ends rioted, 25 years on and they're still keepin up fuckry'. It was the death of his grandmother, Cynthia Jarrett, after the police aggressively and mistakenly raided her home, which sparked the Broadwater Farm riots of 1985 – Scorcher was born the following year.

As the glaziers and magistrates went to work after four nights of extraordinary riots across London and the UK, the search for understanding and the finger of blame were simultaneously pointing towards the MCs and rappers, the 'real Prime Ministers'. Unlike the actual Prime Minister, who was on holiday in Tuscany, they had seen the riots unfold. 'These are sad days man, sad days; it's just … surreal,' Bizzle told me, surveying the wreckage. 'I care because I'm from these places, and I know what happens in these places. I've been through stuff I wouldn't want my kids, my friends, my fans, anyone to go through. It makes you feel lost, like you're in a corner.' Some musicians were reluctant to speak out, posting either short messages on Twitter which carefully balanced support for young people and condemnation for the rioters, or publicising initiatives helping people who suffered in the looting and arson. Their reticence drew the ire of Calvin Harris, who seemed to think the urban music scene should be making some kind of joint public appeal for calm in London's inner cities: these 'role models', he said, 'need to speak the fuck up [and] help stop this'. Harris made a telling assumption. The connection of grime, and of black teenagers, to the riots needs to be heavily caveated: only 39 per cent of those prosecuted in London were black; the number outside the capital was even smaller. And not everyone was young either – of the 3,000 brought to trial across England, 42 per cent were aged 21–39, and a further 5 per cent were over 40.

The one key difference between the fulminations of politicians and media commentators, and of people from the riot-affected areas, was who saw it coming. Everyone in the UK was shocked at the scale of the unrest, but not everyone was surprised at the levels of anger and frustration – the second category applied to the grime scene, as well as the young people I talked to on the streets of Tottenham, Hackney and Peckham. 'It's not just happened out of the blue,' said Bizzle. 'The kids have seen the opportunity to take the piss, [but] they feel like they've been taken the piss out of their whole lives. People come to central London and think "oh this is a lovely place", but you go a couple of miles down the road and you see what's going on. London is not a happy place, and the world can see that now. Robbery. Arson. Theft. Murder: it's been going on for years, but the government's been looking the other way. I see the riots and looting as young people thinking "we've got an opportunity to answer back to the government", even though it's the wrong way to do it – because it's not harming them, it's harming innocent people. But I think they're just frustrated, trying to be heard.'

For Hackney rapper Professor Green, there was the same mixture of affection for his city, and understanding of how suffocating it could be. 'London is a wonderful place to grow up,' he said. 'The fact it's multicultural, the fact we aren't segregated, there's a lot of good that comes from this. The other side to it, is that it is a tough, and for many people a cold place to grow up. As a kid on Northwold Estate, nobody had much, a lot of people went home to a less than ideal familial situation, and there wasn't any avenue to voice the frustration born from this. To see the city I know and love in so much pain and despair is incredibly saddening. It's not really something that can be put into words.'

And yet, in remarkably speedy 'breaking news' style, Britain's MCs and rappers were putting it into words, within a matter of a few days. Chuck D called rap music 'the black CNN' – a means of describing the kind of daily lives which the actual CNN would never care to investigate: the ultimate documentary art form for the marginalised. By this token, grime and UK rap had become the rolling news channel of the British urban working class – a voice for the voiceless, while politicians and media commentators tried to outdo each other in demanding everyone understand a little less, and condemn a little more. Genesis Elijah's captivating a cappella 'UK Riots' alluded to the temporary suspension of postcode wars: 'we all came together last night/for that, I'm grateful – maybe we'll call that a breakthrough'.[6] Bashy and Ed Sheeran's 'Angels Can't Fly' seemed rushed, but then it was, by necessity: 'where I'm from, you don't see angels, man just see rainfall/Slip and you could get a brain-full'.[7] Meanwhile dancehall artist Fresharda's response 'Tottenham Riot', called for 'more ghetto yout' [who] stand firm and stay strong/planning dem future in education'.[8]

The most extraordinary of the bunch was also the most full-on. 'They Will Not Control Us', by a little-known MC called 2KOlderz, was a snarling torrent of dispossessed rage against politicians, police and the media – it's just as well he wasn't more well-known, since he was spitting about firing grenades at parliament. 'Dear Mr Prime Minister,' it began, 'was you travelling on London transport the day the bombs went off?/How about you go and pay rent to the landlord, earn shit money doing a labouring job?/We're living like shit in this country, while you've got your feet up living nice and comfy/Well we know where the problem is, the people acknowledge this: stand up to the politics.'[9]

Others took longer to compose their thoughts. On 'Castles', Skepta spoke of the 'underdog psychosis' of the ends, where 'security guards follow me around like I ain't got £2 to pay for my juice', spelling out what was implicit to a lot of the grime scene's reactions and indirectly addressing the Mayor: 'tell Boris he's lucky that I made it rapping or I would have been looting too'.[10] Six months after the riots, Plan B's track 'Ill Manors' garnered a lot of press attention that the less well-known MCs had missed out on. It was a defence of a young urban underclass who had been backed into a corner, and inevitably lashed out ('There's no such thing as broken Britain, we're just bloody broke in Britain'), but it was also a defence of the margins, or the manor itself: 'New builds keep springing up outta nowhere ... They preserve our natural habitat/Built an entire Olympic village around where we live, without pulling down any flats.'[11] Amid the lyrics about chavs and cops, poverty and violence, another (perhaps accidental) reference point was overlooked. The production for 'Ill Manors' was lifted from a German pop song, but the original source is a stirring violin riff from Shostakovich's Seventh, generally known as the Leningrad Symphony. Shostakovich's Seventh is a perfect example, decades before hardcore or jungle or grime reshaped British culture from the dancefloor upwards, of why political music needn't have vocals explaining exactly why and how they are political. It's a symphony with a direct, descriptive narrative, about the defence of Leningrad from the Nazis during the Second World War; a stirring call to arms in the face of a relentless, brutalising assault on the collective body. It's about a great city under siege, and the ordinary people who suffer in its heart, frantically trying to survive; it was more relevant than perhaps Plan B had realised.

Five years on, Wretch 32's 'Open Conversation & Mark Duggan' offered the most poignant and thoughtful response of all, from an MC who knew Duggan and his family. This two-part track charted Wretch's formative years, growing up in Tottenham's 'concrete jungle', and his experience of being cuffed and arrested, while 'brother Mark never made it to custody'. It was a narrative of hard times and the possibility of redemption, of rising 'from the dungeon' of inner-city hardship. The track finishes with excerpts from a speech from Wretch's uncle Stafford Scott, the local activist who had been a rare voice of community defence on the news in 2011: 'We do this because for generations, they've been killing black people all over the country,' Scott says to a crowd assembled to commemorate Duggan's death. 'Poor and working-class people all over the country – and always getting away with it.'

If the younger rioters and looters were filled with a nihilistic rage directed against all authority figures, then, despite what Calvin Harris had suggested, those authority figures would include their supposed 'role models' too. Wiley, speaking during the riots from a recording studio in Jamaica, expressed the same mixture of empathy and hopelessness which many fellow elders from the grime scene had done: 'These kids won't listen to me. I wish they would, but they won't,' he said. 'In London, they love you so much, but they can hate you in a click of the fingers.' He talked about the Brazilian film *City of God* and its fearless, lawless children; he described a generation who would listen to no one at all. 'The way the kids see it, everyone in this stupid world is out for themselves. I don't even think they're doing it because they want money; they're doing it just because they want to run the place.'

The sad truth, he said, was that as an act of self-empowerment, it was completely empty – running the streets for a few wild nights was meaningless. 'If the Queen does actually get serious and says right, army, go and lick down anyone who's not white who you think is causing a problem, people will start getting shot. But these kids feel like they're ready to go against Robocop. They're testing the patience of the Queen, the government, the police. They're saying, "We're going to do what we want!" – and I'm thinking, "No you're not, because when the police get a grip on it, you're going to be either banged up, or dead."'

With the inevitable nationwide hunt for scapegoats, the articles blaming rap music – not grime; the middle-aged white men leading the charge weren't aware of the distinction – for promoting violence and consumerism were as numerous as they were immediate. First among the self-appointed experts in the relationship between black culture and recent events, Paul Routledge, writing in the *Mirror*, blamed 'the pernicious culture of hatred around rap music, which glorifies violence and loathing of authority (especially the police but including parents), [and] exalts trashy materialism and raves about drugs'. At least Marge Simpson had had the wit to criticise rap music for 'encouraging punching, boastfulness, and rudeness to hoes'.

Underscoring these criticisms was a steadfast refusal to listen or engage with people from the inner-city communities affected by the riots – or to accept the reality of inequality, poverty and racism in those places. They have an 'irrational anger against the world', wrote Routledge. David Goodhart in *Prospect* referred to the 'nihilistic grievance culture of the black inner city, fanned by parts of the hip-hop/rap scene and copied by many white people'. 'It's as if the routine brutalities and racist humiliations of 30 to 40 years ago have been lovingly preserved,' he wrote. According to Graeme Archer in the *Telegraph*, the young people of London's inner cities 'speak in a completely made-up accent based on their idea of how gangsters talk', their heads full of 'a musical subgenre which mixes blatant pornography with violent, egotistical lyrical content'. Even Channel 4 were complicit in the riots, Archer wrote, for running a season of programmes celebrating 'street' culture. Some media commentators blamed 'gang culture' in their op-eds, others were more direct: blaming black culture, multiculturalism, or liberal tolerance in general. It was time to send in the army, to bring back national service, to bring back capital punishment; as the embers died down, the most reactionary voices in Britain were once again the very loudest.

Appearing on BBC *Newsnight* to discuss the riots, historian David Starkey invoked Enoch Powell's rivers of blood speech, and, smiling and rotund, in a red tie to match his face, articulated the views of much of the British establishment. The problem, he said, was 'black culture – it's not skin colour, it's *cultural*'. As if to prove he wasn't a racist, he cited Tottenham MP David Lammy – an archetypical successful black man, he said: 'if you turned the screen off, so you were listening to him on radio, you'd think he was white'. This culture was so corrosive, and yet so potent and contagious, that it was overwhelming sturdy and moral white culture, Starkey claimed – to the consternation of the other *Newsnight* guests. 'What's happened is a substantial section of the chavs have become black: the whites have become black. A particular sort of violent, destructive, nihilistic gangster culture has become the fashion, and black and white, boy and girl, operate in this language together, this language which is wholly false, which is a Jamaican Patois that has been intruded in England – and this is why so many of us have a sense of literally a foreign country.'

Racist scaremongering and fear about the alien cultural 'intrusion' of black culture wasn't limited to Starkey, or even necessarily prompted by the riots. The year before, the *Evening Standard* had sounded the alarm about the nefarious enemy within, in a piece headlined, 'The secret world of gang slang'. The story was that the tragic murder of a north London teenager had been followed by the placing of RIP notes near the crime scene, 'peppered with words such as "liccle" and "peak", street slang terms in common usage among London's gang culture'. The gangs responsible for this sinister plot to confuse the *Standard* weren't doing a great job of keeping it a secret, writing it on notes and placing them in a prominent public place – but it was still 'impenetrable and indecipherable to all but those in the know' warned the newspaper. (Rather like all languages, in fact – that's what a language is.) But this was much worse than any normal slang, because it was spreading beyond 'the inner-city neighbourhoods synonymous with gang culture' – and the popularity of hip-hop, 'Jamaican ragga' and black culture in general meant that even 'white middle-class and Indian kids often sound "black" when they talk. It is often hard to distinguish without looking between the black, brown and white boys and girls sat behind you on the bus.'

There was a lot to choose from, but one of the most offensive accusations in the attack pieces after the riots was the suggestion of an indulgent 'grievance culture': the sense that the 'black inner city' was somehow wallowing in, and enjoying its own oppression, and would never have it any other way. If it does nothing else, the shallow electro-pop which made the likes of Tinchy Stryder, Dizzee Rascal and Tinie Tempah wealthy superstars pointed to a pretty stern determination to rise above disadvantaged beginnings. Lethal Bizzle made a related point: that those looting expensive TVs were most likely doing so in order to sell them to generate cash; numerous accounts of people looting food, and even nappies, suggest a struggle to even survive, rather than a culture of amoral acquisition and a fixation on consumerism for the sake of it.

'People on my Twitter feed were saying to me, "Well you turned your life around,"' he said, 'and sure, I did, but things were a little bit different back then. I remember going to community centres, and going on little trips, staying off the streets. My mum went to college and studied catering and she got a job straight away – she was fortunate then. There are many ways to prevent riots, but the first thing is jobs – I mean fucking hell, where are the jobs? There are no jobs!' He left the question hanging for a split second, the frustration lingering on the phone line. 'My little brother is 20 now, he's never had a job in his life – he's been trying to get a job for four years. And there's no logic at all in taking away the EMA and putting up uni fees: a lot of these kids who are involved in these riots, they're that age, where it's college, before going on to uni. Taking that away is madness.

'They need to start from ground zero, from these unprivileged kids and their unemployed parents,' he said. The timing of the largest unrest in modern British history was especially grim, given that alongside the massive and unnecessary cuts being made by the Tory-Liberal Democrat coalition, £9 billion of tax-payer's money was being spent on the imminent 2012 Olympics. In theory, that meant vast sums pouring into grime's heartlands: the five designated 'Olympic boroughs' were Hackney, Tower Hamlets, Newham, Greenwich and Waltham Forest. 'They've seen none of it,' Bizzle protested, echoing the response of many east Londoners in the aftermath of the riots. 'And now the government have to spend all this money to fix the country – if that money had been spent in the community, they wouldn't have had this problem in the first place.' Far from seeing a much-needed boost in state investment in the pre-Olympic years, grime's home turf was rotting from wilful neglect. Government austerity meant much bigger cuts to budgets in poorer boroughs than richer ones: from 2010 to 2014, Newham and Tower Hamlets topped the charts in cuts to expenditure in London, suffering punishing budget reductions of 26 per cent and 25 per cent respectively; over in affluent Richmond-upon-Thames, the cuts were a much less extreme 12 per cent.

Another familiar icon from the world of grime loomed blinking silently over the burning city below. On 12 August, Sky News ran an interview with teenage gang members who had been involved in looting in south London: they had targeted the specific shops where they had applied for jobs, but never heard back: this had been 'payback', one of them said – they talked about having no future, while the government only helped the richest in society. Hooded, masked up and anonymous, they stood on the shingle in the Thames with the Sky reporter, their backs to the river. As they discussed social exclusion, unemployment, poverty and wealth, one of the looters turned and pointed across the Thames to Canary Wharf. 'That's who the government is looking out for, them people up there. They're not thinking about us, they're thinking about that one pocket that's up there.'

Black youth culture became a focus of discussion after the riots for very different reasons, depending on who was bringing it up: were you looking for explanations, or scapegoats? Was this about them, or you? It's an age-old argument, but the case that music with morally unpalatable messages merely reflects reality, rather than glamorises, or incites amorality, seemed more important than ever. If, as Martin Luther King wrote, 'a riot is the language of the unheard', a result of 'living with the daily ugliness of slum life, educational castration and economic exploitation', then this was Dr King's language rendered as art, and set to music.

'The key to all of this is education and understanding,' reflected Professor Green: 'It's ignorance like that of Paul Routledge that breeds the hate and contempt seen in people during this tragedy. Doing what I do now do has entirely changed my life, as it has done for many of my peers. Why would you want to further silence the already voiceless? I became a lot less angry when I learnt how to communicate, and began to understand exactly where my anger came from, and what I was unhappy with.'

Criticising grime or road rap's negativity and violence might be fair game artistically, but demonising it, of course, achieved nothing. Grime can be as nihilistic as setting a car on fire. As was punk. As was Dadaism. As were Francisco Goya, and Théodore Géricault. It wasn't the first time angry young men – the rioters, like the grime scene, were overwhelmingly male – have screamed 'fuck the world' into the void, using a microphone, a paintbrush, or a brick. The grime kids had been punished and policed with ASBOs, curfews and dispersal orders; they had been surveilled, harassed, kettled and endlessly stopped and searched; their public space had been privatised, their clubs and pirate stations shut down, their youth clubs closed, and their route out of poverty through education barricaded by a political class determined to blame them for their own oppression. Whose streets? Not their streets. Whose city? Not their fucking city.

On the night of Monday 8 August 2011, on the third night of rioting, Logan Sama's weekly grime show on KISS ended with a tune called 'Talk That', by the young MC Rival. First aired in April that year, it felt eerily prophetic all of a sudden, a grim answer to many of the questions being asked. It's a bleak description of a city divided between Buckingham Palace ('that's not London') and the ends, where the inescapable themes are drug dealing, violence, limited horizons and fatalism. 'They want to know why there's all this anger, all this pain/They want to know why I talk that violence, talk that slang,'[12] Rival spits, setting up a chorus that is sung with such stymied emotion that it's somehow all the more poignant, because it's so flat. 'I just say, "It's all I know."'

ELEVEN

GENTRIFICATION AND THE MANOR REMADE

After the long-simmering political eruptions of 2010 and 2011, there followed an inevitable period of no-holds-barred revanchism for the British establishment, a clampdown to end all clampdowns. Within days of the riots, David Cameron was promising a 'fightback'. June 2012 would bring the Queen's diamond jubilee celebrations and August the Olympic games, and this 'Jubilympic' year saw the nexus of state power, feudal servility and corporate might – in the form of rigid brand partnerships – dominate the London landscape. If the demonstrations and riots had amounted to a 'return of the repressed' to the public arena, they were about to return to being repressed: beginning with mass imprisonment of rioters, English courts working through the night, and Conservative politicians happily breaking with democratic protocol to instruct magistrates that they should disregard sentencing guidelines and issue 'exemplary' jail terms – in one case, a student with no criminal record was jailed for six months, for stealing £3.50's worth of bottled water. There was a drastic ramping up of policing and surveillance across London, to prevent the slightest possibility of any security or public order meltdown – or even peaceful protest – in the summer. The state was on manoeuvres, and the city on lockdown.

Dizzee Rascal carries the Olympic torch, 2012

The Met rehearsed for the Jubilympic summer during an anti-austerity demo in November 2011, with a bit of kit held in reserve in case of a major nuclear or chemical attack: a Transformers-style van that opened out into a 10-foot-high steel wall. They cordoned off Trafalgar Square and christened it 'the sterile zone': members of the public could still enter – the entrance monitored by cops repurposed as particularly aggressive bouncers – but only if they discarded any political placards they were carrying. The surprise deployment of what cops called the 'iron horse' made sense for the mood of the anxious post-riots, pre-Olympic period. But it was also a sign of the times in a broader sense. In the same way feudal capitalism relied on enclosing the common public land, the 'commons', to generate profit for its wealthy aristocratic elite, neoliberal capitalism requires putting up walls in our cities, policing and restricting public spaces, and creating enclaves where access is dictated only by wealth and power: including gated communities, securitised blocks of luxury flats, private roads, and shopping malls instead of street markets. While capital must be allowed to move around the world unhindered by the state, the same freedom does not apply to poor people in the west's 'global cities'.[1]

With the threat of terrorism, along with public order, protest, and general human-traffic management, the Olympics provided the justification for turning London into a half-militarised city. Along with 12,500 police officers from 51 different forces, 13,500 army troops were drafted onto the streets of London, along with 1,000 armed US diplomatic and FBI agents. There were also big pay-outs to private security companies: the controversial firm G4S had a £130m Olympic contract alone. The Royal Navy's largest ship, the 22,500-tonne helicopter carrier HMS *Ocean*, was stationed in the Thames. Anarchists were pre-arrested at their homes, just in case they were planning to commit a public order offence. As sweeping government cuts to local council budgets and welfare spending started to take their toll on the poorest families, and use of food banks soared across the capital, the public funds spent on security for the Olympics were £553m in the venues themselves, and over £1 billion overall. All circuses, and no money left for bread.

Most of this security mania was focused on grime's heartlands, east London's five official Olympic boroughs. The Olympic park in Newham, where Deja Vu FM's studio had once stood, was protected by an 11-mile, 5,000-volt electric fence. High-velocity missiles were stationed on the top of strategically located blocks of flats, the closest one positioned on a water tower in the luxury gated community of Bow Quarter, five minutes walk from Roman Road. The Bow Quarter buildings had been the site of the historic match girls' strikes in 1888, and, a century later, a harbinger of the gentrification of the area – transformed into a private residential complex containing 700 flats, a pool, a gym, 24-hour security and a residents-only bar, its constituent buildings named after luxe New York signifiers like Lexington and Manhattan. These gated communities had proliferated in east London around the turn of the millennium, especially in developments aimed at the wealthy new arrivals working in the City of London or Canary Wharf. It was exactly the kind of walling that keeps richer residents from having to interact with poor locals. 'As soon as they get past the gates you can almost see a weight come off people's shoulders, you can almost see them breathe a sigh of relief,' one Bow Quarter resident said of his neighbours in 2004.[2] That same year, Home Secretary David Blunkett had speculated that such gated communities, 'where people contribute towards the security and order within the enclave in which they live', were a model that could be extended much further, across British society, 'for the many' as well as the wealthy few.

The landscape that forged the grime scene was disappearing from the map: pirate-radio signals faded from the FM dial, legendary record shops were replaced with boutique coffee shops, iconic tower blocks were being 'artwashed' by councils and the creative industries, while the less attractive ones were torn down and replaced with luxury flats for the growing influx of young professionals. 'Bow has changed drastically,' says Troy 'A Plus' Miller from Rinse FM. 'Obviously, the gentrification is a problem: there's hardly anything for the younger ones to do, there's no youth clubs anymore, you don't really see anyone hanging out. It's obvious the area's changing, but who do the changes benefit? It's not like they put 20 new studios or media facilities for kids in the Olympic boroughs. The landscape's changed so much, and these establishments are popping up that want to sell you a sandwich for £8. I mean, who's paying that?'

The Olympics were a huge accelerator to the transformation of east London, beginning when the bid was won back in 2005 – but the engine had been started, and the tank filled up much earlier, by New Labour's Urban Renaissance plan. Even in 2004 Wiley was saying of Bow: 'it used to be a very tower block-y area, but the buildings are starting to get knocked down now, so they're making it into more like a suburbs sort of thing.'[3] By the time I spoke to him a decade later about the gentrification of the area, he could scarcely believe it was the same: Labour's estate regenerations, in the name of making the inner city more 'mixed', had taken their toll. 'All I can see is new-builds being chucked up there,' Wiley said, while the market culture of Roman Road ('the nurturer') had weakened considerably as a community hub. 'That market culture was massive,' he said. 'The difference today is people go to flipping Westfield, or Bluewater.'

As for the estates themselves, many of them had been completely overhauled, as per New Labour's plan – but as Miller says, for whose benefit? Crossways Estate, 'the three flats' where Dizzee and Tinchy had lived as children, where Rinse FM had broadcast, backdrop to many grime videos, was undergoing a complete refurbishment. 'They should have been doing that when I was in school,' Wiley said, summing up the entire concept of managed decline. 'Instead they left it until it was actually on the floor, to go in and fix it.'

Today Crossways stands transformed by a substantial gentrification project which refurbished the three tall towers and re-clad them in pastel shades, planting trees and adding new low-rise buildings around them – and brought in a more affluent class of east London migrant. The council-built Crossways Estate is no more, and in its place stands the re-branded Bow Cross. 'Bow is washed, rinsed and looking good – and buyers are impressed,' declared the headline in the *Evening Standard*'s

Homes & Property magazine in June 2011, after 65 per cent of the new privately-owned flats were sold in the first three weeks of sale. Rarely is social cleansing accompanied by such unabashed language about needing to 'wash' and 'rinse' an area of its undesirables.

Before regeneration it had been 'an especially menacing part of east London' the *Standard* explained, where 'any outsider who was brave or foolhardy enough to venture on to the decaying estate' would be 'confronted by intimidating gangs of youths grouped silently on gloomy walkways, the only sound being the crunch of crack vials beneath their feet'. It's a text-book example of the almost gleeful orientalism used about inner-city council estates – and much of east London in general – the *Standard* makes the scene sound like something from Alfred Hitchcock's film *The Birds*. The managing director of Swan New Homes, who took over the estate from Tower Hamlets council in 2004, assured the newspaper that the previous issues, the 'graffiti, grime and crime' had been 'designed out', and instead, the new residents were 'a calm and balanced community'. The *Standard* concluded with the following statement of reassurance to its readers: 'Only about 20 of the original Crossways residents have opted to return to the estate, so the formerly volatile mix of personalities has been dissipated.'

And that's gentrification in a nutshell: the most eye-catching cultural manifestations of urban change, the hipster cereal cafes and pop-up oxygen bars, are never the most influential actors in the process. Indeed, they are a distraction from where the most important decisions are taken. It is the less glamorous and headline-grabbing developments that go under the radar, and where the real pain of gentrification resides: the 'refurbishments' that become de facto mass purging of poor residents; the choking off of the supply of social housing since the 1980s; the granting of planning permission to new luxury blocks; the cynical redefining of 'affordable housing' to mean anything up to 80 per cent of market rate (it used to be more like 50 per cent); developers buying their way out of their legal requirements to build affordable housing by paying cash to struggling councils; the eviction of poor families, most often people of colour, or people with less fluent English, with no access to the media or housing lawyers, and their re-housing further away from the city centre.

Research by Savills estate agents found that, between 2001–11, the most pronounced increases in the proportion of wealthy residents across London were in Stratford, Canary Wharf and Bow, while the London suburbs saw increases in poorer residents and increases in overcrowding in the private rented sector. This 'banlieue-isation' – a reference to the poor suburbs of Paris, the banlieues – has been the story of London's twenty-first century so far. Housing benefit claims were rising every year in outer-London boroughs, and falling in the inner city, as the poor were pushed to the periphery. As the squeeze on affordable housing intensified in inner-London boroughs, poor families were being forced out of their borough more and more: by the end of 2014, 14,000 homeless London households were living in temporary accommodation outside of their home borough – usually in unsafe, unfamiliar, unsuitable hostels or B&Bs, hours away on the outer reaches of the capital, or outside it altogether. This figure had increased 123 per cent in the space of three years, 2011–14.[4] 'No council should be sending tenants en masse to a different part of the country,' a Conservative government spokesman said in December 2014 – which was unfortunate, as that was exactly what was happening.

Even Tory-run London councils like Westminster were complaining about the government's cuts to housing benefit, and the chaos it was creating in an already struggling inner city. There were high-profile cases like that of the 'Focus E15 mothers' from Stratford, a group of single mums in their late teens and early twenties made homeless by the eviction from their social-housing 'foyer' (a building with on-site creche and skills training), whom Newham Council were advising to accept re-housing in Manchester, Birmingham or Hastings, places which they had never even visited and knew nobody – and all while the council marketed, at great expense, huge swathes of the borough to foreign property investment companies as an 'Arc of Opportunity', where a 'Regeneration Supernova' was exploding across the east London sky.

'£9 billion on the Olympics and they're telling us and our babies we have to go live in Hastings,' lamented Focus E15's Adora Chilaisha, only 19 years old, asking why they couldn't be re-housed in the former athletes' village.[5] Although some of the Olympic accommodation was becoming social rented flats for those on the housing register, the overwhelming majority – 1,500 homes – were for private rent, starting at a minimum of £310 per week for a one-bedroom flat.

There were 24,000 people on the waiting list for social housing in Newham alone at the time, but the Labour Mayor Robin Wales wished to prioritise 'those who contribute to society', and in doing so 'drive aspiration and form a stable community where people choose to live, work and stay'. Legally, they didn't have much choice in whether they would stay: if they refused to accept relocation out of the only city they had ever known, they risked being declared 'intentionally homeless', and having all state support withdrawn. And so, the exile of poor families from the inner city continued to gather pace. The critic Jonathan Meades had prophesied the new reality in 2006, as the urban renaissance began to take shape: 'Privilege is centripetal. Want is centrifugal ... in the future, deprivation, crime and riots will be comfortably confined to outside the ring road.'[6]

Along with the 'rinsing' of estates like Crossways, the commercial premises that had been key parts of grime's London were changing too. Rhythm Division on Roman Road in Bow, the shop where 'everyone in grime used to congregate', as Tinchy Stryder put it, as well as the location for Wiley's 'Wot Do U Call It?' video and for countless DVD freestyles, was replaced in 2011 by an artisan coffee shop. 'The record shops were what brought grime together, what made it a scene – people used to link up and just jam; people from different crews and areas,' the shop's former manager, DJ Cheeky told me – and he should know, having been a business associate of Wiley since they were selling vinyl out of the boot of a Vauxhall Corsa. He'd since been back to try one of their flat whites and artisan BLTs. 'I enjoyed the sandwich,' he laughed incredulously, 'but I don't see many people like me in there. These areas were once the breeding grounds for new music. But the area's changed so much; where does everyone go to do their stuff? Or where are you inspired by?'

Other erstwhile social hubs were melting into the air. The Phoenix Arms, a Wilehouse and Roll Deep crew pub on India Dock Road, was closed in 2012, and replaced with a private block of flats. The Stratford Rex, site of some legendary grime nights in the early days, and only a stone's throw from the Olympic site, was repossessed and closed in 2010. A reopening was proposed under new ownership in early 2012, but the Rex's reputation still lingered, and some local residents objected. In an attempt to assuage concerns, a spokesperson for the new owners made it clear it would not be a grimy reopening: 'Don't brand us with the brush of the people that were here before,' she said, 'because we are nothing like them. We are not looking to put on all night hip-hop raves – all clubs will be members only and will target the pop and indie market.'[7]

While working-class people were being decanted from the estates of inner london in the name of the urban renaissance, a strange thing was happening to some of the once-unfashionable concrete blocks they were being forced to leave behind. Erno Goldfinger's 27-storey Balfron Tower and its neighbour and partner, 11-storey Carradale House are five minutes from Langdon Park School, where Dizzee had met his inspirational teacher Tim Smith. They had been left to decline like many postwar brutalist blocks, and in 2007, the council gave up ownership to Poplar Harca, the organisation that would take charge of its long-postponed makeover. Initially, the social-housing tenants were assured they could have right of return, once the lengthy refurbishment was complete – this has failed to materialise, and the homes have been sold off for private purchase; it's a pattern repeated across London's major estate regenerations in the last decade. The heavy involvement of artists in the process of the Balfron and Carradale regeneration has led to accusations of 'artwashing' – both buildings are of architectural interest, and Grade II listed, and a long series of artistic residencies, exhibitions, 'vertical carnivals', artist tours and installations brought further bougie attention. This process reached a nadir with a 12-hour immersive theatrical production of *Macbeth*, and an entire Balfron Season in the empty tower, featuring talks, workshops, an evening of 'East End bingo', a supper-club with a six-course tasting menu, and a Wayne Hemingway-designed retro restoration of one flat in 'authentic' 1960s style.

'We get tourists coming to look at the block every day,' one social-housing tenant said in 2013, as she prepared to be evicted from the Balfron Tower with her five-month-old daughter.[8] 'It feels like you're living in a zoo, [with them] peering through your window and then going back to their nice posh house in the suburbs. They do a little tour round the area – Robin Hood Gardens, Balfron Tower, go look at the Banksy – and then I think they get on the DLR and get out of there.'

Artwashing was not confined to the Balfron, even among other east London estates which had not been listed – Bow Cross had its own artists' residencies, while sections of another huge, decaying Tower Hamlets estate, Robin Hood Gardens, were bought by the Victoria & Albert Museum in 2017, prior to its demolition, as 'an important piece of brutalism, worth preserving for future generations'. Working-class families had no chance of being able to live in any of these mummified husks of affordable social housing, but at least their social betters could study how life used to be before they were displaced by luxury flats and 'mixed communities'. Brutalist estates like the Balfron, and its matching partner in west London, the Trellick Tower, backdrop to many low-budget grime videos in the early days, began cropping up in mainstream pop videos too, as the post-war architectural style became ever more fashionable; you can buy Trellick Tower mugs, plates, T-shirts – even a £150 model for your mantelpiece.

The creative industries had been fetishised by New Labour as the engine of the urban renaissance, as a modernising break from its historic associations with lower-case *labour*, the unfashionable aesthetics of trade-union banners and Jarrow marchers – and now they were playing a part in powering a 'renaissance' which amounted to little more than out-and-out gentrification. Property developers and estate agents love creatives even more than politicians do: 'It's that magical something that [London boroughs] all want,' leading property developer Richard Fagg told me. 'They all want IT businesses and they all want creative industries, because it gives them that young, hip vibe. People take it very seriously, because it creates value.' Council blocks were recuperated as sites of artists' installations and rendered hollow objects of aesthetic appreciation, rather than places where poorer families could live their lives.

Arguably there was a similar process of detachment and depersonalisation happening in grime, in a phase where MCs had largely disappeared from view, and a more carefully produced, experimental instrumental form was developing – the first wave of grime MCs were all reaching their thirties, and most had either given up the mic, or their hearts weren't really in it: their chaotic, youthful exuberance was disappearing along with the London that had produced it. By 2012, even the Brrap Pack's moment of electro-pop grime hits was passing its peak – Wiley finally got a number-one single, with the summery pop song 'Heatwave', but he was the only one, and 2013 saw grime's mainstream pop moment fading from view. A small instrumental underground scene of bedroom producers was beginning to emerge, via club nights like Boxed and label/club-night Butterz, but the MC culture was undeniably waning. 'There is both a curatorial and hauntological dimension to today's grime and the way in which it deploys MC voices,' wrote academic Nabeel Zuberi in 2013, describing the 'cavernous tracks of instrumental grime producers such as Visionist, Wen and Logos, which often feature samples of MC vocal fragments or recall the sonic palette of a decade ago.'[9]

Grime's wild early energy was haunting the new music being made, just like the scene's heartlands and the musicians' childhood homes had been historicised and reduced to museums of its former glory. East London had been haunted by its industrial past for decades, since the factories and docks started to close down. It was there in the place names of the garment district created by immigrant Huguenot weavers (in Shoreditch nightlife hubs such as Curtain Road), and the 'wharves' and 'docks' around Canary Wharf that had not seen a boat in decades. This trend was given a twenty-first-century twist by the cringeworthy co-opting of blue collar work by parts of the emerging 'Silicon

Roundabout' in Shoreditch: most notably the so-called 'White Collar Factory', a pretentious office space for tech start-ups and creative young professionals with portfolio careers.

The way east London housing was developing – or rather, being developed – Crossways was never going to remain as dilapidated as it was during grime's youth, especially given its location: Bow, it bears repeating, stands sandwiched directly between two quintessential twenty-first-century sites of opulence and aspiration, the two biggest regeneration projects in London, two sites that tell the story of our times: the Olympic Park (with its partner in retail, Westfield Stratford), and Canary Wharf. Both were created by government diktat, with piles of tax-payers' money, and managed by arms-length super-quangos (the LDDC and LLDC), but have overwhelmingly benefited private capital: not small-scale local businesses, but some of the richest international property developers on the planet, from the (Australian) Westfield Corporation to the China Investment Corporation, which now owns most of Canary Wharf. A fat lot of good the developments have done for the piggies in the middle. In 2012, schools in Tower Hamlets still had more pupils on free school meals (a reliable poverty indicator, because only low-income families are eligible) than anywhere else in England: 54 per cent compared to a national average of 16 per cent.

London 2012's official slogan, complete with trademark, was *Inspire A Generation*. (The Team GB follow-up slogan for the post-Olympics period was the equally sports brand-like *Better Never Stops*.) Four years after the games' closing ceremony, BBC *Newsnight* invited the former Minister for the Olympics Tessa Jowell, a former Olympic athlete Kelly Holmes, and the London 2012 Director of Sport Debbie Jevans to debate the legacy. Presenter Emily Maitlis put to this panel statistics showing that black and minority ethnic and lower-income groups – both over-represented in the Olympic boroughs – had shown a sharp decline in sporting participation since 2012; the guests had little to say in response. More people were playing handball, they said; terrific – £9 billion of public money well spent. Meanwhile, use of food banks doubled from 2011–12, and a survey for the London Assembly found that 61 per cent of the capital's teachers had fed hungry schoolchildren out of their own pockets – and 41 per cent said they believed hunger had led to fainting or other illnesses. Inspiring a generation only really becomes a possibility when the generation in question have come around from their poverty-induced dizzy spell.

The official narrative across the entire media during the summer of 2012 was 'who could possibly complain about this unalloyed good?' – and any concerns or objections were swaddled in Union Jack bunting and the official logos of the games' corporate partners. In 2017 the London Assembly published a report looking at the impact of the Olympic legacy. Its findings were as predicted by only poorer locals, and a few of us in the media: the gap in most quality-of-life indicators between the impoverished Olympic boroughs and the rest of London had not been closed; incredibly, the gap in terms of sporting or physical activity rates had actually got *worse*. The earnings gap was greater than it had been in 2009: and Tower Hamlets, Newham, Hackney and Barking and Dagenham retained some of the highest levels of child poverty in the entire country.[10]

A full nine years after his clash with Crazy Titch in the Deja Vu FM rooftop studio, Dizzee Rascal returned from Miami to pick up the mic in the same spot – give or take half a mile – for an altogether less humble performance: in the 80,000-capacity, £486-million Olympic Stadium. He was there to perform his number-one party-pop mega-hit 'Bonkers' as a key part of the London 2012 opening ceremony. The ceremony cost £27 million in itself: an arirang mass games-style extravaganza of elaborate choreography, extravagant props and dazzling pyrotechnics, with a supporting cast of 7,500 volunteers, and it was broadcast live to an estimated global TV audience of 900 million people. Dizzee stood proud in his embroidered 'E3' baseball jacket, a single piece of thread connecting this international TV spectacular to the forgotten people and forgotten genre that emerged mere minutes away.

Dizzee was also asked to record one of five official Olympic songs: his contribution, 'Scream', was the kind of thumping sports anthem the situation demanded – 'I feel like Rocky on the steps' – but buried in the final verse of the song, he found room for a fleeting tribute to the roots he had become estranged from, living in Miami: the area he still felt intensely conflicted about, and conflicted about leaving: 'Boy it's lonely at the top, but it's overcrowded at the bottom/And where I come from's overly rotten, I'm from the east side, I ain't forgotten.'[11]

Across the history of the modern Olympic games, there has usually been a fractious relationship with the urban area they land in; even while the official PR rhetoric, parroted by inane broadcasters across the board, always purports that the games make 'a great advert' for that area to the world. The games flatten the reality of everyday life in the host neighbourhood with cheery inspirational slogans, mimicking the sports brands who are the official corporate partners – all smiles, thumbs up, logos and trademarks. Never mind that so many of the people Dizzee had grown up with had been displaced by gentrification, or swept up in the tumult of the previous summer's riots. As a school-aged teenager at the time, the reality of what the games meant for residents of Stratford was not lost on grimy Afrobeats MC J Hus – he and his friends noticed a marked intensification of police harassment. 'They needed to clean things up for the Olympics,' he recalled. 'And about 20 of us, we didn't fit their definition of clean.'[12]

What a great advert for east London, said the talking heads, over and over again. Maybe the statement was true, in and of itself. In May 2013, Newham Council and Mayor Boris Johnson succeeded in selling off a key part of the borough's Arc of Opportunity, the derelict Royal Albert Dock just east of Canary Wharf. The sale was made to a Chinese investment consortium, for £1 billion – so that they could turn the huge, empty site into 'London's third financial centre', after the City of London and Canary Wharf: and create a new 3.2-million-square-foot 'Asian Business Park'.

What a great advert for east London. The question is, what good did the £9-billion advertising campaign – or the £1-billion sell-off of public land – do for the people already living there?

'Now you want to make it a nice, white area, but what happened to the last ten years?' MC Chronik from Slew Dem said, shooting clay pigeons from his sofa on an Olympics computer game.[13] 'It was stabbings here, stabbings there – no one wanted to clean up the area then.'

TWELVE

A TRUE URBAN RENAISSANCE

There is a glaring paradox to grime's relationship with the mainstream over the years. Although its creators regularly talk about fame and fortune, it's a sound that is unapologetically outsider and uncompromising, which – if we play devil's advocate for a minute – is built from beats which are too strange and irregular to dance to, rapping that is too fast to be clear on the radio, lyrics full of slang and swear words, songs not really geared towards hooks and choruses, and artists unwilling to play the industry game, facing up to an industry who were never more than fleetingly interested anyway. How was a genre like this ever meant to cross over?

Grime could never be accused of playing to the gallery, or trying to secure universal appeal. Niche sensibilities were built into the genre's DNA before it even had a name: a motley crew of self-taught mavericks making music full of violent hype talk and hyper-local references, hanging off frantic, awkward beats. This is not what traditional festival headliners are made of. The MCs could talk about stacking grands and being top boy until the cows came back to Tower Hamlets, but the odds piled against them were so overwhelming – and though they were always too proud to complain about it, *so unfair* – that the prospect of commercial

The crowd at Skepta's impromptu show in Shoreditch, 2015

success and cultural dominance becoming a reality seemed remote to the point of absurdity. From about 2006 onwards, writing grime off was probably the smart thing to do, or at least the cool thing to do, if you wanted the precious cultural capital of having pronounced it dead nice and early. In 2007, when Wiley and Skepta both told me that despite the prevailing winds, and the total collapse of its infrastructure, grime was only going to get bigger in the long run, I listened to them, and admired their stoicism and self-belief – but I don't think even they would have predicted the state of play a decade later.

Written off and left for dead, grime would enjoy a renaissance of truly startling proportions, eclipsing all of its achievements in the mid-2000s. Things moved incredibly quickly in 2014 and 2015, but looking closely, there had been clues as to what was coming. Skepta, like Wiley, has long been an incisive lyrical narrator of his own career journey – and his 2012 track 'Ace Hood Flow' documents, with a mixture of bitterness and defiance, the scorn he received for his explicit 'porn music video' (accompanying the mediocre single 'All Over The House'), and the dedication of working on music for no financial return for so long, knowing that 'Rome weren't built in a day', and that redemption was coming. 'I don't care who's got a deal,' he spits, perhaps a bit defensively – but the vindication was just around the corner. That same year, Boy Better Know performed at the four-way live extravaganza, the Red Bull Culture Clash, beating the three other reggae and dance sound systems, whose acts included global stars like Diplo and Usher. The Jamaican soundclash-inspired event is judged at the end by a crowd decibel meter, and BBK were the clear winners. It was, their booking agent Rebecca Prochnik says, a revelation: to see BBK play for a crowd of thousands, for once – in London, for once. Wembley Arena was packed with a generation too young to remember pirate radio in 2003, but who responded to tunes like 'Pow!' and Skepta's 'Duppy' like they were *their* anthems.

Skepta's epiphany, and musical renaissance, emerged from a substantial period of deep self-reflection – from the revealingly titled *Community Payback* mixtape to the bizarre, mumbly 30-minute monologue to camera which the MC uploaded to YouTube in 2014. 'Underdog

Psychosis' describes various periods of depression, alienation and perseverance in his life; doing one live booking every couple of months, for a
£300 cheque, barely scraping by. 'I can remember exactly how I felt,' he
intones: 'I felt like nothing. But I stuck it out, and now I can say I've seen
both sides. I believe in my talent, and I rubbed that "I'm not meant to
be" attitude off my skin.'

When it arrived, the seismic moment for the entire grime scene was
one three-minute single: 'That's Not Me' by Skepta, with Jme as guest
MC – and an old-school, all-star MC line-up on the remix. It was a
disavowal of his past mistakes and a return to the roots of grime, with
Skepta recanting his sins and triumphantly distancing himself from the
trappings of the jet-setter life: 'Sex any girl? That's not me/Lips any girl?
That's not me/Yeah, I used to wear Gucci/Put it all in the bin, cause that's
not me.'[1] It had originally been a back-to-basics freestyle, delivered on
the street while his crew stood around, hands-in-pockets, idling in the
ends, in the middle of a grainy, seven-minute VHS video, made just for
YouTube. It was only then decided to pluck the diamond out of the
rough, and turn the freestyle into a proper studio single.

'That's Not Me' rejuvenated grime by taking it back to its roots: the
bouncy rhythm track built around a riff from the same Plugsounds
sample preset ('Bagoo') that formed the backbone of classic grime
instrumentals like 'What' by Wonder and 'Jam Pie' by Wiley. Skepta's
instrumental is incredibly similar in sound and effect to that made by
Wiley for his 2004 single 'Pies': a connection tacitly acknowledged in the
lyrics, when Skepta quotes the line, 'See I come from the roads, pricks
want to put Wiley on hold'[2] – swapping in his own name instead. Like a
true prodigal son returning home, after years wandering lost in a gaudy
electro wilderness, Skepta needed to locate the talisman that had given
him his powers in the first place: specifically, Jammer's old Korg Trinity
keyboard. It was the keyboard that had been responsible for countless
classic early grime instrumentals made in Jammer's basement, not just
by him, but by Wiley and Skepta too – and, lending the keyboard an
even more Holy Grail-like quality, it was pre-loaded with 'all the old
grime sounds,'[3] as Skepta put it, obscure software plug-ins not available

anywhere else, unique building blocks that had long vanished from the internet. Jammer had given the keyboard away to a kid from the estate some years before, much to Skepta's initial alarm – but after a few panicked phone calls, they tracked it down.

To Skepta's surprise, having made an uncompromising old-school grime single, just for the hardcore fans – just for himself, in a sense – it sold brilliantly, entered the charts at 21, and, at a point when this was unprecedented, got played on daytime Radio 1. 'It's crazy that it's blown up,' he said, shortly after its release.[4] It formed the basis of a whole new ethos, and a new confidence: 'I've made more commercial songs which have had much less radio support. It's mad. I've seen now that merking and keeping it grimy is what I should do. I'm not trying to live in the past; I'm doing yesterday in HD.'

The official music video for 'That's Not Me' followed the same 100 per cent DIY path: made for just £80, with Skepta and his DJ, Maximum, performing against a green screen, on which was projected the same 'nostalgic backdrop', as Jme puts it in his verse: grainy shots of Jammer's famous basement studio and the gritty street freestyle. The video for the song's all-star remix took the 'returning heroes' theme a stage further, with sections shot by Roony 'Risky Roadz' Keefe on an old lo-fidelity VHS camera, with the cast of MCs (D Double E, Tempz, President T, Jaykae and Sox) lined up to deliver their bars in front of Lanfranc Estate on Roman Road, directly opposite where Rhythm Division used to be, before it became a coffee shop. As a measure of how much grime's epicentre had changed in its lifetime, one typical two-bedroom flat in the 1970s estate was sold for £462,000 in 2016. Less than 20 years earlier, in 1997, the exact same flat sold for less than a tenth of the price, £46,000.

It was a righteous return to the source – and even if the source looked substantially different to how it had been, something of the spirit had been resurrected: the best kind of cheesy redemption story, in which the hero discovers he had the qualities he needed inside him all along. And with that epiphany about their internal mentality came a need for grime to reaffirm its external self, its uniform, as well.

Compared to some genres, grime has never been overly concerned with fashion as part of its self-identity – the lyrical content is assertively quotidian, and so are the clothes; there is generally less name-checking of particular brands than in American hip-hop – but Skepta's awakening was embodied in his re-christening of his team as the 'tracksuit mafia': a key emblem of the humility and authenticity of grime's origins, and the fact that re-embracing those origins had brought him new life, as it would for the scene. Skepta had previously spent time shouting out the hideously garish Ed Hardy brand (he even wrote a song about it, 'Ed Hardy Party'), or fetishising prestigious labels, but in this period he made being 'dressed like I just come from PE' the pinnacle of cool again. He was featured on numerous 'best-dressed' lists, and American style site *High Snobiety* even compiled a collection of his 'best tracksuit moments'.

The black tracksuit had long been an unofficial grime uniform, part of the same logic of the need to 'move low-key',[5] to assert a degree of privacy and maintain personal security in a city full of eyes (rivals, enemies, cops, cameras) watching your movements for all the wrong reasons. Even back in 2006, Tinchy was spitting bars about wearing 'trackies black, Huaraches black, all because I want to blend in with night'. In grime's early days, both Dizzee and Wiley had lyrics attesting they would never wear 'shiny suits' ('I'm a rudeboy, still buy goods from the Loot' continued Wiley, summoning the spirit of East End wheeler-dealing) – perhaps a rejection of the suited and booted City boys raking it in on Canary Wharf, or of UK garage's strict club-dress codes, or perhaps a reference to the (very shiny) multicoloured baggy suits US rappers like Mase and Puff Daddy had been wearing in their multimillion-dollar videos. Either way, it was a reaction to the ostentation, glitz and glamour of a world far away from grime. Why, Skepta wondered, had he spent so long aspiring to be a part of a wealthy, white global fashion elite that had only contempt for him and his friends? 'I just had a wake-up call,' he said to me in 2015. 'I feel like the last two years, I've been becoming a man, and growing up has made me realise: why the fuck am I buying Louis Vuitton and Gucci, when none of their adverts, none of their fucking posters or campaigns ain't got no hood ni**ers? They ain't got no black people wearing their clothes. It's just about working with the people that are working with you – the people that acknowledge you.'

In January 2015, with the tracksuit mafia's confidence in their own self-sufficiency taking hold, Wiley had given hotly tipped teenage MC Novelist – 18 years his junior – a piece of avuncular advice: don't wear a tracksuit to the MOBO Awards, he said. The implication was 'don't make the mistakes we made,' and bring the street attitude of the ends into the industry, because it will backfire on you. Try and play the game, at least a bit. The younger MC's response was to (respectfully) tell the godfather of grime to fuck off. 'People like me for being me,' Novelist told me at the time. He compared it to telling a punk to get rid of their tattoos. 'Telling me to take off my tracksuit, it's like telling me to change my skin colour or something. It's just who I am: I'm from the ends, that's what I wear.' He laughed. 'Even mum's wedding, I might just get a white tracksuit.'

An iconic moment in the trajectory of grime's renaissance came, ironically, with the appearance of an American rap superstar at the 2015 Brit Awards. Debuting his new track 'All Day', Kanye West was backed by a Greek chorus of about 40 men in black tracksuits and hoodies, two of them holding giant flame-throwers. Among this backing line, keen eyes noticed, were British MCs Skepta, Jammer, Shorty, Krept and Konan, Novelist, Stormzy and Fekky. It was a stage show which managed, presumably deliberately, to flush out more than a few racists; Kanye was condemned for 'promoting gang culture', according to some critics on Twitter – as if anything he has ever done has been as straightforward as that.

For many in the UK, it was a moment to be celebrated – 'Kanye brought the whole grime scene to the Brits!' was a common response – a triumphant mobbing of the stage by some of the biggest names in a scene that had for so long been ignored, humbled or watered down by the British music industry. Two fingers up to the suits, on their biggest night out of the year. The irony was simple and powerful: there was no way any of those MCs would be invited to perform on that stage under

their own steam; the British music industry had never been a meritoc-
racy, and this was further proof. The fact that the British MCs got their
'break' at the invitation of someone as flighty as Kanye didn't matter – he
recognised that they deserved to be there: it seemed that the black
Atlantic bond was stronger than black British music's foothold on its
own soil. For Wiley, enthusiastically cheering proceedings on from his
sofa, 'a statement was made', adding on Twitter, 'Kanye Knows The Brits
Ain't letting dons in there like that so he kicked off the door for us.'

What a way to use the bully pulpit, right? Not if no one really knows
you're there. 'The literally fiery performance featured Kanye with a crew
of people, all dressed in black' reported US rap magazine *Complex* to
hundreds of thousands of YouTube viewers. Some of the very people
that the likes of Skepta might have hoped to impress did not even notice
they were there, let alone use it as an entry point to discover what their
music might be like. Writing in the *Voice*, Remel London expressed
scepticism about whether this really was such a great landmark for black
British music. The performance 'helped placate my longing to see people
who look like me on stage', she wrote, '[but] why do we need validation
from a US artist on a British platform? Don't treat my brothers like
back-up dancers.' It was to be the first of several moments of deep
ambivalence about the mixed blessing of support – or co-signs, to use
what was, ironically, originally a US rap term – from American rap
superstars. At the heart of this debate was Drake, who was suddenly
posting old grime clips from *Lord of the Mics* and SBTV to his 39m
Instagram followers, adopting London 'roadman' slang ('top boy getting
waved with the man dem'), getting a BBK tattoo, and eventually
announcing he had signed to BBK in 2016 – although this turned out to
be entirely symbolic. In 2017, he announced he would be executive
producer on a new season of his favourite TV show, *Top Boy*, the grimy
London drama series starring Kano, Scorcher and Asher D.

For Novelist, at 18 the youngest of the British MCs to join Kanye
onstage, the idea of grime playing second fiddle to its multimillionaire
endorsers never occurred. Like the rest of his generation, he had been
raised on the idea of the grime scene's DIY self-sufficiency – it had

survived for almost his entire life without American patronage: why change that now? 'The US has got nothing to do with what we're doing,' he said. 'On the UK scene we take influence from each other. We're closer to bashment artists than Americans.' On the night of the show, he had been chilling in Skepta's house – the grime scene's tendency to socialise together, and for older MCs to take the youngers under their wing, was as strong as it had been when Wiley was taking Dizzee to More Fire Crew's studio in 2002 – and Kanye rang Skepta and asked 'can you get some of your guys to come down?' So Skepta brought the people he was with – the MCs. 'It was very spontaneous,' Novelist said. 'It was only an hour before the show. I liked the fact that I was onstage with people like myself in my tracksuit, that was sick.'

*

It's a mild evening in the spring of 2015, and about a thousand young Londoners, summoned only by a social media announcement made that morning, have gathered on the uneven gravel and dirt of the Holywell Lane car park in Shoreditch, beer cans and spliffs in hand, ready to go completely berserk to grime. It's a show with no tickets, no guestlist, no VIP area, and no permit, just a borrowed sound system set up on the back of a truck, parked underneath a railway overpass. The gates at the entrance have been swung shut, so scores of hyped-up fans arriving late are climbing over the 10-foot-high wire fence to get in. Police vans are parked at either end of the street, but wary of intervening. 'I gave the car park guy some money,' laughs Skepta's manager. 'He said "I don't want to know what you're doing, just lock up when you leave."' For an illegal show, it's not exactly in the most remote or covert location: the car park is five minutes from Liverpool Street station, and in the centre of London's busiest area for nightlife and youth culture – which is entirely the point.

At 8 p.m., after an escalating clamour of excitement, Skepta bounds onto the makeshift stage, wearing a long black trench-coat with the words 'anarchy is the key' written several times across the back. He is soon encouraging an already raucous crowd to raise their middle fingers to the sky and shout, 'Fuck the police!' over and over again. They are only too happy to oblige. Boy Better Know's DJ Maximum has already warmed things up with a starter-pack of raucous grime anthems. Ubiquitous crowd-pleasing instrumental 'Rebound X' is wheeled out, Jammer does 'Murkle Man', and Skepta performs 'That's Not Me'. 'It's a British thing, it's a London thing, it's a shutdown thing,' Skepta bellows. 'And we're going on until they shut us down.'

He's revving up the audience for his brand new single, 'Shutdown', a triumphant three-minute ode to his own rising profile. 'Want to know how I did it with no label, no A-list songs?/I told them: blud, I just shut-down,'[6] he spits over a grinding bassline, brash keyboard riff, and sparsely placed knock-out drums. The mosh pit erupts, and the record is pulled back. With the world watching after 'That's Not Me', Skepta's next move was vital: 'Shutdown', while not ostensibly *about* anything, managed to perfectly sum up the grime scene's mood-shift, and its renaissance – built around a trinity of self-confidence, independence, and a back-to-basics DIY aesthetic.

'They have to come on my wave,' Skepta says the next day, talking about the growing interest from the likes of Drake and Kanye: 'I understand the objective now, and like, I ain't going to fucking America to shoot a video. They need to come to the roads with me.' This was exactly what had happened with the video for 'It Ain't Safe', which was shot on the Tottenham estate Skepta grew up on, Meridian Walk – ASAP Mob's Young Lord, the guest rapper, flew in for the video, donned a tracksuit, and hung out on a north London council estate. Skepta summoned Roony Keefe to shoot the video, and asked him to bring the original *Risky Roadz* camera – 'it's got a lot more feeling,' Keefe said later. 'You can hide behind crazy studio lighting, and a load of gloss or a stage set, but put someone in front of a VHS camera and a standard lens, and you're going to get something a lot more real.'

After 40 minutes of mayhem at the 'Shutdown' guerrilla gig, the police do finally enter to break up the party, but before any names are taken or arrests are made, Skepta and BBK are already slipping offstage and disappearing into the mass of bodies and clouds of weed smoke, their mission complete.

The car park is only a five-minute walk from Cargo, the venue where Skepta launched his debut album, *Greatest Hits*, in 2007. Within three years of that gig, Cargo's management had banned DJs and promoters from booking grime acts, or even playing grime records. It is also a three-minute walk from Plastic People, the legendary basement dive once home to Rinse FM's FWD>> party, the long-running club night that helped incubate dubstep and grime, often with Skepta on the mic. Plastic People had closed in 2014, after several years of undue harassment from the police and local authorities, noise complaints from new neighbours, trumped-up charges and fans' petitions to save it. It was a new high-water mark in a tide of gentrification which turned Shoreditch into corporate-hipster ground zero, an area full of overpriced street food markets and fashion tourists, and shipping container pop-up shops for brands like Gap and Nike.

The 'Shutdown' launch had been a victory party on enemy territory, a game of capture the flag played and won, in the same renegade, DIY style that grime itself was built on. That enemy territory – for centuries, impoverished slums and textile factories – had been transformed beyond all recognition since the millennium. It's ironic that the infamous Old Nicol slum, and Charles Booth's pivotal studies of urban poverty were both located in Shoreditch too: the area that, more than any other, exemplified twenty-first-century youth culture-led gentrification (parodied in the peak New Labour-era TV series *Nathan Barley*). For better or worse, Shoreditch and Hoxton were responsible for 'east London' finally coming to symbolise something in popular vernacular beyond hardship, industry and cockney clichés: specifically, self-consciously youth-orientated, irreverent art and culture, post-everything cool, and new media and tech industries (Old Street is now 'Silicon Roundabout'): a mixture of actually existing new culture (in the gigs, clubs, clothes shops and artists' studios), and the big money corporate hipsterism that quickly swooped in to capitalise on it: expensive restaurants, members' clubs, and corporate shabby-chic enterprises like Boxpark. Ten years before the 'Shutdown' launch, Skepta spat his 'god forgive me if I buss my nine' reload bars over Skream's anthemic

'Midnight Request Line' at FWD>>, and now he was back, spitting them on the last grimey bit of land left in Shoreditch, in front of a crowd's flashing lighters and gunfingers held aloft once again.

The next day, hanging out with his team in a friend's studio, ostensibly to get advice on the structure of his forthcoming album, *Konnichiwa*, hood pulled down low over his hangover, Skepta had become obsessed with a photo posted of the gig on social media: a photo of fans climbing the ten-foot wire fence to get in. He said aloud to his manager more than once, 'We've got to do something with this picture.' I asked him why he was so fixated. 'I just feel like it captures what yesterday was about. It captured what *I'm* doing in the music industry: if you can't get in, climb the fence. I just love it man – the fact we made this happen.'

Skepta wasn't the only one from the old guard to have discovered that a dogged commitment to independence could be the key to success, and artistic fulfilment. His brother Jme, for one, had been a devout industry refusenik since the beginning – and happily so – but now it was paying off: his Boy Better Know T-shirts continued to sell out, but in ever larger quantities, to the point he eventually stopped queuing at the local Post Office to mail it to his fans and bought a 'Drop and Go' card for bulk mailing. ('They kept seeing me there, and one day one of them said "Jamie, you know you don't have to queue up every time, if you've got this much post?"') His self-released 2015 album *Integrity* went to number 12 in the charts, a remarkable achievement from an MC who rarely does interviews, or promotion of any kind. His Twitter bio at the time offered a kind of potted BBK manifesto: 'No label, No pr, No publisher, No manager, No pa, No stylist, No Instagram, No meat, No dairy, No egg & No Fluoride.' On the evening Kanye invited Skepta et al to join him onstage at the Brits, Jme was there in the Adenugas' family home too, but he'd just finished a long day in the studio, and was hungry, so he excused himself and went for a bite to eat instead – you make your own limelight, on your own terms. As one way of measuring grime's resurgence, Boy Better Know Limited's filings to Companies House record fixed assets of £11,000 in 2013, £12,000 in 2014, and £127,000 in 2015. By 2016 the crew were headlining the Wireless festival main stage in front of 50,000 people, and by 2017 headlining Glastonbury's Other Stage, and hosting an unprecedented, day-long, Boy Better Know themed 'takeover' of the biggest corporate entertainment venue in the country, the O2 complex.

BBK are the most obvious avatars of grime's DIY-led commercial resurgence, and its reach beyond the inner city to teenagers in suburbs and small towns across the country, but other first-wave MCs had seen serious financial success pushing their own merchandise brands too – Tinchy Stryder's Takeover Entertainment record label, founded as far back as 2006, was, by the time of the Brrap Pack pop moment a few years later, seeing an annual turnover worth millions, diversifying into artist management, music publishing, and doing major deals for the Star in the Hood clothing line to be stocked in hundreds of branches of JD Sports nationwide. Tinchy's business empire would eventually partner with Jay-Z's Roc Nation and EMI, relocate to Macau in China (home of various tax-avoidance schemes), and expand into headphones and other tech, via a subsidiary called Goji Electronics, co-owned with the multi-billion-pound monolith Dixons Carphone plc. It's not quite the same as the straight-edge vegan self-sufficiency of BBK, but it has certainly worked for Stryder.

Lethal Bizzle had also pursued a uniquely independent creative path since the mid-2000s, collaborating with rock bands like Gallows and Babyshambles, courting the *NME*-reading crowd and pulling in rock festival cheques when Form 696 had killed the London scene. Bizzle also developed a thriving social media 'personality brand' several years before it became de rigueur for every artist, and indeed for every faceless corporation, to follow suit: bypassing traditional media outlets and communicating directly to young fans on Snapchat, Instagram and Twitter, talking about football, cars and clothes as well as music. Being himself, but publicly. This pioneering approach helped Bizzle cut out the industry middlemen, cultivating a fanbase for his music, but also for his clothing brand Dench (a Bizzle neologism meaning, broadly, 'amazing'), which launched in 2011, with the help of his cousin, footballer Emmanuel Frimpong. He told me in 2015 that his focus had been established when

More Fire Crew were dropped by Polydor, more than a decade earlier: 'The whole journey of having to rely on other people to determine your destination, of having something and then getting it taken away from you, just made me think: I don't want to have to wait for someone else to say yes, in order for me to proceed.'

His business hustle had started when he was still at school: going to Walthamstow market to buy fake Armani jeans, and selling them on to his peers at triple the price. When we met, that summer, he was also enjoying the vindication of success entirely on his terms. He had followed his thumping single 'Rari Workout' (featuring the shy and retiring Tempz, as well as Jme) reaching number 11 in the charts by signing a deal hooking Dench Records into a collaborative deal with Virgin EMI – whereby they would take care only of the distribution. Bizzle and his team celebrated with chicken and chips, and champagne. The Dench brand moved beyond T-shirts and hoodies to bags, hats, fragrances and even children's clothes. It acquired its own warehouse and team of permanent staff, and expanded into various light-hearted experiments in hype: including a Facebook and London Underground poster campaign to get the word 'dench' in the *Oxford English Dictionary* (they succeeded with the Scrabble and Macmillan dictionaries), and an appropriately ridiculous meeting with Dame Judi Dench – the name was just a coincidence – in which the MC taught the revered actress to rap.

The problem with the renaissance narrative is that grime never vanished altogether during the 2009–14 period – and the people who were pushing the scene, developing the sound and putting in practice hours on the mic or the decks during that period felt understandably chagrined to learn that grime had suddenly come back from the dead. Indeed some people who were latterly regarded as 'veterans' only began establishing themselves during this difficult period, long after the industry had written off grime: MCs like P Money and Little Dee and DJ-producers like Spyro. Equally important was the establishment of a sustainable grassroots infrastructure, that did not look for widespread commercial success, or expect it: Jammer kept working on his *Lord of the Mics* series, generating some much-needed hype and controversy via

MC clashes; the pages of the GrimeForum kept turning; and the imagination and hard work of pillars of the scene like Elijah and Skilliam was invaluable – the two Rinse FM DJs set up a Butterz label in 2010, releasing new grime when almost no one else was, and cultivated a passionate fanbase at their often instrumental-led club nights and residencies, winning over a new generation of ravers – a hardcore who would become the nucleus of grime's fanbase when it unexpectedly exploded into the mainstream again. The rationale was that great new instrumentals were emerging thick and fast, often from bedroom producers who'd grown up on first-wave grime, didn't know any MCs, and weren't part of a crew. Grassroots independent labels, club nights and radio shows like Butterz and Boxed gave a platform (not to mention record releases) to a new generation of producers, the likes of Swindle, Royal-T, Faze Miyake, TRC, S-X, Preditah, Mr Mitch, Spyro, Slackk, Logos and Murlo, as well as releasing new material from long-standing fan favourites like Terror Danjah and Spooky.

The scene's infrastructure had been built up around these independent labels and club nights, too – not by big money invested by established titans of industry, but by young fans with the same passion for the music, and DIY spirit, that had sustained grime and its burgeoning sibling, road rap. Following in the spirit of Channel U and the grime DVD cottage industry, YouTube channels such as SBTV (970,000 subscribers at time of writing), Link Up TV (930,000) and GRM Daily (810,000) used the new medium to record MC freestyles, interviews, and eventually to produce artists' music videos too. If MTV was the evangelical tool that launched Dr Dre and Snoop Dogg into suburban households in the American midwest, these YouTube channels were, unnoticed by traditional gatekeepers, doing the same for everyone from Skepta and Stormzy to Giggs and J Hus. The possibility of instant online discovery greatly enhanced the spread of grime and UK rap beyond London, and beyond the increasingly confident scenes in Birmingham and Manchester. More than ever before, British MCs were becoming stars beyond the hood, which goes some way to explaining why grime was reaching its 'US rap in 1992' moment.

In the space of a few years, the YouTube channels started as teenage passion projects became major commercial ventures: SBTV's founder Jamal Edwards (the SB stands for Smokey Barz, his MC name) was soon a household name in his own right because of his success as an entrepreneur: appearing in adverts for Google Chrome, receiving an MBE at the age of 24, and, in 2013, partnering with investment firm Miroma Ventures, who valued the company at £8 million. GRM Daily launched their own annual awards show, the Rated Awards, with soft drinks brand Ka, and Link Up TV expanded into publishing a print magazine. What was notable, given that these three companies were ostensibly in direct competition with each other, was their determinedly collective attitude. 'Everyone that's in-charge of something in this scene right now has a role to play,' Link Up founder Rashid Kasirye told *Complex* magazine.[7] 'The Rated Awards [aren't] just GRM's – it's all of ours. The Link Up mag isn't just Link Up's – it's everyone's magazine. That's my thought process when it comes to diversifying and building that infrastructure. It's very important to support everything everyone is doing.' The imperative to 'support the scene' is so commonplace in the lexicon of grime fans and artists alike that it just sounds banal, like it has no real meaning – but few other successful genres have ever functioned on this level of instinctive collective solidarity and enterprise. It's hard to imagine Johnny Rotten talking about the vital importance of supporting and sustaining the punk scene as a whole.

The titans of industry were soon struggling to catch up with the grime scene's DIY heroes. Following the embarrassment of the Kanye episode at the Brits, the BPI, the music industry body responsible for the ceremony, loaned GRM Daily some of their team to help run the Rated Awards, and also invited GRM's founders onto the BPI's newly – some would say belatedly – formed diversity board, as well as broadening out the Brits voting panel. Other small but significant acknowledgements from mainstream gatekeepers, like iTunes giving grime its own section, distinct from 'rap' or 'electro', helped a little. Spotify, meanwhile, signed up long-standing BBC 1Xtra supremo Austin Daboh in 2016, and invested in high-profile initiatives – such as a 10,000-capacity grime and rap one-day festival at Alexandra Palace – to pull younger listeners obsessed with grime and rap away from their reliance on YouTube (teenagers are less inclined to sign up to services like Spotify, let alone pay to subscribe). 'We want to represent street culture, council-estate culture,' Daboh said.[8] 'It's not a black or white thing, it's a working-class thing embodied by people like Giggs, J Hus and Dizzee Rascal.'

In his new role at Spotify, Daboh was as optimistic about the future for British MC-led music as the artists were. This wave of interest was not comparable to the 2005 gold rush, he thought: too much had changed for the better – not just the shape of the industry itself, but the personnel in key positions. 'It's so much more sustainable this time,' he told me. 'The landscape of the gatekeepers that control the music has changed. At the point at which grime was first coming through, a decade and a half ago, it was reliant on a handful of people – literally just a couple of label bosses, a few people in radio, press and TV, and that was it: a cabal of ten or 15 people at major corporations who held the fate of grime in their hands. And if a record label boss felt as though grime wasn't the in thing, then grime wasn't going to be supported financially. My story is mirrored across the industry; so in publishing you've got people who understand and grew up in the culture, you've got people who are now running record labels who understand it. And if you look at someone like Mistajam at Radio 1, even in traditional media you've got DJs in positions of power who want to push the genre forward.'

The 'Grime Shutdown' playlist Daboh curated – named after the Skepta single, of course – was getting close to 10 million streams a month: tellingly, the top ten locations for streams included Hertfordshire and Kent, as well as London, Birmingham and Croydon. 'I think grime has kind of replaced US rap as the go-to sound for young disaffected youths of all colours, creeds and religions,' Daboh said.

And with the new zeitgeist that emerged after 'That's Not Me', other A-list MCs who had strayed began following Skepta's path back home again. Kano took it all the way back, musically, thematically and spiritually, with an entire album dedicated to his roots, *Made in the Manor*. Chip signalled his return from the world of schmaltzy pop-rap, and years collaborating with big American stars, with a number of high-profile clashes with UK MCs in 2015 and 2016, and remonstrated about his lost years with Columbia-Sony. His single 'Sonic Boom' opened with a portentous clip from *The Matrix*: 'You are a slave – you were born into bondage, born inside a prison that you cannot smell, taste, or touch,'[9] before going on to spit that the industry had 'chewed me up, then it spat me out – now I'm spitting back.' The messages, like those surrounding Roll Deep's foray into light-hearted poppy grime in 2005, were mixed. 'Bruv, no one put a gun to my head and told me to make anything,' he said subsequently of songs like 'Oopsy Daisy'. 'Every song I've done, I wanted to do.'[10]

Everyone was returning home for a bite of the fatted calf. In May 2016, lured by Red Bull (because Big Taurine had become a major player in music by this point), Dizzee Rascal performed his epochal debut album *Boy in da Corner* in full, in New York City. Scandalised that an album so decidedly about London, and so clearly a product of it, was being given this historic treatment on the wrong side of the Atlantic, a petition was started to bring the show to London, and a 7,500-capacity show was booked for later that year (and immediately sold out) in the Copperbox Arena on the Olympic site – just metres away from where Deja Vu's studio had been. I met Dizzee, rehearsing his debut in the same Bermondsey studio where he had recorded it 13 years previously. After the best part of a decade performing tracks like 'Bonkers' and 'Holiday' to festival crowds around the world, collaborating with the likes of Shirley Bassey, Robbie Williams and Shakira, he was genuinely surprised that people felt so strongly about the music he had summoned out of his troubled teenage mind.

'I was like *rah* – I didn't think it was that deep. I understand what it means now to this country. But it was never meant as a fuck you to the UK. I didn't realise they wanted it that much here.'

He was in the middle of making an album, and was knocked off-course, artistically – and maybe even existentially – by the upsurge in interest in grime. In his understanding, he had moved away from the sound of his first two albums because it didn't really make sense for him anymore. He was touring the world, playing rock festivals, and living in Miami – it would be weird, perhaps even *wrong*, for him to keep talking about depression, petty crime and high-rise tower blocks, and moreover, he didn't think people wanted to hear strange, off-kilter beats and rhymes too fast to sing along with. 'It's all crazy to me, but it seems like this is what people want,' he said, 'and it's made me think, rah, maybe I should just give them what they want? No one's in a hurry for me to fling out an album right now, and if this is what the wave is, and grime's really big right now, it's like getting a second chance to come and put your foot down, and say "This is how it started."'

One of the many things that made this renaissance remarkable, and distinct from earlier mainstream high-points for black British music – distinct from the UK garage days, or the brief grime wave of 2004–05, or the Brrap Pack in 2009–11 – was that a new generation of MCs were quickly picking up chart hits, daytime radio play and mainstream media interest without ever signing to a label at all, let alone a major label. They were bypassing the potential hindrances the industry had created in the past: pressure for artistic compromise, restrictive bureaucracy and scheduling, marketing positioning, or the threat of being sidelined in favour of more easily saleable imported American acts. The learned wisdom was that the established industry didn't understand the grime and UK rap scenes, or the appeal of the music – whereas, who understood what grime fans wanted better than the artists who had created it? The example set by the likes of Skepta, Jme and Lethal Bizzle were filtering down to the next generation: qualities of perseverance, self-knowledge and self-confidence, choosing your own path and making the most of the increasingly democratic 'distributional aesthetics'[11] of Web 2.0 and social media, where you could release music not just independently but instantaneously, and promote it through your own channels, directly to your fans.

Maybe in the future, young MCs will actually want to work with major labels, Jme said to me, trying to be even-handed – that would be their call; he wasn't about to preach how they should approach their music. 'But I'm just pleased we've given them an example of how to do it themselves,' he said, 'because, when we were coming out, there were no options. There was no choice. And that's what forced us to start going to pirate radio, to start going to raves, to start MCing in the streets and filming it ourselves, and making DVDs. We had to do that, because MTV were not putting us on their channel, Radio 1 were not putting us on their radio station. And the next generation, they can see us doing things for ourselves and achieving all this. They can look at us and say, "Rah, Skepta's got flipping, his own Nike trainers? Rah, them lot took over the whole O2? No one's took over the whole O2 before! Rah, them man headlined Wireless twice in a row? Rah, Skepta did bloody Ally Pally on his own?"

'We've let them know that, even if you haven't got any support, other than just you and your mates, that's enough.'

They were paying attention. Many of the top MCs rising to prominence in the 2010s self-released their music on their own labels – and significantly, many of them steered their way to the top with a manager who was an old friend they had come up with, rather than a long-standing experienced industry professional: including Stormzy, J Hus, Giggs, Wretch 32 and rap crew, 67.

'We're from a close friendship group where we're so similar people even say we sound alike,' Stormzy's manager Tobe Onwuka told *Music Week*. 'The beauty of it is, it never has to be that formal – some of the biggest decisions could be made over us eating Nando's.'

The no-messing-about DIY mentality of the grime scene was suddenly not just running up against the music business, but increasingly, running rings around it, resulting in some amusing culture clashes. 'Why is there so much faffing?' Onwuka asked the *Music Week* interviewer. 'I'm anti-boardrooms almost, sometimes a group text can work.'[12] Boy Better Know, similarly, continued to coordinate massive enterprises like their O2 Takeover, and a clothing collaboration with Nike, via group chat on their mobile phones.

For all this DIY hustle and self-sufficiency, the artists weren't operating in creative silos, working for themselves and themselves alone – Wiley's approach of 'running things like a youth club' still held: a network of artists hanging out (as so many of them were, in the Adenugas' house, on a random Wednesday evening in February when Kanye texted), endlessly collaborating and sharing ideas, inspiration and contacts. I have never encountered any other group of people, in the smartphone era, who still use the telephone to *phone* each other, so much and so often – often short calls, but with incredible regularity. It's part of an ethic of getting shit done, not leaving possible collaborations, ideas or messages hanging, not leaving anything to chance. Skepta told me in 2015 he talked to Wiley 'every day'.

At that point, Novelist was recording and performing with his Lewisham crew The Square. In their early and mid-teens – i.e. the early 2010s – it had been 'kind of uncool to be doing grime', he told me; the slower, gritty nihilism of road rap was in the ascendant, using YouTube instead of pirate radio. But grime was more their speed, so they assembled a crew of all the local MCs who wanted to spit on grime, and bunked off school to write beats and bars, saving their pocket money to record in local 'bedroom studios' for £10 an hour, honing their skills. Novelist would eventually go solo, but at this critical stage, a revival of the collective mentality was working well for them. 'It's good because you get energy from the people in your crew,' he said. 'I know this might sound funny, but you've got more to live for as well, when you've got guys to support. It's quite communal.'

The feedback loop of inspiration and hype that came from honing their raw talent together harked back to grime's first wave, and would, a couple of years later, come through in the tightly knit web of south London's drill-rap crews. There was still great value in standing together, on the margins, united against more powerful foes and institutions. 'The music I make is rebellious,' Novelist said: 'Fuck the feds, fuck the government, big up the man dem. That's where the energy comes from.'

As 2015 proceeded, the increasingly intertwined grime and rap scenes seemed to be undergoing something like a mass epiphany, and the infectious confidence imparted from elders like Skepta, Jme and Wiley were resonating ever louder with an energetic new generation. Hotly tipped young MCs like Stormzy had built up a huge head of steam without any of the old 'raves, radio, riddims' infrastructure: but instead, with a series of videoed freestyles delivered in parks and car parks, over classic early instrumentals made when he was still in primary school: Ruff Sqwad's 'Pied Piper' and Jme's 'Serious'. 'I was on the roads when Dizzee made "I Luv U"', he spat on his breakthrough single, 'Know Me From' – in fact, he would have been eight years old, so 'on the swings' might be more accurate. By the time of his freestyle 'Wicked Skengman 4', later in 2014, he was surrounded not just by his crew, but Section Boyz, Krept, comedian Michael Dapaah (aka Big Shaq), and fans who had travelled from around the country. 'Man are saying that I blew up too fast, man are saying that I came up too quick,' he mocked; 'Rudeboy, look on the YouTube, darg: man dem are putting in the graveyard shift.'[13] He had done his Web 2.0-enabled practice hours: churning out low-key hood singles and road freestyles on SBTV five years earlier, in 2010, when he was still barely 17.

In person, Stormzy was full of the effervescence that comes with knowing everyone is hyping you as the 'next to blow', mixed with the innate good humour that would help make him such a huge star. 'I don't want to take my foot off the gas,' he said when we met early in 2015, 'you have the breakthrough year, and that's sick, but I want to have another breakthrough year.' He had nothing but admiration for the pioneering MCs he had grown up listening to, but he also knew he was a new breed: that the rules had changed. 'Even Chipmunk, Ice Kid and Griminal are like three or four years older than me, and they were the *youngers*,' he emphasised. 'They were the last of that pirate-radio era. I was in the playground spitting lyrics over mobile phones: Sony Ericssons, Walkmans, W810is, the Teardrop Nokia phones, all of that Bluetooth infrared. Vital equipment! I missed the vinyl era too. I knew about it all, but I didn't ever get to experience it. I never had a DJ set where a DJ's playing vinyl and I'm spitting. I was MCing in the playground instead.'

This new generation had seen the remarkable journey to redemption their elders had been on, and it was having a huge effect on their mentality. There was an emerging piece of received wisdom that black British music had finally emerged from the shadow of the American rap imports that had loomed over the 1990s and early 2000s. Even Krept and Konan, who made rap music at US tempos, took their first MC inspiration to pick up the mic from So Solid, before they'd even hit their teens. 'I wanted to be one of the So Solid Kids,' Krept told me – 'you couldn't get any cooler than the "21 Seconds" video.' Likewise, Fuse ODG, who had four Top 10 singles in 2013–14 with his poppy iteration of Afrobeats, told me he started rapping by practising So Solid lyrics and recording them to tape in his bedroom, too. By the mid-2010s, a thousand flowers were blooming from the roots of London's pirate radio heyday.

'The Americans have their way of talking, their way of dressing, their way of doing things, and we have ours,' Stormzy said, gesturing to Krept and Konan and Lil Simz in the background. 'This whole UK underground thing has become sick, because everyone from the ends has finally said, "Yeah yeah, Drake is sick – but we're sick as well." People ask me, "Who's your favourite rapper of all time?" and I know they're expecting a Biggie, or a Nas, or a Tupac, but I say, "You know what, my favourite rapper of all time is Skepta, or Wiley." Because *these* are the guys over here. Who's the best up and coming talent? It's not flippin' Chance The Rapper, or Kendrick Lemar, or whoever's coming out of America – it's flippin' … it's me! It's Novelist. It's Lil Simz. We've got our own thing going on over here, that we need to focus on, and nurture.'

A decade after Kano had wondered aloud if the underground could go mainstream, and a decade after most critics, and the British music industry, had held its sides and belly laughed its way through a resounding 'no', the most unlikely of revivals had occurred – and it was built on the astonishing perseverance and DIY hustle of musicians defiantly charting their own course, to reach far beyond inner-city London with a sound and a personality that was completely unique to it. And when you've realised that you can thrive artistically, reach new fans, and even make a decent living, without compromising one bit, entirely on your own terms, with your own team, why would you ever do it any other way? Something monumental had changed in the grime scene, and it would change black underground music's terms of engagement with the wider world – indeed it would change British pop culture – forever.

'It's about confidence,' said Stormzy, confidently. 'It's like everyone's just clocked at once: hang on, fuck *that*, we're sick – *we* are sick. My tracksuit is sick. My grime freestyle is sick. The way I do things is sick. And when you have that self-confidence and that belief, it just oozes onto people. It's really authentic – and the energy is right.'

THIRTEEN

THE REAL PRIME MINISTERS

By the start of 2016, the grime scene was garnering attention far beyond the manor. In January, a new head of BBC Radio 1 and 1Xtra was appointed. Chris Price, like his predecessor of ten years, George Ergatoudis, was keen to emphasise his support for grassroots British music in interviews: in particular, he wanted to talk about grime. In an interview with the *Guardian* upon taking over, Price suggested that 2016 would be a turning point for the genre: that after years of unfulfilled potential, with albums from Skepta and Stormzy on the way, it could become the UK's next 'big cultural export … our hip-hop'. It was important, he said, that the world – pointed the right way by the likes of Drake and Kanye – suddenly seemed to be watching. Crucially for its long-term sustainability, it had finally reached the suburbs in significant numbers, just like rap did in the US. Grime was suddenly hailed as a proudly British triumph by cultural gatekeepers and politicians, after they had spent years blaming its protagonists for urban unrest and social decay.

When Skepta won the 2016 Mercury Prize for *Konnichiwa* it confirmed a perfect redemption story – that through its independence, grime had finally thrived on its own terms, a decade after it had supposedly been

Jeremy Corbyn poses with Jme during the 2017 general election campaign

killed off for good. 'I really did this for people to see freedom,' he said on receiving the award – he wanted to inspire others to reject the industry as well. 'I want this to get into people's heads. This is real. I'm not signed. This is independent.' Tory Culture Minister Matt Hancock met Skepta at the Mercury after-party, and told the *Daily Mirror* that he and his team listened to grime in the back of the ministerial car – though asked to name his favourite track, he couldn't think of a single one, and turned to his aide for help. Hancock went on to spin grime's resurgence as a triumph of Thatcherite values: 'He tells a story of his background, but the thing that excites me is he can break through. I don't like to wallow in poverty. I think wherever you come from, you can make it. Grime represents modern Britain – the entrepreneurial, go-getting nature. It speaks that wherever you come from you can make it.' (Hancock, to his credit, had never wallowed in poverty, doggedly building a political career in spite of the hindrances of a £13,000-a-year private school and degrees from both Oxford and Cambridge.)

This kind of desperate lunge for the bandwagon only served to highlight how fast it was moving. Just when it seemed like Britain's last big pirate radio sound had spluttered its last, it came back stronger than ever before. Grime's revival and meteoric rise since 2014 was as unexpected as it was overwhelming. Even prior to Skepta's Mercury win, the scene's resurgence was deemed newsworthy in its own right: there were items on both Channel 4 and *BBC News at Six*. 'It's bold, it's British, it's driven by social media, and it's taking the world by storm,' ran BBC News anchor Sophie Raworth's opening to the four-minute news package, introducing relative newcomers Elf Kid and Lady Leshurr to the nation's viewers, as well as Mercury nominees Skepta and Kano. Leshurr told the BBC reporter what was now becoming a piece of received wisdom: that social media had transformed things for aspiring artists – that autonomy came from having 'all your supporters in your phone'.

With new levels of success come new audiences – for better, and sometimes worse. Everyone had a damn good laugh when the *Evening Standard* published its review of Skepta's landmark homecoming show at Alexandra Palace (ten years earlier he had delivered bars reminiscing about being an 'Ally Pally jungle raver' as a teen). The reviewer didn't understand what a rewind was, and thought they had been technical hitches. 'Frustratingly,' wrote John Aizlewood, 'not everything went to plan: songs were re-started ... and the audience sloped home unsatisfied.' While some of the older members of her majesty's press were trying to catch up with decades of Jamaican music heritage, and the pop zeitgeist, all at once, beneath the surface, some invisible shifts were occurring in the tectonic plates of British pop culture. While the structure of Skepta's performance might have confused a middle-aged rock critic, it didn't confuse the 10,000 or so mostly new, very young fans present; the same generation that were buying the tickets to Kano's, Wiley's and Dizzee's sold-out shows, or who made Stormzy a superstar before he'd released an album, or who propelled Jme and Skepta's records to numbers 12 and 2 respectively.

The live scene was suddenly flourishing, and a decade of practice hours, combined with the surging mainstream interest in them as pop stars, set the scene perfectly. Skepta was booked for a coveted and unprecedented slot on Glastonbury's Pyramid Stage that summer, and 'wanted to bring his world with him', Boy Better Know's long-standing live booking agent Rebecca Prochnik recalled: to that end, they built a festival-sized stage set with a CCTV rig, a London phone box and a street scene reminiscent of a *Risky Roadz* or *Practice Hours* DVD freestyle.[1] 'It was a lovely punk moment in a universe of anodyne predictability ... (the) zeitgeist isn't something you can plan. The floodgates opened for the scene afterwards, everyone's getting booked for places they've never been booked before. It was a real "you can" moment.'

Grime had become established as a festival soundtrack – even if some of its least musically interesting iterations were the ones that worked particularly well: the jump-up, chant-along choruses of tracks like Solo 45's brainless 'Feed Em To The Lions' fulfilled the same kind of role that nu-metal once had, in terms of offering 20,000 festival-goers some cheap headbanging thrills. But this only constituted a minority of the songs, and they were getting paid – and getting to play live – at last, after decades of being effectively barred from performing by racist policing, and struggling to eke slivers of CD-mixtape income off a generation raised on Limewire, BitTorrent and later YouTube and Spotify. It is hard to compute how occasional Ruff Sqwad member XTC must have felt, seeing tens of thousands of Glastonbury revellers joining Stormzy in a singalong of the melody from his cult 2004 B-side 'Functions On The Low' on the BBC, 13 years later – but it was a marker of how far grime had come.

Substantial sold-out London concerts and nationwide tours became the norm, subverting Form 696 by appearing at venues run by large entertainment chains, who had their own arrangements with the police, in a concert rather than a club slot (since 696 was only supposed to apply to DJ and MC nights 10 p.m–4 a.m.). At his headline shows at Koko and the Roundhouse, Wiley's audience were split 10:90 between ageing pirate-era fans in their late thirties (as he was too), and 16–22-year-olds of all races, though predominantly white. In 2017 he was asked about whether he considered grime to be black music. 'Predominantly black, yeah. The raves were all black. When it went white, I was a bit shocked. I love whoever loves grime – you could be black, blue, pink. But when that happened I was like, "Wow, where have all the black people gone?"'

While the likes of BBK were playing to massive festival crowds, some of the other 'day one's who hadn't seen much of a mic in the intervening decade or more decided to pick it up again. In 2017, Sharky Major started a night called Grime Originals, with a line-up packed with pirate radio legends, some of whom hadn't been heard from much in years – MCs like Jamakabi, Nasty Jack, Bruza, Jookie Mundo, Lioness and Fuda Guy – at a tiny underground dive venue called Birthdays. 'Many, including myself, fell off for a while and some never returned,' Sharky Major reflected later that year, explaining his motivation. He was happy for the success of the likes of Stormzy, he said, and appreciated that the game had changed since the pirate days, but wanted to remind people that the genre 'grew from the bars and instrumentals': from a different, more organic kind of live energy than a pre-ordained setlist of clearly demarcated, already-familiar *songs*.[2]

On Grime Originals' third outing, on a hot Sunday night in July 2017, a crowd of less than a hundred gathered for exactly this kind of 'rollage', and the vibe was exuberantly old school – energetic, joyous, unpretentious – as MCs hovered with intent, passing the mic as DJs mixed and blended the instrumentals. Though not billed, Jammer, D Double E, Riko Dan and Skepta also showed up, with no fanfare, to spit their reload bars, just like they would have done in the old days. Skepta's presence felt particularly poignant, simply because, the previous night, he had headlined Wireless in front of a sell-out crowd of 37,500 revellers in a north London park. Now he was spitting to about 80 people in a windowless basement with a low ceiling, with 17 people crammed onto the tiny stage, one MC for every four punters. When he'd done some of his classic bars, Jammer – always the scene's cheerleader and champion, as much as its participant – stood on the side of the stage watching his peers as the mic was passed, every 16 or 32 bars – he was grinning blissfully, hands in prayer-pose as if in worship of the microphone itself.

'Birthdays was a spur of the moment thing,' said D Double E, who turned up that night with Skepta, 13 years after he had appeared on the latter's 'Thuggish Ruggish' 12-inch – but it was also emblematic of the prevailing attitude: a fervent need to 'stay connected to the ground, and represent something that is a part of the music's history, something that helped the growth of a community. 'Them things there are *earthly*,' D Double said. At all these shows, there was a striking unity: a manifestation of the pass-the-mic, finish-each-other's-bars pirate radio and rave mentality that was intrinsic to the genre's early development – and perhaps also a mitigation of the agoraphobia that would come otherwise. Staying humble, or earthly, was a pressing concern. 'Boy better know man went to the Brits on the train,' Skepta spat on the title track from *Konnichiwa*, 'Think it's a game?/Man shut down Wireless, then I walked home in the rain.'[3]

In the summer of 2017, Boy Better Know took over the entire O2 complex – the corporate mega-venue formerly known as the Millennium Dome – and put on a multi-faceted one-day festival that filled not just the 20,000-capacity main arena, but its many side-rooms, alcoves and cubby holes too; everything but the Harvester and the All Bar One. There was a five-a-side football competition, an outdoor stage for up-and-coming MCs and DJs, a 'tropical' roller disco with legendary DJs like Todd Edwards and new favourites like TQD, film screenings, and the opportunity to play computer games against Jme. For the main arena show, Boy Better Know's DJ Maximum had been responsible for managing the Boy Better Know setlist – just like at a Sidewinder or Eskimo Dance in 2003, the DJ was ultimately in control of proceedings: they brought out guests Lethal Bizzle, Giggs and Drake. 'Obviously you've got to be pretty selective about what tunes you're going to do,' Maximum said afterwards. 'It's a bit of a negotiation, like, "I want to perform that tune", "Nah, you're not performing that one." The timing has to be perfect. We go into it with the same mentality as an old-school grime rave though.' While the mindset informing the stagecraft was the same, the presence of nine-year-old children in baggy Wiley T-shirts, accompanied by their parents, on a nice Sunday outing on a bank holiday weekend, was, it is fair to say, somewhat different. Even a couple of years prior, it was an utterly inconceivable concept. 'Hard work pays off,' Jme announced to the sell-out crowd, introducing his song 'Work'. It was difficult to disagree.

With commercial chart success came ever wider cultural influence: following the *Daily Telegraph*'s earlier adventures in embarrassing themselves, glossaries of grime slang cropped up across the media, from American rap magazines to the *Sunday Times*, to academic website the *Conversation* – with varying levels of accuracy and cringeworthiness. 'Know your Wasteman from your Roadman?' asked the *Daily Mail*. 'As grime music takes the world by Storm(zy), a guide to how YOU can keep up with today's underground lingo.'

The commenters were unsurprisingly unimpressed. 'No thank you, the Queens English is good enough for me,' was one of the more polite responses. It did at least give linguistics professors the chance to talk about MLE (Multicultural London English) in the press – and even to argue that its spread beyond London meant it might now better be referred to as 'Urban *British* English, a "multiethnolect", as even young people far away from London are often familiar with some of the core terms, such as peng and creps.'[4] Linguists had been noting white working-class schoolchildren in London using 'recreolised lexis' (or 'Jafaican', or 'blaccents', in press shorthand) back in the 1990s, but, given a wider platform through grime and its pop cultural siblings in the 2000s, it spread outwards to young people beyond – until *Daily Mail* journalists were lamenting in print that their children were using 'alien' language, 'indecipherable code-speak … delivered in an accent I could only place as somewhere between south London, downtown Los Angeles and Kingston, Jamaica. It certainly isn't indigenous to our home village of Ashtead, in the rolling Surrey hills.'[5] When Stormzy called Theresa May a 'paigon' at the 2017 GQ awards, former New Labour spin doctor Alastair Campbell misunderstood it as 'pig', later apologising for his confusion, adding that it was 'good to learn new words'. The BBC's *Daily Politics* programme ran an audience quiz the next day, asking what he had called her: peng, paigon, mandem or bossman. 'You lot are so embarrassing,' responded Stormzy on Twitter. 'Young black men have a vocabulary that spans beyond those buzz words.'

While this collision of the ends with the mainstream threw up new tensions, and misunderstandings, an atmosphere of overdue arrival, or of closure even, seemed to pervade the elder statesmen of the scene. It was appropriate that after 11 official studio albums and somewhere between 14 and 29 mixtapes (depending on how you count them), not to mention Roll Deep's output and countless vinyl releases, Wiley was putting out an album worthy of his talent at last, and at this point – it was even called *The Godfather*, as if to mark his graduation, and recognition beyond the faithful. When I went to interview him for the fifth time, in August 2016, even after all these changes, he was still putting his album together in a makeshift homemade studio in someone's flat, in a humble terraced house in Hackney, sitting on a plastic fake leather sofa, and arranging his own press via text message. He has always been philosophical, but there was a lot more to be philosophical about this time. Wiley spent large portions of the interview talking down his own work, and strategy, and declining to claim credit for 'carrying the whole scene on my back', as he once spat – or for having predicted grime would succeed eventually, as he had done a decade earlier. 'It's not a fad, obviously,' Wiley said, 'and it will get taken more seriously this time, because it's persevered.' He was happy to be playing 'the Zidane role' – *he wasn't 19 anymore*, he kept emphasising, and it was 'time to let the ball do the work' – pulling strings and controlling the play. 'I'm not going to break my neck about this,' he said, as we discussed his tendency to 'push the button marked PANIC' and rush-release another mixtape or six. 'There are periods of time where less is more.' But he was looking back on 15 years of grime, and 20 or more making music – trying to get a sense of it all, forensically studying his own back catalogue, and others – in particular Skepta's *Konnichiwa* – to try and ascertain what worked, and what didn't. Grime, he reflected, had been a happy accident. 'It's music that was trying to be garage, that didn't actually fit in. But we carried on, we made the beats that we wanted to spit on, and now we're sitting on top of everything.'

His album reflected this sense of composure, and self-knowledge. The lead single, 'Bring Them All/Holy Grime', featuring Devlin as guest MC, one of his many former lyrical opponents, was a triumphant announcement of this belated confidence, on a bombastic instrumental jointly produced by Mr Virgo and Preditah. The latter had only released his first production in 2011, itself almost a decade after 'Eskimo' and 'Pulse X'. Even though Wiley was 'letting the ball do the work', and slowing down a little, there was no prospect that *The Godfather* was a retirement album – from the figure who had stuck with grime through thick and thin, who was still releasing grime albums in 2010 when almost everyone else had given up. 'Wiley's dream has always been that grime would be taken seriously,' his oldest collaborator Target said to me. 'That grime artists could just come through and do as well as any other genre artist. That was always Wiley's thing. And because Wiley can see it's actually happening now, with Skepta, Stormzy, Kano's back, all the new exciting artists – there's no way he's not going to be involved in that happening.'

Recognition is all the sweeter when it's been deferred for such a ludicrously long time. In 2015 the MOBOs unveiled a Wiley plaque in the pavement outside Bow School, where he and his father had both attended, paying tribute to him for 'Paving the Way' for the next generation – he hadn't even received a single MOBO Award until 2013, as a measure of how seriously even the black music establishment had taken grime over the preceding decade (the MOBOs changed their annual Hip Hop award to 'Hip Hop/Grime' in 2010 – the winners were the not-very-grimy Professor Green, Tinie Tempah, Plan B and then Tinie Tempah again, before grime was finally given its own standalone award in 2014). In 2017 Wiley won the Outstanding Contribution to Music prize at the *NME* Awards and the Innovation In Sound prize at the *Q* Awards – two publications who had barely acknowledged his existence prior to this point – and in the 2018 New Year's honours, he was awarded an MBE.

A few years earlier, there had even been a petition proposing a statue of Wiley be erected in Bow, receiving 5,000 signatures and a great deal of press attention. He waved it away. 'Look, a statue in anyone's area, you're gonna have to be in some war – not a lyrical war! – like a war hero, you know for your country, in a tank; you've lost a leg or something deep.' He was typically self-effacing about the idea of taking sole credit for a scene built by a community; one reliant on the musicians who didn't ever make it, as much as the ones who did. 'I would rather people treat it like a shrine to grime,' he told me. 'You know that picture of me and Dizzee sitting outside the three flats? That should be the statue. I don't want to sit here and say I single-handedly carried hundreds of kids onto the moon. I worked with everyone – and some of us blew, and some of us never.'

The brands were coming calling too. High-street clothing chain H&M stocked T-shirts with *GRIME* emblazoned on them; Skepta became Uniqlo's cultural ambassador, and also partnered with Levis, Selfridges and Sports Direct (drinking out of their mugs in the video for 'It Ain't Safe', and wearing a Sports Direct T-shirt to perform), as well as designing his own Nike Air Max shoe, the SkAIR. Ghetts advertised Clarks shoes, Wiley worked with Puma, and Stormzy, extensively, with Adidas – indeed, his involvement was so substantial that when Paul Pogba signed to Manchester United for a world-record fee of £89 million, the transfer was announced by an exclusive video featuring the two of them.[6] AJ Tracey launched the Tottenham Hotspurs kit for Nike with a special gig, Tinchy Stryder collaborated with Premier Inn, producing a new track in one of their new hotel rooms, and Chip, Kano and Wretch 32 did the same for KFC, producing a music video in an hour, as part of their campaign to 'pack more into lunch'. Lethal Bizzle loaned his song 'Dude', and some of grime's anti-establishment essence, to processed-meat producer Mattessons, for an excruciating campaign called 'the Snackarchist', about a rebellious nerdy white boy who likes processed meat snacks: 'no one tells him what to chew', indeed.

In 2016, as part of their expansion beyond the simple if highly controversial business of renting out rooms and apartments to tourists – in a city beset by an ever-worsening housing crisis – Airbnb began offering a £190, three-day 'grime experience' to visitors to London, with a dedicated tour guide who would introduce them to a grime producer, take them out to clubs and show them what remained of the grimy inner city. Parts of London once deemed 'no-go areas' by a certain section of the population were now deemed worthy of visiting for exactly the same reason. The moment in *Withnail and I* when Danny intones sadly, 'They're selling hippie wigs in Woolworth's, man,' had arrived for grime, as it does for all genres that cross over.

Such was the commercial potential that in August 2017, *Music Week* ran a special issue devoted to – as the cover put it – The Business of Grime, which congratulated the scene on 'tearing music industry traditions apart while bursting further into the mainstream than ever before'. *GQ* magazine produced a 20-minute documentary, also called *The Business of Grime* – which benefited from having the likes of Ruff Sqwad and Lethal Bizzle at the front and centre, explaining just how grassroots and DIY the industry had been in the early days. Everyone wanted the recipe for the genre's magic potion. Red Bull and Vice made a series of documentaries about grime's phoenix-like rise, as did Channel 4 and the BBC. And even though corporate endorsements, sponsorships and partnerships were supposed to be the main source of income in the digital age, where 'most of us make our money out of thin air', the actual sales of the music were flourishing too. In June 2017, music industry body the BPI published a report which found that grime sales and streams across all formats had risen a staggering 93 per cent in the previous year, massively outperforming the rest of the market (which had seen an increase in sales of 6 per cent overall). It was no wonder that the music business was interested at last – it wasn't just a distracting fad, but a fillip for the entire industry. 'It's not only helping to shape domestic consumption and trends, it is becoming a flag-bearer for Britain's global reputation as a hub of musical innovation,' said the chief executive of the BPI, Geoff Taylor. 'Grime sales are officially doing a madness', ran the GRM Daily headline. It certainly helped grime's status as a national treasure, rather than a London one, that bubbling underground scenes in other British cities were producing their own crossover stars, and the success of MCs like Bugzy Malone from Manchester and Lady Leshurr from Birmingham were inspiring other local talents.[7]

In its breakdown of the newfound commercial success of grime, *Music Week* noted that Skepta's *Konnichiwa* (140,000 copies sold at that point, 15 months after release) and Stormzy's *Gang Signs & Prayer* (200,000 after just six months) were both released independently, on Boy Better Know and Merky, respectively – but both were signed to 'label services' deals, a kind of industry bolt-on of all the admin, distribution and fiddly bits, but with zero label intervention in the creative process. 'They give you all the infrastructure you want from a label but they're not there to A&R things,' John Woolf, Wiley's manager told the magazine. It was the same deal with Wiley's *The Godfather* album. It was a way of maintaining total artistic independence, but maximising the reach of the music by using the industry's infrastructure.

Grime had come to dominate the worlds of marketing and fashion, the live-music scene they had been shut out from, and the music industry that had forsaken them. And then, in what would turn out to be a cataclysmic decision, in April 2017, Conservative Prime Minister Theresa May called a snap general election, with the aim of shoring up her flimsy Brexit negotiating position, and destroying a crisis-hit Labour

Party in the same move. The grime scene had other ideas. With Jeremy Corbyn's newly left-wing Labour Party beginning the election campaign a staggering 24 per cent behind the Conservatives in the opinion polls, and with the press and the majority of Corbyn's own MPs against him, it was going to need an almost inconceivable turnaround for Labour to avoid shedding scores, possibly hundreds of seats, and wiping out the British left for decades. To make matters worse, Corbyn's apparent strength, his popularity with the young people who wore bootleg Corbyn Nike T-shirts, or called him a legend on Twitter, was derided as a hollow consolation – because they wouldn't bother to vote, when the vital day came, let alone unplug themselves from social media for long enough to campaign for him. In the previous general election, two years earlier, only 43 per cent of 18–24-year-olds had voted, compared to a national figure of 66 per cent.

Within a few days of the election announcement, a surprising cascade of endorsements followed, from grime MCs and DJs instructing their followers to vote Labour – in some cases, specifically for Corbyn. Support from Novelist was not surprising – he had been Deputy Young Mayor of Lewisham as a 16-year-old, and had already publicly announced he had joined the Labour Party; when Corbyn was under pressure from his own MPs to stand down in 2016, he tweeted directly to the leader of the opposition: 'Do not resign, the mandem need you'. Novelist had made anti-Tory songs and led chants of 'Fuck David Cameron' at raves. The best of his political tracks, 'Street Politician', gave a typically powerful, if bleak account of 'black boys stuck in the system', set to swirling police sirens. Initially, Novelist had seemed like an outlier: grime had long been political music, but artists had rarely voiced opinions on British party politics or elections – the political classes were wilfully detached from grime's milieu, and dismissive of the 'real Prime Ministers' who Lethal Bizzle had spoken of in 2011, never mind their music. MCs like Durrty Goodz, Bashy, Jammer and Ghetts (who once sampled Martin Luther King's 'I have a dream' speech and Dire Straits on the same song) had long ago made homages to figures such as Malcolm X, Marcus Garvey and Nelson Mandela in their bars, but contemporary politicians and the grime scene had always held each other in mutual contempt.

But the tectonic plates of British culture and society had shifted – grime had ascended from the underground to become a new form of pop culture, and Jeremy Corbyn was a new kind of political leader. The specific appeal of Corbyn to the grime scene – a teetotal, vegetarian, 68-year-old cyclist who spent his spare time tending his allotment; on the face of it, somewhat apart from his new cheerleaders – was owing to a shared spirit. He had a down-to-earth sensibility that was familiar – he knew inner-city London, he understood poverty and marginality, and he listened when ordinary people told him their problems. 'I know people who Corbyn has personally intervened to help, writing support- ing letters to help with housing, immigration and other legal matters,' Ruff Sqwad's Slix said, explaining his reason for voting Labour – Slix's cousin was one of Corbyn's constituents in Islington. 'He has been putting in a lot of work at a community level for many, many years.' Something about his durability and authenticity chimed with the perse- verance and self-belief of the grime scene at this point in its history, too. 'He has been on the backbench not seeking power for 30 years,' wrote Novelist during the election campaign. 'For him standing up for what's right is more important than promotion.'

The likes of Plastician, Logan Sama and Big Zuu joined in the calls to vote Labour. Jme explained to his 700,000 Twitter followers how to register to vote for Corbyn. Hackney rapper Professor Green did the same to his 700,000 Instagram followers, and MC and self-described 'third-world internationalist' Akala wrote a piece for the *Guardian* drawing out another key side of the Labour leader's appeal: that 'for those of us that still have family in the global south', Corbyn's anti-apart- heid history and anti-war, anti-racist approach to foreign policy marked a break with Labour's past as an unapologetic party of empire. As a result, Akala explained that he would be voting in a general election for the first time in his life. Young MC AJ Tracey went one step further, and made an official Labour campaign video, grinning broadly as he talked about how Labour would 'support the youth', defend the NHS and build new council homes, before lamenting the massive tuition-fee debt he had incurred doing a criminology degree. (Labour had pledged to abolish tuition fees.)

After the rush of endorsements, and a rush of media interest, there was a note of caution. Jme, who had previously worn a T-shirt with the slogan 'David Cameron hates the mandem', backed away from endorsing a particular party, saying he wanted everyone to do their own research and come to their own decision – it was a smart move, given that he was already attracting a lot of unwanted attention: a *Daily Mail* hit-piece on the MC soon followed. But the link had been made, and activist-fans proceeded to take it into their own hands: the Twitter hashtag #grime4corbyn went viral, and a new website, grime4corbyn.com, compiled the many MC and DJ endorsements together, with a new 'Corbyn Riddim' that sampled speeches from the Labour leader, and promised free tickets to a secret grime show for anyone registering to vote. On the same day it launched, halfway through the campaign, Jme went to meet the Labour leader for a high-profile filmed conversation about youth engagement with politics. They talked about giving young people the space to be creative – but also about poverty, education and housing. 'Political change doesn't always come from politicians, does it?' Corbyn asked, and the Tottenham MC agreed. The grassroots energy that had brought both men to that cafe table in Islington seemed to suggest that he was right – and grime's DIY spirit was to prove incredibly influential in the campaign. The initial rallying call was around youth voter registration: the surge to get young people registered before the 22 May deadline was phenomenally successful, with about a million people under 25 registering to vote in a matter of weeks.[8]

Unofficial 'Vote Labour' posters appeared in London featuring photos of AJ Tracey, Jme, Akala, Novelist and Corbyn – and an image of a tweet from Akala that read, 'Homie Jeremy Corbyn was anti-apartheid back when the Tories had Mandela down as a terrorist. Safe.'

Stormzy, the big star of the moment, the MC with the first ever number-one grime album, had enthusiastically praised 'My man, Jeremy!' in an interview in 2016, saying that 'he gets what the ethnic minorities are going through and the homeless and the working class'. But the coverage that followed made him play down the connection, and he stayed quiet throughout the 2017 election campaign. In Stormzy's hometown of Croydon, where one local constituency was a fiercely contested marginal seat, unofficial leaflets started appearing across the borough, featuring an image of the MC, and an entirely unofficial message. 'The Tories hold Croydon by 165 votes (that's literally it). Even your dad's got more Facebook friends. Stormzy says VOTE LABOUR.' Stormzy didn't comment, and behind the scenes, his lawyers quietly sent a cease-and-desist letter. But it didn't matter: the other MCs' spontaneous support, the DIY posters and the online #grime4corbyn campaign had generated its own headlines across the mainstream press, becoming one of the key themes of the campaign – like grime itself, starting out as something organic and networked, and filtering up into traditional media institutions. 'What we've done is reach into a cultural hinterland that's never been reached before by political parties. There's something happening,' Corbyn said in an interview with grassroots football website Copa90 on Hackney Marshes, with one week to go. 'There are people on the street talking about him constantly – people I've never known to be interested in politics before,' P Money observed.[9] 'Last week, every day I was getting Whatsapp messages from people going: "Vote Corbyn! Vote Corbyn!" I've never known anything like it before.'

When the results came in on the night of 8 June 2017, it was a political earthquake, the most remarkable turnaround in post-war British history. Labour had surpassed all expectations – narrowing a 24 per cent poll deficit at the start of the campaign to just 2 per cent – and while Labour still lost the election, they had actually won seats, humbling Theresa May's Conservatives, and depriving them of a majority in parliament. 'Give yourselves a pat on the back,' Jme responded, imploring his followers to stay involved in politics. Novelist did the same, telling them to find out their MPs' details, contact them and get involved in their local communities: 'It doesn't stop at voting,' he said. It had been an election in which grime could very plausibly be said to have made the difference.

Turnout nationally was at a 25-year high – and this was driven by an unprecedented surge of young and BAME voters. Ipsos Mori polling suggested the 18–24 vote increased 16 percentage points on 2015, while turnout among BAME Britons increased 6 points: the substantial majority of new voters, those who had not voted in the 2015 election, had chosen Labour.[10]

In Croydon Central, home of the unauthorised Stormzy leaflets, Sarah Jones won her seat from the former Conservative Housing Minister Gavin Barwell with a 9.7 per cent swing, turning a deficit of 165 votes into a 7,000 majority. Jones was by no means a Corbyn supporter, coming from the opposite wing of the Labour Party, but she explained that it was unofficial, grassroots peer-to-peer campaigning, and Corbyn's popularity with previous non-voters, which had made the difference. 'It was a completely different kind of campaign,' she told me afterwards. Visiting Croydon College the day after the election, she asked the young students what had motivated them to vote. 'They said they really liked Corbyn because he had stuck to his guns for so long, for so many years, that he'd been out campaigning against apartheid years and years ago.' She asked where they had got their information. 'Snapchat – they all said Snapchat! In Croydon there were people putting out leaflets to young people, and putting things on social media, that were nothing to do with the Labour Party. There was a reach beyond what we would normally be capable of: lots of young people voted in this election, and we didn't talk to all those people.'

Not everyone in the grime scene had been on board. A few protective fans thought political activists had co-opted grime's popularity for their own ends (spurious, given that it had begun with a spontaneous flurry of endorsements from the musicians themselves). Skepta, meanwhile, seemed to fall out with his brother during a BBK group interview later that summer: it was the first time the two had discussed Jme's meeting with Corbyn, and Skepta stood by his insistence on not listening to 'no politician', as he had said on 'Shutdown': 'You know why grime exists? Because of the pain that they've put us through,' he said. 'That makes me sick. Everyone was telling everyone, all the youth to "vote for my man".

I'm not watching them, I'm laughing at them, bruv ... Everybody should run theirself.'[11]

Jme dismissed his brother's nihilistic, libertarian attitude. Dropping out and condemning all political activity was a cop out, he said. 'I'm all right if the NHS gets privatised. I'll just spit two bars, get a bit of money and go fix my ribs. But people that grow up with nothing – like I did – I'm doing it for them. I thought: "You know what? I'm gonna make them have a voice."'

Less than one week after the election, at 1 a.m. on Wednesday 14 June, a fire started in the Grenfell Tower, a 24-storey, 1970s tower block in west London containing 120 flats – it spread with terrifying and unusual speed, accelerated by external cladding applied in a refurbishment the previous year, and quickly engulfed the entire building, making rescue efforts near impossible. In desperation, some residents jumped to their deaths. Others made phone calls to loved ones and the emergency services, or screamed for help out of the window, but they could not escape, and died in their flats, or trying to escape the inferno. Parents were forced to throw their children out of windows. It took the best part of 24 hours, and at its peak more than 200 firefighters, to tackle the fire – leaving a blackened tombstone on the west London skyline. Hundreds of people from the lower floors were successfully evacuated, but for a long time, few victims were found and identified. After weeks of intense public anger, grief and confusion over what had happened, and how, and the number of victims there had been, the police eventually said they believed 71 people had died in the fire, and 223 had escaped.

Grime's world, an inner city riven by poverty and affluence, gentrification and hostility to the poor, was back in the headlines. The Royal Borough of Kensington and Chelsea has long been one of the wealthiest in Britain, and the average salary there at the time of the fire was a staggering £123,000 a year. Earlier in 2017, the EU's data organisation Eurostat had found that 'Inner London West', incorporating Kensington, Chelsea and Notting Hill, was the richest area in the whole of Europe, comfortably beating the Grand Duchy of

Luxembourg into second place. One and a half miles away from Grenfell was the most expensive street in the country, home to mansions worth an average of £41m each. And yet, alongside these obscene riches, was intense poverty: the Notting Dale ward in which Grenfell was located was one of the ten most deprived wards in the entire country. Grenfell had been home to poor families and individuals of all races – the first victim identified from the blaze was Mohammed Alhajali, a Syrian refugee. Kensington was, its new Labour MP said, 'a place where inequality has become a gross spectacle'. Planning documents seemed to show that the building's new external cladding, which had created the chimney-like effect that made the blaze so devastating, had been chosen in part so that the tower would look better when seen from nearby luxury flats.

It was both a microcosm and an indictment of an entire political culture, of attitudes that had held sway since the late 1970s: in particular, the prioritising of market principles over housing security for Britain's working-class communities. The stability and affordability intrinsic to the post-war social housing ideal – that everyone had the right to a decent home – had been allowed to melt away by successive governments. As New Labour's then Housing Minister, Nick Raynsford, announced in 2000, they had 'left behind the twentieth-century framework where, on the whole, the ethos was based on assumptions that the state would provide and people should be grateful for being allocated the benefit of a home'.[12] This market-led mantra in theory offered tenants greater choice, and participation in the management of their estates, in exchange for security, and yet the people living in what remained of Britain's social-housing had ended up with none of the above. The Grenfell Action Group, a residents' association, had repeatedly warned a catastrophe of exactly this kind was possible, in the absence of a building-wide fire alarm or sprinkler system, and they were ignored. Their words, written on a blog only eight months before the disaster, were chilling. 'It is a truly terrifying thought but the Grenfell Action Group firmly believe that only a catastrophic event will expose the ineptitude and incompetence of our landlord.'

There followed the usual pseudo-pious calls that the tragedy should not be 'politicised', from people worried about the consequences – from people with guilty consciences. They fell on deaf ears. In one sense the Grenfell fire was impossible to politicise, because it was so obviously, nakedly political: a consequence not of some act of god, but of direct political decisions. Decades of mismanagement of social housing, managed decline, swingeing cuts, and partial or wholesale privatisation – underpinned by a contempt for Britain's poorest communities, conscious or otherwise – had produced this tragedy.

In his Labour election-campaign video a few weeks earlier, AJ Tracey had talked about soaring house prices in his native west London, and Labour's plans to build more council houses – at last. 'I've grown up here,' he said, 'and I don't know if I ever will be able to buy a house here.' He did so on a glorious late spring day, and as he spoke, the camera cut away to what looked like a gleaming new tower block above his head. It was the Grenfell Tower, wearing its fresh new cladding. 'We need places to live,' Tracey said.

A few days after the fire, with London still reeling, and community-relief efforts filling the chasm of state support on the ground in Kensington, AJ Tracey and his brother did a video interview with the *Guardian*. Tracey walked past Grenfell every day of his life, he said – he looked out his window and could see the tower. They talked about the housing crisis, and the way it was undeniably racialised – that people of colour would never be able to afford to buy a house in their own neighbourhood. 'It's unheard of,' Tracey said. And slowly but surely, they were being pushed out in favour of 'the Chelsea set', or buy-to-leave millionaires looking to use properties as part of their investment portfolio, instead of homes. It was, he said, part of the exact same mentality that led the Tory-run borough's desire to shut down Notting Hill Carnival, 'one of the gems of the UK', a totem to London's multiculturalism, 'a celebration of culture, colours, happiness'. The inner city was being wrenched away from the people who lived there.

This was grime's milieu, and once again grime MCs were in the thick of its community activity, amplifying calls for charitable donations and the search for missing residents, arranging and playing benefit gigs, and helping with relief efforts on the ground, along with thousands of other ordinary people of all races – a grassroots effort that was essential, in the absence of any immediate support for the survivors from the Tory council, or the Tory government.

The distance between the people the grime scene represented, the kinds of people who had lived in Grenfell Tower, and their political masters, seemed wider than ever. The difference was that the former, much larger group, were finally being heard – and they had a new cadre of spokespeople, who had been used to airing their views into a microphone since they were teenagers. In a BBC News discussion after the election about the Grime 4 Corbyn phenomenon, east London MC Saskilla, who had performed at the Grime 4 Corbyn gig, gave the same interpretation Lethal Bizzle had done, seven years earlier, about a political class who did not understand life as it was lived by the majority of British people – a life of struggling to make ends meet, poor quality and overpriced housing, insecure, low-paid jobs, food banks and budget supermarkets. 'Has Theresa May ever been to Aldi?' Saskilla asked. 'Has she ever been to Lidl in her life? If she can tell me what Lidl looks like from the inside, I'll listen to what Theresa May has to say.'

Within 48 hours of the fire, a hotly tipped young west London grime MC, Big Zuu, who had also been intimately involved in the relief efforts, had released a 'Grenfell Tower Tribute' song and video, as part of a fundraising effort for the victims. Grief and shock were mixed with an intense, rational anger. He bigged up the 'community, the people power', concluding they should 'bun the government, the city's ours'. South London rapper Dave's seven-minute epic 'Question Time' probed the same issues with incredible lucidity, addressing Theresa May at length about her cowardice and silence in the wake of the catastrophe. 'Everyone who knew about that cladding should really be going prison under rule of joint enterprise/But if it ain't a little kid with a knife, I bet that judge is going easy when he's giving him time.'[13] The real Prime Ministers had spoken.

In the ensuing debate in parliament about the Grenfell fire, the new Labour MP for Kensington, Emma Dent Coad – the first Labour MP ever elected in the constituency, reflecting the pivotal moment London was living through – made a speech that pointed to the newfound pre-eminence the grime scene had found in public debate. 'At times of national disaster,' she said, 'poets laureate are often called on to commemorate and reflect on events. In north Kensington, we have our own Ben Jonsons and Alfred, Lord Tennysons. Our poets laureate are Akala, AJ Tracey, Lowkey and Peaky. We have Stormzy, and Potent Whisper calling out what he calls "Grenfell Britain" in gut-wrenching prose.'

They assumed this new role with grace and humility. Coming off the back of his remarkable number-one album, *Gang Signs and Prayer*, Stormzy played a triumphant set at Glastonbury, and in among the heart-rending gospel and head-spinning grime energy, he used his platform to call for justice for the victims of the Grenfell fire. 'We are urging the authorities to tell the fucking truth, first and foremost,' he said, unzipping his jacket to reveal a T-shirt with 'Grenfell' written on a heart-shaped London Underground logo. 'We're urging the fucking government to be held accountable for the fuckery, and we ain't gonna stop until we get what we deserve.' The stage set behind him seemed to resemble an assembly of black tower blocks. After his speech, the crowd began chanting 'Oh, Jeremy Corbyn', to the tune of the White Stripes' 'Seven Nation Army', and he joined in. He went on to perform his verse from the official Grenfell charity single, the fastest-selling record in a decade, which he had opened, with the words, 'I refuse to forget you, I refuse to be silenced, I refuse to neglect you ... that could have been my mum's house, that could have been my nephew.'[14]

At the tail end of that strange, feverish summer, on a baking hot day in September, I took a train out to Woodford in Essex, where Boy Better Know had gathered at a local athletics track to record a new music video. It was intended to promote a new Nike football shirt produced in collaboration with the grime crew, designed by Jme. The crew's O2 Takeover had only been a few weeks earlier, and they had just recovered and begun to take stock of the scale of it all. They seemed tired by a long summer of festival headline slots, but happy, blinking in the bright Indian-summer sunshine.

'It was surreal,' said Jammer, slightly awed, of the BBK Takeover. 'It was like a dream – it was something you never could have scripted. It was inspirational, I think – to UK music, and to everyone that's been following us since the beginning, to see what you can build, if you stick to something you believe in. That's really what's important to me about it: seeing a vision to come to life, and seeing that progress – being there with all the people who were there on the underground, people I've spent so much time with, creating music. The respect that's now being paid to us and to the music is amazing.'

Far from atomising the new stars, grime's newfound commercial success seemed to have enhanced its collectivism, if anything. Instead of spinning off into silos of self-indulgence, where they counted their money like cartoon villains, cavorted with celebrities and developed ruinous drug habits, the artists had pulled their peers in closer, almost by way of protection against degeneracy – but also out of habit. The years on the underground, passing the mic in youth clubs and pirate stations, had incubated a collaborative spirit no one wanted to shake off. When one of the 'day one' MCs had a gig on in London now, as they so often did, it was understood that everyone else would turn up and spit their reload bars, or perform their big hit, by way of peer support. The stage was a shared space. Jammer said they were making sure to indoctrinate the younger generation of MCs into this principle too; and judging by the number of guest MCs at all of Stormzy, J Hus, Dave and Mostack's gigs in 2017, they were listening.

'This all started with those pirate-radio days,' Jammer continued, 'people bringing each other along to the studio, or to my basement, or to a pirate station, that's where it's all from – kids hanging out together, making something they enjoy. And now, because we believed in it, and we stuck to it … now *this* happened.' He gestured out to the athletics track, where a hundred teenage extras in black tracksuits were performing their roles for the video, moving in formation as teams of camera people – watched over by Jme – tracked their movements. 'The fact that everyone's been able to watch our story play out on the big screen, since they were growing up, it's like it's their film too – they believe in it because they saw it develop. Sometimes in other genres, you see an artist suddenly blow up out of nowhere and get big – and that can be kind of cool I guess, but there's no story behind them, there's nothing to follow. Everybody loves a good story, and that's what's amazing about this one. It's like a film.'

Grime had drawn its power from a rupture at the start of a new millennium. It was a sonically violent enactment of the claustrophobia of the inner city, and a confrontation with the society that was determined grime's creators would remain on the margins, unheard. It was a stunning exercise in collective alchemy that this anger and alienation so often manifested itself in joy and irreverence, but there was no denying that it was all born from poverty, and all born from pain, as Skepta had said.

But what now? Wasn't there a chance that the trappings of fame and fortune would go to their heads? Jammer waved the suggestion away – 'grime's not flossy,' he said: 'it's more tracksuits and trainers, not gold chains'. They'd spent so long on the underground, doing things for themselves and each other, that they weren't about to change now – not when there was work to be done.

'Our principle has always been to make your music, get it out there, and crack on – and we're cracking on.'

EPILOGUE

BACK YOUR CITY

With the urban renaissance begun by New Labour fully underway, London stands transformed, if not exactly reborn. Its skyline is crenellated with a growing assembly of cranes and obelisks, and underneath them, masquerades of privately owned plazas patrolled by security guards and ringed with a glitzy simulacrum of cosmopolitanism, branches of Wahaca, Wagamama and Le Pain Quotidien. It is a city where working-class mobility is restrained by the most expensive public transport in the world,[1] and where the public realm is served by only one specific newspaper, the *Evening Standard* – owned by a Russian billionaire and edited by the former Conservative Chancellor responsible for wounding London's poorest with six years of brutal austerity. Perhaps it is their city now.

One Ballardian vignette from 2013 seemed to sum up the spirit of the new capital: when the sun hit the new lump of glass and metal that is 20 Fenchurch Street, the City of London skyscraper known by its cutesy sobriquet 'the Walkie Talkie', it reflected the rays upon a parked car on the street below in such a way that the car began to melt, causing almost a grand's worth of damage.

Grenfell Tower, 2017

In common with what some urbanists call the 'luxified skies' developing in cities across the world, vertical sprawls of elite tower blocks such as the Shard look set to become commonplace. According to New London Architecture's '2017 Tall Buildings Report', there are more of London's 455 high-rise towers currently proposed, approved, or already under construction in Tower Hamlets than in any other borough – 77, altogether – and nearly half of the overall total are in east London. 27 of the total will be 50 storeys or higher, in other words, as tall or taller than Canary Wharf. The overwhelming majority of these new skyscrapers will be residential, and while the report does not seek to estimate what proportion will be social housing, it is safe to assume it will be minuscule. These vertical gated communities threaten a new incarnation of the urban class system, where the very rich are elevated above the din, and offered a god-like gaze on the tumult of the undistinguished and indistinguishable masses below. The view that was once prized by the likes of Slimzee and Geeneus, when they were putting up Rinse FM's aerials on the council blocks of Bow, will belong to a very different class of Londoner.

It is a pattern repeated in cities across the world. One new super-elitist, high-rise residential tower block in Mumbai, the Indiabulls 'Sky' Tower, made the Icarian hubris explicit: its marketing bumph offered the opportunity to 'possess your piece of the sky ... rise up to the city's most elite residences' and 'share the same address as God'.

London's property marketeers may be slightly more subtle, but barely – and the offer to escape from the ordinary people, the noise and the grime of city life is the same. Back in 1924, Le Corbusier had written of the utopian possibilities offered by a 'vertical city', 'a city which will pile up the cells which have for so long been crushed on the ground, and set them high above the earth, bathed in light and air ... clear and radiant and sparkling'.

On the occasions where London's new luxury blocks have been forced to fulfil their 'section 106' legal requirement to build a small quota of affordable housing (often, they have bought themselves out or otherwise fudged their already minimal obligations), property developers have often done so using 'poor doors': separate entrances for the 'affordable' dregs. In the case of One Commercial Street in east London, the main entrance for wealthy owners is through a 'bespoke entrance lobby with the ambience of a stylish hotel reception area' – meanwhile, the affordable-housing tenants enter through the poor door, tucked away in an alleyway around the corner, opposite the trade entrance to a branch of Pret a Manger.

Cities, like music genres, always change, and they should change. The question is always the same: how are they changing, and for whose benefit? The influx of foreign investment into the London property market has received a growing amount of attention in the last decade – indeed the financial speculation in housing as a commodity has even prompted concerned reports from the United Nations, who have felt compelled to reiterate that adequate housing is a human right. In 2014, research by the firm Molior Consulting found that ten international investment consortia own sites for 30,000 new homes in the centre of London. These investments were characterised as 'buy-to-leave' investments, or 'safety deposit boxes' – the idea being that wealthy overseas investors will buy up expensive flats safe in the knowledge that their value will continue to increase, and rarely (if ever) actually inhabit them. The asking prices for these luxury flats are, of course, far beyond the reach of the overwhelming majority of Londoners.

London's relationship with the wider world (and its money) is complex – since it was founded by the Romans in 43AD, the city has never been a monoculture, and would never have thrived if it had been. More than 300 languages are spoken in London, and 37 per cent of the city's population were born outside the UK. In spite of this, there is still an occasional whiff of xenophobia visible in some of the British media coverage of the capital's evolution; coverage which assumes that archetypes like the Russian oil baron or Saudi prince are singly responsible for the crisis in affordable housing in the capital, when of course the truth lies much closer to home. Apart from anything else, the overwhelming majority of new housing developments in London are bought by Brits (87 per cent, according to a York University study[2]), and are generally pitched at the same wealthy strata of society as the scapegoated foreign oligarchs – to the exclusion of the majority of Londoners, whatever their heritage.

The glare given off by London's new skyscrapers can blind us to some murky truths: in spite of the £9 billion spent on the 2012 London Olympics, and the general impression that the capital is the striking exception to the rule of British economic stagnation, the statistics tell another story. The British government's own figures show working-age poverty among Londoners rose from 22 per cent in 2003 to 25 per cent in 2016 – as real wages fall and house prices, rents and living costs soar. Child poverty in the same period fell, but only from 39 per cent to 37: still a figure to shame a city home to grime's neighbours in Canary Wharf, with their champagne receptions and multimillion-pound annual bonuses. According to figures published in 2014 by the Child Poverty Action Group, London contains 14 out of the 20 local authorities with the highest rates of child poverty in the entire UK.

Research into levels of poverty in London consistently indicate one significant new trend: they are rising in the periphery and falling in the centre. Child poverty in inner London fell from 51 per cent to 42 per cent in 2003–16, but rose from 28 per cent to 34 per cent in outer London. This process of hollowing out is crucial to understanding the dynamics of supply and demand in the global cities of the near future. The replacement of post-war social housing with high-end new developments is seeing inner London's poorest families being pushed further and further out: rehoused up to two hours away from their schools, jobs and support networks, and struggling accordingly. 'The emphasis is different now,' a housing charity worker in Westminster explained to me, in between counselling dismayed, tired mothers and fathers on how to adapt to the capital's new reality: 'We have to tell them, if you can't afford the accommodation, you've got to move.'

It's not that politicians hadn't noticed it happening, but too few have had the will or the power to do anything about it. In response to the 2014 Molior report about foreign-owned buy-to-leave flats, one London Labour MP, Joan Ruddock, called for government intervention in the market to create more affordable housing: 'The capital will not be sustainable unless people in the public services can afford to live here. We are pricing them out.' Her intentions were good, but where her wording was slightly off the mark, is that whatever happens, the capital will be sustained, but the people who are being 'priced out' will stay, and suffer. People desperately need the jobs that concentrate in cities like London, and are flocking to major urban centres around the world in vast numbers for precisely this reason.

What seems far more likely than an exodus from London by lower-paid workers – where would they go? – and a consequent shortfall in the working population, is that they will remain – but they will be forced to live further away from the jobs in the centre, in more cramped and poorer quality accommodation, and will have to spend more of their wages on rent and travel, commute for longer hours, and their finances, their social and personal lives, and their physical and mental health will all suffer accordingly. In the intense clamour for urban space, something has got to give, and unless something drastic changes, it will give way at the bottom.

Grime's inner city has changed so much since its beginnings that when you ask its pioneers about how the ends look now, they mostly just shake their heads in disbelief. On Dizzee Rascal's sixth album, *Raskit*, he revisited on two key tracks the east London that had made him. The first, 'Everything Must Go', talked of east London youth 'swept off of their feet before them condos are complete', and – in the name of high-lighting their hypocrisy – excerpted speeches from Margaret Thatcher and Boris Johnson. The quote from the latter, as Mayor, playing over Dizzee's bass-quake outro, had Johnson insisting to the press that he would 'emphatically resist' a London 'in which the rich and poor can't live together', and London becoming more like Paris, where poorer and immigrant communities were contained in crime and drug-ridden suburban ghettos, and where 'the less well-off are pushed to the suburbs: that is not going to happen in London'. It was a perfect description of exactly what was happening in London on his watch, and it was happening in part thanks to his fellow old Etonian and Oxford University

Bullingdon Club member, his fellow senior Conservative, Prime Minister David Cameron.

The second, the pinnacle of Dizzee's long-awaited return to a 'hard' sound, was 'Slow Your Roll', a poignant reflection on the futile youth violence he'd seen in E3 and the Isle of Dogs as a teenager, and what had happened to east London while he'd been away. It was ironic that it took the MC who became a global superstar and moved to Miami – and more recently, to Kent – to really address the gentrification of the manor. The central message of 'slowing your roll' is to abandon foolish and 'numbing' gangster pretensions and postcode beefs over streets where the kids risking their lives 'don't even own yards'. In a stunning second verse, Dizzee describes the entire process of gentrification with devastating clarity over swooning, sad-eyed synths and chipmunked background vocal wails. 'The developers rocked up ... and the hood got chopped and the natives cropped and the ends got boxed up, then the price got knocked up/Foreign investment raising the stock up, so the rent got propped up, and it kept getting topped up/So the heart got ripped out, and rinsed out: some got shipped out, got kicked out ... Power, money and big clout's what it's about.'[3] Dizzee had been reading Anna Minton's book *Big Capital*, which is about exactly this.

'Look at all the housing they built: it's this whole new postcode, this whole new clinical little town,' he said.[4] He was talking about E20, the postcode created for the housing going up around the Olympic site – the same bit of marshy land where he had squared up to Crazy Titch on Deja Vu FM, all those years ago. The marketing people had christened the area 'East Village', a piece of place-branding uniting two of the most telling trends of modern gentrification aesthetics: fetishisation of New York (connotations: foreign glamour, urbane sophistication, hyper-gentrification), and fetishisation of 'the village' (connotations: cosy, English, white). Don't worry, reassured the advertising campaign for the expensive new rental properties in East Village, you'll still have the social capital of being in transport Zone 2, i.e. relatively central, so your status among your snobbish 'I don't do Zone 3' friends will not be under threat.

As rich in pathos as grime's extraordinary triumph over the odds has been, the question facing future generations of teenage DJs, producers and MCs is whether the same community-driven youth sub-cultures can still flourish, when the informal city from which they once emerged is being erased. The stunning self-belief and creative autonomy of such artists as Wiley, Jme and Skepta have certainly inspired the current generation of MCs emerging from London's council estates, and the foundations they have laid in moving the underground into the mainstream seems to offer great new opportunities for AJ Tracey, Novelist, Big Zuu and their peers. But with these opportunities come a whole new set of questions and challenges. When the sound of the inner city is finally at the heart of UK pop culture, what does it mean when the places that produced it have changed beyond all recognition? And if the young Londoners who were once demonised are suddenly being held up by Tory MPs and media gatekeepers as paragons of British values, where does either side go next? If deprivation, crime and riots are confined to outside the ring road in the future, as Jonathan Meades predicted, does that point to the suburbs as the future incubator of rebellious working-class music and youth culture, whatever form this takes? And where do these changes leave the culture of the inner city? Will it simply reproduce the homogeneous and glossy feel of the property billboards going up across 'regenerated' inner London?

The increasing pervasiveness of the internet over our lives has prompted both nostalgia and hand-wringing – about the death of the youth sub-cultures and tribes that had sustained pop culture since the 1950s. The lesson some observers drew from grime's speedy rise and fall between 2003–06 was that both youth culture and the media were fragmenting into ever-smaller pieces. New music scenes were much more likely to be flashes in the pan, as new scenes became ever more disposable and commodified – young people had too many choices, they complained, and too much instant gratification. Our attention spans were all being shot to pieces, and as a result new genres were not being allowed to grow and flourish. If it does nothing else, the story of grime rips a hole in these gloomy prophecies.

It is an ironic function of grime's renaissance that, after years of not being able to persuade the industry and the mainstream media that it even existed ('British hip-hop', they would usually say), they now have the opposite problem. For years, grime was being called rap. Now, UK rap – and drill, and dancehall, and Afrobeats, and the new, slippery hybrid that some are calling Afroswing, or Afrowave, or Afrobashment – is being called grime. When *Music Week* ran their special issue on 'The Business of Grime', the cover star was J Hus, a terrific MC whose music bears almost no relation to grime. A lot of fans of black British music rolled their eyes at the mislabelling, others gnashed their teeth. Always a pragmatist, Jme was ambivalent about this new confusion emanating from the industry:

'Labelling Giggs, J Hus and all these people as grime is a mistake – but it's up to Giggs and J Hus, and if they don't mind, it's fine. I would never say "Giggs isn't grime!" It's nothing to do with me. Me and him are on the same songs, spitting at the same speed, so … what do you call that, you know? Some people say to the artists, "You need to tell them to stop calling you grime," but it's nothing to do with the artists. The industry are out of touch and they're trying to catch up with what's going on – it's a learning curve, but whatever, I don't mind. If anything, calling J Hus's music grime is good for grime, because he's merking, he's sick.'

The octopus of MC-led scenes thriving during grime's renaissance has prompted a new kind of identity crisis in some quarters: what is grime? Is it, as most fans have always maintained, a unique genre in the dance-hall and UK garage tradition, at approximately 140 beats per minute, with big sub-bass and double-time spitting? Or is it more abstract than that: something more like an attitude, and a vibe, that can take on different musical forms? Interviewed on a YouTube chat show in 2015, Scorcher talked about the continuing rise of road rap, and success of rappers like Giggs and Krept and Konan: 'We're entering a place where there's people giving people the same feeling that grime does, via rap,' Scorcher said, pointing to south London rapper Fekky as an example.[5] Fekky's best-known track at the time was a reworking of Dizzee Rascal's 'Sittin' Here', featuring no fewer than ten guest grime MCs. One of young rapper Dave's first major break-out hits was a single called 'Thiago Silva', a pairing with AJ Tracey, spitting at grime speed, on a grime riddim – a slightly reworked Ruff Sqwad instrumental from a decade earlier. Krept and Konan released a single with Stormzy. Jme's biggest single, if you use YouTube views as a measure, is a track featuring Giggs, and so is Kano's. The lines are becoming ever more blurred.

Another issue raised by the scene's dominance is the possibility of it calcifying and stagnating through the over-exposure of the scene's biggest (and eldest) names hogging the limelight. Fortunately, fresh blood doesn't seem to stop coming through. Roony Keefe from *Risky Roadz* was keen to ensure that a sound that had always been predicated on newness – the latest riddim, the freshest banger, the hottest new MC, the most dazzling sound – didn't stop evolving. 'Without new talent, the scene doesn't move forward, it just fades away,' he said. 'When Ghetts done *Fuck Radio* a decade ago, it was to make sure the under-18s, the new kids, had a chance. That sort of mentality – I think it's an old-school grime mentality, where you always have to look for the new generation. From when we started I always felt a bit like *Risky Roadz* was like a kind of low-key A&R. I didn't work for a label or anything – but I kept finding these people. That's the fun part of it. I love seeing someone MC for the first time and just being like, "Fuuuck, people need to hear this!"' A healthy disrespect for one's elders is no bad thing. At the tail end of 2017, as Wiley and Dizzee beefed pettily but furiously with one another on Twitter, Big Zuu responded airily: 'Don't really care about Dizzie and Wiley arguing about the 2000s, man was like 5 years old.'

In November 2017, it was announced that Form 696 would be scrapped, a stunning and long overdue victory, after a decade of police obfuscation and fudged tweaks to a racist policy that had never been fit-for-purpose. 'The landscape of the night-time economy in London has changed,' said a Met spokesman. Fans congratulated Mayor Sadiq Khan and his Night Tsar, Amy Lamé – though really they should have been congratulating the Conservative Culture Minister's special advisor, Jonathan Badyal, who had set the ball rolling, and the likes of Stephen 'Cheeky' Cee from Eskimo Dance, and the Arts Council-funded NGO

British Underground, responsible for much of the behind the scenes lobbying. Ultimately, it took commercial success to achieve a modicum of justice, rather than the other way around, but some cautious optimism seems justified – at last, the Met are promising to communicate with promoters, via a regular Promoters' Forum. 'There's lots of work to do but it's really great to see that my colleagues in the industry can shape something we didn't have a say in when 696 was formed,' wrote DJ Funk Butcher, after attending the first meeting. Ultimately, it took commercial success for people involved in black British music to actually be listened to, as well.

Grime is not only being allowed to breathe, and to exist in a live context, but it's even being listened to outside the manor, and engaged with by the music industry, the media, politicians and cops. This is what victory looks like, right? But what about the inner city that grime came from?

While the turbo-gentrification of inner London since grime's inception has pushed poor people further and further out, as their estates are methodically demolished or sold off, and rents soar to prohibitive new heights, the urban renaissance is also making life harder for those who remain, in the inner city's increasingly isolated social-housing blocks. With this process – not to mention Tory cuts to benefits, youth services and the removal of EMA – has come a further narrowing of opportunities and horizons for young people from poor backgrounds, and a further intensification of postcode wars, youth violence and territorialism. 2017 saw the highest number of teenage murders in London since 2008, and a 47 per cent rise in knife crime incidents. Four teenagers were stabbed to death in London on New Year's Eve alone.

Inevitably, you can hear this in the music being made on inner London's council estates, most notably in the rise of drill, a branch of the rap family tree that originated in the south side of Chicago, and has been thriving on the UK underground in the last couple of years – if 'thriving' is an appropriate word for a genre as dark and nihilistic as drill. Grime lyrics, especially in the genre's early days, were home to a certain amount of gun and knife talk – only some of which, it is fair to assume, bore a relationship to the MCs' direct real life experience. Drill crews talk about almost nothing else: virtually every track centres on a world of postcode wars, drug dealing and violent crime.

'The roads ain't fun any more,' 67's Y.SJ spits on 'Lambeth Maps', capturing the mood. There is even a bleak, dead-eyed austerity to the artists' choice of names: on that track, 67's Y.SJ, R6 and ST address their three local 'opps', or rival crews – 410, 150 and 17. The cover artwork for the *Lambeth Maps* EP depicts a kids'-book-style treasure map of the borough, with piles of gold bullion, guns, snakes and treasure chests. The musical accounts of leaving their opps 'dripping in sauce' are slightly less playful, and lend the map a much more ominous aspect.

Another young south London drill crew, Harlem Spartans, have channelled the grandstanding sonics and epic energy of grime more than most. In 'Kent Nizzy' and 'Kennington Where It Started', two stunning neighbourhood anthems released within a month of each other in early 2017, drill's intensification of the hyper-localism and claustrophobia of grime is at its most startling, and lucid. They pay tribute to 'Kennington, where my heart is' – but, like most drill, it is a defensive pride, accompanied by a richly poetic but nonetheless grim enumeration of drug dealing, knives and guns, where they 'scrap fast at Waterloo like Wellington, try and rip holes and touch man's skeleton', and where 'CCTV can vouch for the squady'.[6]

If grime is claustrophobic, this sound is positively smothering, and the sense of proprietorial angst in defence of the ends – now so hemmed in that we are talking about just a single estate, the Kennington Park Estate, not even a postcode – make songs like SLK's 'North Weezy' or 'Southside Allstars' seem like joyful party anthems, by comparison.

This intensity reaches its apex in the breathtaking chorus of 'Kent Nizzy', a rallying cry for the ever-tighter geography of their manor, backed by an instrumental which is both chilling and cinematic, as if they are indeed riding into battle: 'CID's trying to lock my city/But fuck Trident, we all violent/Man, back your city/Kennington: where it's fucking sticky'.[7] It's a stark and stultifying worldview, but not if you consider the position of Kennington Park Estate in regards to the London that now surrounds it, and how that might have changed in the Spartans' young lives. As one measure of how the area has changed, average house prices in Kennington have more than tripled since the millennium. On one side of the Kennington Park Estate is Elephant and Castle, where Labour-run Southwark Council have joined forces with two of the world's biggest property developers, Lendlease and Delancey, to wilfully socially cleanse the area, demolish the Heygate Estate, the Aylesbury Estate (where Blair made his 'forgotten people' speech) and Elephant's 'town centre', sending working-class and ethnic minority communities scattering to the outer zones of London, to make way for luxury flats. On the other side, Vauxhall and Nine Elms constitutes one of Europe's biggest regeneration zones, where a 'major new cultural quarter' is apparently planned, but which is most effectively symbolised by the fifty-storey St George Wharf Tower, home to 214 flats costing up to £51 million, not one of them affordable, and few of them even occupied – most of the lights are never on.

Is it any wonder that 'we all violent, man, back your city' emerges as a motto from teenagers in that environment? Young people who have been forced up against the wall of their estate, boys in the corner, whose whole life constitutes a seemingly inescapable position. They are effectively under siege – not from tanks and air raids, but from poverty and youth violence, inequality, institutional and societal racism. *Bank scams, street robbery, shotters, blotters or HMP.*[8]

The power of grime comes from transmuting the anxiety, pain and joy of inner-city life into music. That power shifts and bends its form as the world around it changes, and it will continue to do so. Man, back your city.